Immigration and International Relations

Proceedings of a Conference on the
International Effects of the 1986
Immigration Reform and Control Act
(IRCA)

Georges Vernez, editor

May 1990

The RAND Corporation

JRI-02

The Urban Institute

UI Report 90-7

The RAND Corporation was chartered in 1948 as a nonprofit institution to "further and promote scientific, educational, and charitable purposes, all for the public welfare and security of the United States of America." To meet these objectives, RAND conducts rigorous analyses of significant national problems to provide decisionmakers and the public with a better understanding of the policy issues involved.

RAND's research is analytic, objective, and interdisciplinary. National security programs focus on the planning, development, acquisition, deployment, support, and protection of military forces, and include international matters that may affect U.S. defense policy and strategy. Domestic programs include civil and criminal justice, education and human resources, health sciences, international economic studies, labor and population, and regulatory policies.

The Urban Institute is a nonprofit policy research and educational organization established in Washington, D.C., in 1968. Its staff investigates the social and economic problems confronting the nation and government policies and programs designed to alleviate such problems. The Institute has two goals for work in each of its research areas: to help shape thinking about societal problems and efforts to solve them, and to improve government decisions and performance by providing better information and analytic tools.

Through work that ranges from broad conceptual studies to administrative and technical assistance, Institute researchers contribute to the stock of knowledge available to public officials and private individuals and groups concerned with formulating and implementing more efficient and effective government policy.

PREFACE

As part of their research and convening activities under the Program for Research on Immigration Policy, The RAND Corporation and The Urban Institute hosted a conference on *The International Effects of IRCA* (Immigration Reform and Control Act of 1986) in May 1989 in Guadalajara, Mexico.

The conference had several objectives. First, it provided an opportunity to discuss ongoing research on the implementation of IRCA and to review early information on IRCA's actual and potential international effects. Second, it gave participants from Mexico and the United States a unique opportunity to begin what is hoped will be a continuing dialogue and exchange of information on IRCA and its effects and, more generally, on immigration issues. The third objective was to explore the growing links between immigration and other important policy arenas, including foreign investment, national security, and other foreign policy issues.

Some 50 scholars and public officials from Mexico, the United States, and Canada participated in the conference. They addressed the effects of IRCA on four areas: illegal immigration, U.S.-Mexico relations, Mexico, and the West Indies and inter-American relations. This report summarizes the discussions in these areas. It also includes 11 papers that were presented at the conference as resource materials.

The Program for Research on Immigration Policy was established in February 1988, with initial core funding from The Ford Foundation, to provide analysis that will help inform immigration and immigrant policies. The program has three basic goals:

- To study the domestic and international issues raised by IRCA;
- To address the larger questions and problems that continue to characterize immigration and immigrant policies;
- To disseminate and exchange information about IRCA and immigration through publications, working groups, and conferences.

The program publishes books and immigration policy reports. The program's research will help policymakers identify the degree to which IRCA is achieving its objectives. The research should also help practitioners assess the effectiveness of several previously untested "tools" of immigration policy.

Conclusions or opinions expressed are those of the authors and do not necessarily reflect the views of other staff members, officers, trustees, or advisory groups of either The RAND Corporation or The Urban Institute, or any organizations that provide either of them with financial support.

The program also aims to disseminate and exchange information about immigration and immigrant policies. Researchers interested in receiving the program's publications or in attending its working groups or conferences should address inquiries to either of the program's co-directors:

Frank D. Bean
The Urban Institute
2100 M Street, N.W.
Washington, DC 20037
Telephone: (202) 833-7200

Georges Vernez
The RAND Corporation
1700 Main Street, P.O. Box 2138
Santa Monica, CA 90406-2138
Telephone: (213) 393-0411

ACKNOWLEDGMENTS

Organizing an international conference is a major undertaking that requires the cooperation and assistance of many.

Special thanks are owed to Victor Palmieri, chairman of the Advisory Board to the Program for Research on Immigration Policy, for his support and for presiding over most of the conference deliberations. His good humor and perfect sense of timing contributed greatly to the success of the conference.

We are grateful to Jorge Bustamante of the Colegio de la Frontera Norte and to David F. Ronfeldt of The RAND Corporation for assistance in identifying and inviting key officials and scholars from Mexico and for many helpful suggestions.

The conference was a joint undertaking of The RAND Corporation and The Urban Institute involving financial support from The Ford Foundation in New York and in Mexico City. A special debt of gratitude is owed to Frank D. Bean, the Program's co-director, for his helpful suggestions. We thank The Ford Foundation for its financial support and express our appreciation to Paul Balaran, Bill Diaz, and Raul Sanchez for their support and for their continuing interest in researching immigration issues.

The conference preparation and logistics fell primarily on the shoulders of Jacqueline Bowens and Connie Moreno of The RAND Corporation. Their relentless efforts and attention to details before, during, and after the conference assured that everything ran smoothly, and we owe them many thanks.

We are indebted to Joyce Peterson, who made useful suggestions for organizing this report and helped summarize the presentations and discussions succinctly and directly, and to Judith Westbury, who edited the report.

Finally, special thanks are owed to Jacqueline Bowens for her hard work in helping organize the conference, in keeping the preparation of these Proceedings on track, and in typing much of this report.

CONTENTS

PART I

INTRODUCTION

OVERVIEW
Georges Vernez

In November 1986, the U.S. Congress passed the Immigration Reform and Control Act (IRCA) following long, often intense debate. As with the debate, the intentions and provisions of the law have raised complex issues and questions. Among the most complex, from a policy standpoint, are the ways in which IRCA will affect other countries and U.S. relations with those countries. In May 1989, The RAND Corporation and The Urban Institute hosted a conference in Guadalajara, Mexico, that brought together scholars, policy analysts, and government officials from Canada, Mexico, and the United States to discuss *The International Effects of IRCA*. This report presents the Proceedings of that conference.

This section describes the background of the conference, its objectives, its participants, how it was organized, the topics it addressed, and its highlights.

CONFERENCE BACKGROUND

IRCA's Context, Objectives, and Main Provisions

Over the past two decades, patterns of immigration to the United States have changed dramatically. Besides an increasing number of legal immigrants and refugees, an increasingly greater number of undocumented immigrants have entered and remained in the country. Further, more and more of these immigrants have come from Mexico, Central America, and Asia, and fewer from Europe, the traditional place of origin. These changes have led to an ongoing reassessment of U.S. immigration and refugee policies.[1]

In 1981, a blue ribbon Select Commission on Immigration and Refugee Policy submitted its final report to the President, recommending a comprehensive overhaul of immigration law and policy. Then, after nearly six years of deliberation and review of various proposals, Congress passed the Immigration Reform and Control Act. The President signed it into law on November 6, 1986.

The primary intention of IRCA is to reduce illegal (undocumented) immigration to the United States. The law relies primarily on two mechanisms to control illegal immigration: (a) a provision prohibiting employers from hiring undocumented workers, and (b) a provision for imposing civil and criminal sanctions for noncompliance. These provisions are complemented by an authorized 50 percent increase in resources allocated to the Border Patrol of the U.S. Immigration and Naturalization Service (INS).

Other key provisions reflect other objectives of the law:

- A legalization program that grants temporary and then permanent U.S. residence to undocumented immigrants who have resided continuously in the United States since 1982;

---

[1]See Frank D. Bean, Georges Vernez, and Charles B. Keely, *Opening and Closing the Doors: Evaluating Immigration Reform and Control*, The RAND Corporation and The Urban Institute, JRI-01, 1989.

4

- When employers hire and fire, prohibition against discrimination on the basis of national origin or citizenship; and
- A number of special provisions designed to benefit U.S. agriculture.

The Initial Reactions to IRCA

The passage of IRCA immediately generated concerns that were vocalized in both the United States and the key countries of origin, particularly Mexico, the Caribbean Islands, and Central America.

In the United States, critics expressed concerns about the effects of "employer sanctions." The concerns were varied: Sanctions would not reduce illegal entry into the country. Sanctions would lead to increased discrimination against "foreign-looking" workers—whether documented or not. Further, sanctions would make undocumented workers more vulnerable to exploitation. There were also concerns that the INS would not have the necessary administrative capability and would prove too insensitive to implement an efficient and equitable legalization program. This would leave many eligible undocumented aliens worse off than before IRCA. Finally, some expressed concerns that IRCA would lead to major labor shortages in the United States, which would, in the end, be more costly than beneficial to the U.S. economy and its international competitiveness.

In the countries of origin, governments and the popular press focused immediately on the prospects of "mass deportation" and of absorbing large numbers of returnees. This was expected to exacerbate already difficult economic and political conditions and even undermine the political stability of some of these countries.

IRCA's effects have not yet been sorted out. However, they have not been as immediate or as drastic and visible as some thought they would be.[2] This is partly because IRCA has more than 50 provisions being phased in over a five-year period, and enforcement of some key provisions is only beginning.

It is possible that IRCA may become less significant for its immediate effects than for its catalytic effect on immigration and immigrant policy. It has set in motion a long-term redefinition of the rules under which the movement of labor between the United States and other nations ought to take place. It may also alter the perceptions in both the United States and countries of origin about the range of policy options available in this critical area.

IRCA's International Implications

IRCA is not an isolated event unique to the United States. It actually reflects a trend in Western Europe that began in the 1970s with the passage of laws having objectives and means similar to those of Simpson-Rodino. Over time, many European countries have enhanced the enforcement of those laws and increased the penalties for breaking them. This propensity toward increased control over who and how many can enter the most developed countries is important not only in its own right but also because it seemingly bucks three important worldwide trends.

The first is economic. Simply put, the population of the more developed nations is expected to stagnate, if not decline, in the near future, while that of the less developed nations will continue to increase. For some, population may increase at a rate exceeding their ability to create jobs for the new entrants into the labor force. Also, the disparity in relative wages

[2]Bean, Vernez, and Keely, *Opening and Closing the Doors.*

between developed and developing countries is likely to continue to increase. These push-pull factors are likely to converge to increase international migratory pressures.

The second is the much-heralded increasing economic interdependence of nations, with its current drive toward freer movement of goods and services, capital, and even technology. This trend tends to blur previous comfortable distinctions between domestic and foreign policies. At the very least, it increases the possibility that changes in domestic policies will have significant consequences affecting other nations. In this context, it is no accident that IRCA explicitly recognizes the potentially negative effects it may have on countries of origin: IRCA established a mechanism—the Commission for the Study of International Migration and Cooperative Economic Development—to explore this question.

A third trend is the burgeoning development of regional economic and (at least in one case) political integration, e.g., the European Common Market, the Canada-U.S. trade agreements, and the Central American Common Market. This trend raises new questions about linkages and tradeoffs among capital, technology, and labor as factors of production. If the trend continues or accelerates, it may require new kinds of agreements concerning regional labor markets and immigration flows. Foremost among the labor issues will be how freely labor is to move across member nations and—the most controversial issue—the extent to which labor will be allowed to move into the regional community from outside.

The Institutional Background of the Conference

To address these trends, understand IRCA's implementation process, and analyze the full range of IRCA's outcomes, The RAND Corporation and The Urban Institute established the Program for Research on Immigration Policy. This program was instituted in 1988, with initial funding from The Ford Foundation.

The program will follow IRCA over its five-year implementation period, as well as investigate broader and continuing issues of U.S. immigration and immigrant policies and their effects on countries of origin and on their relations with the United States. The program will also offer continuing opportunities for exchanging research results and viewpoints both in the United States and abroad. The intent is to foster and encourage a debate on international immigration issues that takes place in a setting as objective and nonpartisan as possible.

THE NATURE OF THE CONFERENCE

As part of its continuing agenda of workshops, seminars, and conferences, the program hosted this conference on *The International Effects of IRCA* in May 1988 in Guadalajara, Mexico. Approximately 50 participants heard presentations made by scholars and policy analysts and joined in conference discussions over a two-day period. To encourage frank exchange of views on sensitive issues, the conference was closed to the press.

Objectives

The conference had several objectives. First, it provided an opportunity to discuss ongoing research on the implementation of IRCA and to review early information on IRCA's actual and potential international effects. Second, it gave participants from Mexico and the United States a unique opportunity to begin what we hope will be a continuing dialogue and exchange of information on IRCA and its effects and, more generally, on immigration issues. The third objective was to explore the growing links between immigration and other important policy arenas, including foreign investment, national security, and other foreign policy issues.

Participants

The conference brought together government officials and scholars from the United States (19), Mexico (29), and Canada (1). Thirty of the 49 participants were scholars or policy analysts representing more than 15 different universities or nonprofit organizations in the United States and Mexico. Twelve represented various legislative and executive agencies of the United States government, including the U.S. Senate, the Commission for the Study of International Migration and Cooperative Economic Development, the U.S. Embassy in Mexico, the U.S. General Accounting Office, the INS, and the Department of State. Mexico's participants came from its House of Representatives, its national planning agency (CONAPO), and Consular Affairs. The appendix lists the conference participants.

THE STRUCTURE AND SUBSTANCE OF THE CONFERENCE

Setting the Tone

The conference began with an opening statement from a prominent Mexican policymaker and keynote remarks from an important participant in the formulation of the IRCA legislation. Our intent was to provide the participants with the currently prevailing views and perceptions on immigration issues in both the Mexican and U.S. Congresses.

Opening remarks were offered by the Honorable Guadalupe Gomez Maganda de Anaya, president of the Mexican Congressional Commission on Foreign Relations. She discussed how IRCA has affected Mexico's perceptions of its policy options regarding emigration and other policy issues vis-à-vis the United States; whether IRCA has made bilateral consultations and/or negotiations easier or more difficult; and whether consultations at the legislative level between Mexico and the United States are feasible and/or desirable, and if so, how they could be accomplished.

The keynote address was delivered by Mr. Richard W. Day, former Chief of Staff to Senator Simpson and now Minority Chief Counsel to the Senate Subcommittee on Immigration and Refugee Affairs. Mr. Day discussed IRCA's implementation and the Congressional view of its effectiveness, what Congress might consider if employer sanctions prove ineffective, and what the Congressional agenda on immigration matters might be over the next several years. He also addressed the issue of bilateral negotiations between the United States and Mexico on immigration issues.

Another address was delivered by the Honorable Flora MacDonald, member of the Canadian Parliament from 1972 to 1988, former Secretary of State for External Affairs, and former Minister of Employment and Immigration. She described the Canadian perspective on immigration issues and policies.

The Working Sessions

The major conference activities consisted of four working sessions, each focused on a topic central to the international effects of IRCA:

- Effects of IRCA on illegal immigration
- Effects of IRCA on U.S.-Mexico relations
- Effects of IRCA on Mexico
- IRCA and inter-American relations.

In each session, presentations were made by scholars and policy analysts conducting ongoing research in the relevant area. In all, we commissioned 12 resource papers. To minimize overlap and maximize complementarity, we asked each author to address a defined set of questions. The authors were encouraged to expand beyond these core questions or to amend them as they thought appropriate. Many expanded on them; few modified them. The presentations were followed by discussions open to all participants. All deliberations were conducted in the language preferred by the presenter (either English or Spanish). Simultaneous translation was provided for those who were not bilingual. Eleven papers are reproduced in Part III of these Proceedings (the twelfth paper was printed separately; see footnote 3 below). As we note there, the papers represent the views of only the authors.

Below we briefly summarize the questions and issues addressed in each session and list the papers presented.

Session 1: Effects of IRCA on Illegal Immigration. Reducing the number of immigrants illegally entering or staying in the United States is the primary objective of IRCA. Is the law having the effect intended? Is it inducing changes in the composition of undocumented immigrants entering and/or staying in the country? To the extent that such changes are occurring, to which provision of IRCA can they be attributed—the two legalization programs, "employer sanctions," and/or increased border enforcement?

The presentations were based on the following resource papers:

- *The Effects of IRCA on the Pattern of Apprehensions at the Border* by Michael J. White, Frank D. Bean, and Thomas J. Espenshade from The Urban Institute in Washington, D.C.
- *Migración Indocumentada México–Estados Unidos: Hallazgos Preliminares del Proyecto Cañon Zapata* by Jorge A. Bustamante, President of the Colegio de la Frontera Norte in Tijuana.
- *The Effect of Employer Sanctions on the Flow of Undocumented Immigrants to the United States* by Beth J. Asch and Keith W. Crane from The RAND Corporation.[3]

Session 2: Effects of IRCA on U.S.-Mexico Relations. Although undocumented immigrants to the United States come from nearly every country in the world, no one country is expected to be more affected by IRCA than Mexico. It has been estimated that more than half of the undocumented immigrants residing in the United States are Mexicans; and more than two out of three of the 3.1 million applicants to IRCA's legalization programs are Mexicans. How is IRCA affecting (or anticipated to affect) U.S.-Mexico relations? Is it affecting the perceptions of Mexican elites about immigration and other important issues in U.S.-Mexican relations? What is the significance for Mexico, for the United States, and for the future of their bilateral relations of the legalization (and eventual naturalization) of nearly 2 million Mexicans residing in the United States? What new institutional arrangements between the two countries might be desirable and feasible to help address issues of immigration?

---

[3]For a complete study, see Keith W. Crane, Beth J. Asch, Joanna Zorn Heilbrunn, and Danielle Cullinane, *The Effect of Employer Sanctions on the Flow of Undocumented Immigrants to the United States*, The RAND Corporation and The Urban Institute, JRI-03, April 1990.

The presentations were based on the following resource papers:

- *The Anticipated Effects of IRCA on U.S. Relations with Mexico* by the Honorable Diego C. Asencio, former Assistant Secretary of State and Chairman of the Commission for the Study of International Migration and Cooperative Economic Development.
- *The Immigration Reform and Control Act of 1986 and Mexican Perceptions of Bilateral Approaches to Immigration Issues* by Carlos Rico F., professor of political science at the Colegio de México.
- *Mexican Immigration, U.S. Investment, and U.S.-Mexican Relations* by David F. Ronfeldt and Monica Ortíz de Oppermann from The RAND Corporation.
- *Emigration as a Safety Valve for Mexico's Labor Market: A Post-IRCA Approximation* by Manuel García y Griego, professor and historian at the Center for International Studies at the Colegio de México.
- *The Domestic and Foreign Policy Consequences of Mexican and Central American Immigration: Mexican-American Perspectives* by Rodolfo O. de la Garza, professor of government at the University of Texas, Nestor Rodríguez, professor of sociology at the University of Houston, and Harry Pachon, professor of political science at Pitzer College.

Session 3: Effects of IRCA on Mexico. How U.S.-Mexico relations are affected may depend in part on how IRCA affects the domestic economic and social conditions in Mexico. It has been estimated that up to one-third of new entrants into the labor forces of several Mexican states are immigrating to the United States, either permanently or temporarily. How many immigrants not eligible for legalization in the United States have returned to Mexico? How is IRCA affecting the perceptions and behavior of would-be immigrants and their families? How is it affecting (or might it affect) "revolving" migratory patterns and, in turn, the pattern of remittances to families remaining in Mexico and the pattern of spending in Mexico by immigrants to the United States?

The presentations were based on the following resource papers:

- *Algunos Impactos de La Ley de Reforma y Control de Inmigración (IRCA) en Una Región de Jalisco de Fuerte Emigración Hacia Estados Unidos de Norteamérica* by Jesús Arroyo Alejandre, Director of the Institute of Regional and Economic Studies at the University of Guadalajara.
- *La Ley Simpson-Rodino: El Punto de Vista de Los Pueblos Expulsores* by Gustavo López Castro, professor of anthropology at the Colegio de Michoacán.

Session 4: IRCA and Inter-American Relations. After Mexico, the Caribbean Islands and Central America are the regions most likely to be affected by U.S. changes in immigration policies. This session was designed to explore the significance of IRCA for these regions. How have the governments in the regions responded to the enactment and implementation of IRCA? What domestic consequences might be expected were IRCA effective in reducing undocumented immigration? What new issues is IRCA raising for these regions?

The presentations were based on the following resource papers:

- *United States–Caribbean Immigration Relations* by Anthony P. Maingot, professor of political science at the Florida International University at Miami.
- *Changing the Rules: The Impact of the Simpson/Rodino Act on Inter-American Diplomacy* by Christopher Mitchell, professor of political science at New York University.

Closing Remarks

We asked two participants to make closing remarks based on what they had heard during the conference and on their considerable experience and understanding of immigration and foreign policy. They were Mario Ojeda Gomez, President of the Colegio de México and member of the Bi-Lateral Commission on the Future of United States–Mexico Relations, and the Honorable Flora MacDonald, Canada's Secretary of State for External Affairs from 1972 to 1980 and Minister of Employment and Immigration from 1984 to 1986. Their closing remarks are reproduced at the end of Part II of these Proceedings.

CONFERENCE HIGHLIGHTS

Because IRCA is being phased in over several years, the conference reached definite conclusions about only a few of the questions initially posed to the presenters. Nevertheless, it generated important insights into the attitudes and concerns of scholars and policymakers about IRCA and about migration in the United States and countries of origin. Here, we highlight only a few prominent points. The individual papers and the summaries of discussion provide details of these and the many other points that arose during the sessions.

Effects on Illegal Immigration

The participants seemed to agree that IRCA had decreased the gross flow of undocumented immigrants across the U.S.-Mexican border. This was attributed primarily to the legalization of some 3 million previously undocumented immigrants who can now cross the border legally. However, there was skepticism about IRCA's deterrent effect on first-time undocumented immigrants—and hence about the effectiveness to date of employer sanctions. This skepticism was tempered somewhat by the awareness that, at the time of the conference, the INS had barely begun enforcing employer sanctions.

Some participants also noted that IRCA itself might induce changes in migratory behavior that could be confused with the effects of employer sanctions on first-time undocumented immigrants. One such change could be the desire for family reunification among the 3 million legalized migrants (40 percent of whom are married), which might increase undocumented immigration independent of labor market considerations. Another change might be increased difficulties crossing the border (perceived or real), which could increase the length of time undocumented immigrants stay in the United States between crossings.

Effects on Countries of Origin and U.S. Bilateral Relations

Considering their subsequent consternation, sending countries, particularly Mexico, acted curiously in not seeking to influence the debate preceding IRCA's passage. The conferees suggested that this restraint was based on at least three factors: (1) the principle of nonintervention in legislative affairs of another nation; (2) the belief that the U.S. Congress would not be able to enact the legislation; and (3) the perception that the status quo was preferable to anything that might result from IRCA.

Once IRCA was enacted (to the surprise of many), fears of mass deportations prompted the governments of Guatemala, El Salvador, and the Dominican Republic to ask the U.S. Administration and Congress for special treatment of their citizens. No such deportations or mass voluntary returns have occurred, and these fears have been replaced, at least in Mexico, by another scenario. Information presented at the conference, although limited, supported the basic premise of a "win-win" scenario: The now legalized population will have a positive effect on sending regions since it will return more frequently, boosting local spending. At the same time, IRCA is expected to have little or no deterrent effect on potential first-time undocumented migrants.

Under the circumstances, the conferees expected Mexico to take a "wait and see" attitude toward IRCA. However, they noted areas of Mexican concern that may strain bilateral relations: (1) the human rights of undocumented immigrants remaining in the United States; (2) the increased violence against would-be undocumented crossers on both sides of the border; and (3) the unilateral implementation of the Replenishment Agricultural Worker (RAW) program, including recruitment and selection of workers in Mexico, which bypasses Mexican governmental channels.

Both Mexican and American conferees were not sanguine about the potential for bilateral negotiations on immigration issues between the United States and Mexico. This skepticism reflected three interrelated considerations. First, Mexico is likely to continue honoring the principle of nonintervention in U.S. affairs. Second, Mexico does not wish to be perceived as encouraging out-migration of its citizens. Third, such negotiations require changes in attitudes about these issues in both countries. However, the conferees recognized the potential for limited consultations in specific areas, for example: information and data exchange; human rights; Central American undocumented immigrants; the RAW program; and issues affecting the "push" factors for would-be emigrants, including trade and foreign debt.

Looking Beyond IRCA

Looking beyond IRCA's immediate effects, the conferees considered its possible long-term legacy and its relationship to other policy domains. The latter included legal immigrants and international affairs.

Conferees expected that the large number of newly legalized immigrants and their concentration in U.S. border states (California, Texas, and Florida) would accelerate and reinforce two already existing trends in the United States:

- Emerging competition between Mexican and Central American workers, since the latter has begun to displace the former in some occupations.
- Growing political influence of the Mexican-American community in local and national affairs.

The latter is expected to eventually lead to greater involvement by the Mexican-American community in Mexico's electoral process and in U.S. policy formulation toward Mexico and Central America. This expectation is generated by two major factors: (1) the potential for increased movement of people back and forth across the border (particularly of the more than 2 million legalized immigrants now residing in the border states); and (2) the fact that two key regions, southern California in the United States and Baja California in Mexico, are among the fastest growing regions in the two nations.

The conferees also considered the motivations behind IRCA and considered proposed changes in legal immigration policy. The latter are designed to increase the number of independent immigrants selected on criteria related to the labor market. At one extreme, some conferees from both sides of the border characterized these efforts as "racist." Others saw them as attempts to build support for a continued "liberal" immigration policy in the United

States. This discussion underlined very real sociocultural issues in the United States, Canada, and the countries of the European Community, which permeate the contemporary immigration debate. These issues range from increasingly restrictionist immigration policies and English-only laws to what kind of assistance, if any, immigrants should receive to help them adjust to a new society. The discussion also included the question of whether immigrants who have never been discriminated against in the United States should benefit from U.S. civil rights legislation and affirmative action. Regardless of positions, the consensus was that these issues cannot be ignored and should be openly discussed.

Finally, the conferees noted that IRCA had placed migration on the foreign policy agenda of sending countries as never before and that this effect was expected to persist. They also noted a trend in policy discussions toward linking immigration, particularly illegal immigration, to drugs and to issues of national security. Migration, legal or illegal, was seen as a permanent feature not only of U.S.-Mexican relations but of relations between industrialized countries and the third world. In this global context, the concern was that introducing restrictive measures to stem flows of people from third-world countries might create an explosive situation, given third-world demographic and economic realities.

ORGANIZATION OF THE REPORT

Part I of these Proceedings presents the opening and keynote addresses and an address summarizing Canada's perspective. Part II contains the summaries of the presentations and discussions of each of the four sessions. The summaries were prepared by the editor of the Proceedings based on the recorded transcript of the conference deliberations, so they may differ in emphasis from the resource papers. Part II also contains the two Closing Remarks addresses. Finally, Part III contains the resource papers, some of which were revised by the authors after the conference.

PALABRAS DE ABIERTA
Guadalupe Gomez Maganda de Anaya

Agradezco a la Corporación RAND y al Instituto Urbano, el haberme distinguido con su invitación como ponente a esta importante reunión, en la que se discutirá un tema de gran trascendencia para nuestro país que es el de la migración de los trabajadores mexicanos, dentro del programa para la investigación de la política de inmigración.

Iniciaré mis comentarios con una breve reflexión sobre algunos aspectos que considero fundamentales en la relación bilateral México–Estados Unidos.

Tal vez pocas naciones en la comunidad internacional tengan la gama de contactos y de interrelación que observamos entre ambos países. La vecindad propicia un enorme campo para la cooperación; no obstante, no está exento de conflictos dados los diferentes niveles de vida de nuestras respectivas sociedades, lo que aunado a la gran asimetría entre ambas naciones, explica la diversidad de enfoques que a veces surgen en torno a un mismo problema.

Es indudable la relevancia del tema de los trabajadores migratorios, dado el interés que suscita en los diversos sectores de la opinión pública de México y de los Estados Unidos. Prueba de ello ha sido la recurrencia en su análisis a través de los años, por las respectivas reuniones interparlamentarias. Pareciera que ya se ha aceptado que el fenómeno es de carácter económico, que corresponde a un mercado internacional de fuerza de trabajo, conformado por las condiciones de oferta en México y las de demanda por parte de la Unión Americana.

La frontera de aproximadamente 3,000 kilómetros entre nuestros países, la necesidad de mano de obra de sectores críticos de la economía de los Estados Unidos y el creciente desempleo de la Mexicana, derivado de la difícil situación económica por la que atraviesa nuestro país, constituyen factores que favorecen el flujo migratorio.

La naturaleza preponderantemente económica del fenómeno obliga a reconocerlo como una cuestión de caracter bilateral, cuyo tratamiento debe tener como punto de partida el respeto a los derechos humanos y laborales de los trabajadores migratorios.

La Asamblea General de las Naciones Unidas, en su resolución del 16 de diciembre de 1977, recomendó a los países miembros: "Adoptar todas las medidas necesarias y apropiadas a fin de que se respeten plenamente en el marco de su legislación nacional, los derechos humanos fundamentales y los derechos sociales adquiridos de todos los trabajadores migratorios, sea cual fuere su situación desde el punto de vista de la inmigración."

De la misma manera que los convenios de braceros que operaron entre 1947 y 1964, no resolvieron el problema y propiciaron maniobras inconvenientes para nuestros trabajadores, ya que al expirar su vigencia, no se dio la sustitución de mano de obra Mexicana por la local, sino que se aprovechó la ventaja de la permanencia de nuestros compatriotas para reducir todavía más los salarios y minimizar las condiciones de trabajo de los contratados; no consideramos tampoco, que la Ley de Reforma y Control a la Inmigración, mejor conocida como Ley Simpson-Rodino, de noviembre de 1986, vaya a alcanzar mejores resultados.

En su primera etapa de recepción de solicitudes de regularización de la calidad migratoria, que concluyo el 4 de mayo de 1988, según datos del Servicio de Inmigración y Naturalizacion, se recibieron 1,601,200 solicitudes, de las cuales 1,138,400 (71 por ciento) correspondieron a México. No conocemos el numero de las solicitudes aceptadas y ahora se encuentra en la segunda etapa, de examenes de idioma e historia de los Estados Unidos, para obtener la tarjeta de residencia permanente. Estaremos pendientes de los avances de la ejecución de la ley.

Es necesaria la comprensión y el apoyo de todos los sectores de la opinion estadounidense, a fin de obtener facilidades para los familiares de aquellos trabajadores que han presentado su solicitud, y por razon de la diferencia de fechas de llegada al país no pueden acogerse a los beneficios de la ley, propiciándose así la desintegración familiar.

Se sabe que en el Congreso estadounidense se han presentado diversas iniciativas para la modificación de la Ley Simpson-Rodino, a fin de que se incluya la clausula de unidad familiar que permita a los familiares de los trabajadores la oportunidad de reunirse.

Ahora bien, en cumplimiento de la Ley Simpson-Rodino se creo la "Comisión para el estudio de la migración internacional y el dessarollo económico cooperativo." También, como resultado de las visitas del señor Comisionada, Alan Nelson, se creó un "Grupo de trabajo México–Estados Unidos sobre migración," que han logrado algunos avances, para solucionar conjuntamente problemas vinculados a la migración de trabajadores mexicanos.

Durante la Reunión Interparlamentaria celebrada en Nueva Orleans en 1988, me correspondió, a nombre de los legisladores mexicanos, proponer la constitución de una comisión parlamentaria bilateral que trabajara sobre los asuntos de migración; por seguir siendo importante objectivo a alcanzar, insistí en la XXIX Reunión con los congresistas estadounidense, que tuvo lugar recientemente en Ixtapa-Zihuatanejo, Gro., para reafirmar la necesidad de su creación.

Hacemos votos porque así sea, pues fundamentalmente nos interesa, como dijo el Presidente de México, Carlos Salinas de Gortari, al inaugurar dicho encuentro: "Asegurar el respeto a los derechos humanos del emigrante y a su dignidad y calidad como trabajador."

Es necesario que se eviten los abusos, los actos de violencia y discriminación contra los trabajadores mexicanos que se internan en los Estados Unidos sin documentos, que desafortunadamente han seguido presentádose y que todos lamentamos.

Hacemos un llamado a los cientificos estadounidenses para que se sumen a nuestros esfuerzos en la búsqueda de la salida del círculo vicioso: Deuda externa, exportación de capitales y estancamiento económico; lo que sin duda alguna nos permitíra crecer y ofrecer así más oportunidades de empleo a los mexicanos, que ya no tendrían que abandonar el país, sino trabajar para México, como es lo deseable.

Son evidentes los beneficios de la migración para México y para los Estados Unidos. Los investigadores estadounidenses han demostrado las ventajas que acarrea para ese país la presencia de los trabajadores. Coincidieron con ello los legisládores estadounidenses en la pasada reunión, uno de ellos originario de California, al firmar que sería difícil imaginar a su estado sin la mano de obra de los indocumentados.

Probablemente el verdadero desafío para los especialistas en migración sea lograr comunicar a la sociedad estadounidense, los resultados de sus investigaciones, que han demostrado que los estereotipos en relacion a los indocumentados, son sólo eso, estereotipos. Se sabe del grado de dificultad que presenta el equilibrar informaciones inexactas. El doctor Jorge Bustamante, Director el Colegio de la Frontera Norte, nos ha comentado la verdadera dimensión del proyecto de la zanja de Otay; magnificada por el representante estadounidense ante la Comision Internacional de Limites y Aguas.

Tal vez la clave para los científicos estadounidenses esté en el acceso a los medios de comunicación masiva y no sólo a los especializados, por los menos en una proporción semenjante a los espacios dedicados a difundir conceptos erróneos del discurso político superficial como: "La amenaza cafe," "La invasion silenciosa," "Recuperar el control de la fronteras" o que los emigrantes mexicanos sólo ingresan a los Estados Unidos para recibir los beneficios del "welfare."

En este sentido, los hallazgos de los investigadores David North y Marion Houston han sido reveladores en cuanto a que la gran mayoria de los inmigrantes indocumentados pagan impuestos y cuotas del seguro social en Estados Unidos, sin tener acceso o sin recibir los beneficios derivados del pago, previstos por las leyes estadounidenses. Otra conclusión interesante es aquella a la que llego Clark Reynolds, sobre la necesidad de un flujo más libre de bienes, capitales y trabajadores.

Por nuestra parte, creemos que se hace necesario precisar con claridad los marcos adecuados para encontrar soluciones conjuntas en materia de migración. Pensamos también que el análisis de problemas comunes favorece el intercambio de información y propicia su resolución.

Basándose en ese intercambio ¿por qué no empezar a cambiar la semántica relativa al tema? Y, por ejemplo, referirnos a los inmigrantes como indocumentados y no como ilegales, dadas las consecuencias jurídicas que el último término conlleva? De un reciente ensayo de Manuel García, del Colegio de México, y James Wilkie, de la Universidad de California, se desprende que no es ilegal buscar trabajo.

Estamos ciertos de que si a las extensas investigaciones realizadas en la materia, agregamos sociedades conscientes de todas las implicaciones y voluntad política en ambos países, seguramente estaríamos muy cercanos al principio de la solución del asunto migratorio. El verdadero desafío para ambas naciones será vencer obstaculos, zanjas y escollos que reduzcan los puntos de conflicto y permitan avanzar en la búsqueda de soluciones.

Los nuevos dirigentes de ambas naciones, con espíritu de dialogo y cooperación, dan margen al optimismo, las acciones concretas lo ratificarán.

OPENING REMARKS
(English Summary)
Guadalupe Gomez Maganda de Anaya

Few nations in the international community have the range of contacts and relationships that we observe between Mexico and the United States. The geographic proximity of our two nations offers a great opportunity for cooperation, while at the same time our differences in economic welfare often contribute to our perceiving the same problems in quite different terms.

It seems there is a consensus about the economic nature of migration and its relationship to an international labor market that is governed by demand for labor from critical sectors of the U.S. economy and by supply of labor from Mexico. Because of its economic nature, the phenomenon should be recognized as a bilateral issue, based on respect of human and labor rights for migrant workers.

Just as the Bracero program—which operated between 1947 and 1964 and did not adequately address the human rights of migrant workers—led to unfavorable actions toward Mexican workers, IRCA is unlikely to achieve positive human rights results. This is an issue that requires the understanding and support of American public opinion. Mexico has repeatedly supported the creation of a Bilateral Parliamentary Commission on Immigration to better ensure the respect of migrants' human rights as workers.

Mexico will monitor closely the process of legalization of undocumented migrants and the steps taken to avoid their separation from family members who are not eligible for legalization. We are aware that the U.S. Congress is presently reviewing different proposals in an effort to include a family-unity clause in its immigration law. In addition, we call on American scientists to join our efforts to find solutions to our problems of external debt and economic stagnation. Once we improve these areas, Mexico will be able to grow and offer more employment opportunities to Mexicans in Mexico so that they will not have to leave their country in search of such opportunities.

The benefits of migration for both countries are evident. American scholars have documented the benefits that the migrants' presence represents for the U.S. economy. Perhaps the real challenge for immigration specialists is to communicate these findings to the American people.

As far as Mexico is concerned, we believe it is necessary to develop appropriate frameworks for finding joint solutions to the various dimensions of the immigration problem. Joint analysis of problems will also assist in their resolution. We suggest that one starting point would be to modify the semantics in the area of immigration, using the term "undocumented," rather than "illegal," when referring to migrant worker status.

The ultimate challenge for both nations is to surpass obstacles and difficulties in order to reduce the points of conflict and to advance the search for solutions.

KEYNOTE ADDRESS
Richard W. Day

Georges Vernez suggested that I discuss how the U.S. Congress views the implementation and effectiveness of the Immigration Reform and Control Act (IRCA) of 1986; what Congress might consider if employer sanctions are ineffective; and what an immigration agenda for Congress might look like over the next several years. He also suggested addressing the issue of bilateral negotiations between the United States and Mexico on immigration issues.

First, to discuss whether or not Congress would view IRCA as effective, we have to understand what Congress intended by it. I can tell you what I understand Senator Simpson and the Senate intended and I also believe I know fairly well what Congressman Mazzoli intended.

Simpson and Mazzoli and their staffs worked together for hours in a room in the center of the capitol. It is called S100 because it is in the exact center—on one side are the bells and lights for activities on the House floor, and on the other side are the bells and lights for activities on the Senate floor. We all sat at a table right in the middle, Mazzoli and his people on the House side and we on the other. And we sat there for hours, day after day, negotiating the original Simpson/Mazzoli bill, which was introduced into both chambers of Congress.

I believe Senator Simpson and Congressman Mazzoli began with an understanding that illegal migration was a phenomenon to be dealt with, not a problem that could be solved. I believe that they saw Mexico, Western agriculture, and some of what Senator Simpson referred to as the executive directors of the national Hispanic organizations as preferring the status quo. The Senator and Congressman knew that this was a political minefield. I heard Senator Simpson say many times that this is an issue that is equal parts emotion, racism, guilt, and fear. And it is.

Did the Senator and Congressman believe that the United States had lost control of its borders? I know that Attorney General Smith used to say that and I think that President Reagan also said it when he came out in support of the Simpson/Mazzoli bill. But what Senator Simpson usually said was that the first duty of a sovereign nation is to control its borders and we do not do that; that is different from saying that we have lost control.

The main intention that Congress had with the bill was to withdraw the magnet of jobs attracting unauthorized workers into the United States. As Senator Simpson would put it, only in America would we have a law stipulating that it is illegal for the worker to enter the country without documents and work but not illegal for the American employer to hire him. And in fact, we were practically the only Western democracy that did not have a law prohibiting the employment of unauthorized workers.

It is true that Congress expected most employers to voluntarily comply with the law. Somebody mentioned 90 or 95 percent today;[1] I think the figure they used to use was 75 percent, which they thought was probably the same number of people that complied with the tax laws. Congress thought that most employers, probably three out of four, would want to do the right thing. If the law said that you were not supposed to hire unauthorized workers, employers would try to determine whether their workers were authorized.

Congress intended that the new law not be an unreasonable burden on employers. I put that on the list of high priorities because Congress, at least Senator Simpson, considered that

---

[1]This keynote address was delivered in the evening after the first day of conference deliberations.

to be an important aspect of the law. The employers should not become policemen. It is not their fault that there are unauthorized people in the country looking for work.

Congress also intended that the law disallow new employment discrimination against lawful workers. It intended that any impact on the labor market resulting from this law should be alleviated as much as possible; hence the "grandfathering" provision. We felt that if we put in such a provision—that employers could keep on their rolls, without risk of penalty, any undocumented workers they had at the time the bill passed—the law would not cause any great disruption in the labor market.

Congress did not intend to have mass deportations or create mass departures (in this country we do not deport people, we allow them to voluntarily depart). Simpson often said that the U.S. Immigration and Naturalization Service (INS) can best use its limited resources by preventing new illegal entries at the border rather than by trying to ferret out long-term illegal residents in the United States. And he frequently reflected that he did not want to be part of a country that was, so to speak, on the hunt for people.

Nor was there an intent to stop Mexican immigration into the United States. In fact, the original Simpson/Mazzoli bill included substantial increases for legal Mexican immigration. The idea was to close the back door but keep the front door open, and in Mexico's case, open it even wider. The original bill doubled the immigration quota for Mexico, doubled it for Canada, and provided that any unused visas by either country would go to the other. We knew that Canada was not going to use any more than 8,000 to 12,000 visas a year—at least they had not in the past—so that, by doubling them from 20,000 to 40,000 a year, the bill gave Mexico a tremendous increase in the number of visas available.

Congress intended that immigration enforcement increase both in the interior and at the border. Congress always suspected that there were many more visa overstayers than was generally assumed and that many more than assumed were non-Mexican. We knew that we were issuing 7 million or more nonimmigrant visas a year, and we used to say that if only 1 percent of those overstayed their visas, there would be a lot of people in the country illegally from all over the world. And the telephone calls we received, during those years when it looked like the bill might be moving, from persons interested in the amnesty program sounded a lot more like they were from Canadians than from Mexicans and other Latin Americans.

Has the bill been effective in carrying out the intentions of Congress? We are spending a lot of time and energy in this area, but really it is much too early to tell. I think we all know that. This is partly because the bill stipulates that the General Accounting Office (GAO) must make certain reports at certain times about the bills' possible effect on employment discrimination, so people have to look at this sooner than they really should. We know the European experience. It took them years to develop a degree of effectiveness. You have to convince the enforcement officials that this is a serious law, that Congress really cares about it. You have to convince judges that fines must be substantial or they are not going to be more than the cost of doing business. And you have to be ready to put resources toward the enforcement. We have not really done any of that yet.

Let me discuss increased enforcement. So far we have not been able to implement that. The bill gives lip service to it. The House even put in an amendment that we would increase the Border Patrol by 50 percent. However, this year's budget from the White House would decrease the INS by, I think, 1,500 positions. Just after we passed this bill intending to beef up enforcement, we got caught with the budget deficit problem, and the INS has had to take its lumps just like everybody else. The Border Patrol tells me that there has actually been a 25 percent reduction in border patrolmen on linewatch, and that means we have not done what we had intended.

Has the bill reduced legal migration from Mexico? I said that Congress did not intend that, and no, the bill has not. Mexican immigration to the United States continues to grow, and Mexico continues to be the largest migrant-sending nation. As you know, more immigrants come every year from Mexico than from all the countries of Europe. As far as I can see, Mexico will be the largest sender of migrants to the United States for the foreseeable future, whether a new legal immigration bill passes or not.

Have there been mass deportations? I think we have all agreed today there have not, but it has been interesting. When the bill was moving, the Mexican news media wrote about expectations that 4 million Mexicans would be deported. We also had President Duarte of El Salvador asking first the President and later Senator Robert Byrd to exclude Salvadorans from employer sanctions. And Elliot Abrams (Department of State) told Senator Simpson that he thought we should exclude El Salvador because we had put a lot of money into that country to keep it afloat over the years, and if it was going to lose its remittances, everything done could be lost. Senator Simpson could not believe this attitude and immediately called Secretary of State Shultz to point out that if we excluded El Salvador, who would be next? Mexico? The same day that Senator Simpson was talking to Secretary Shultz, the United States received a letter from the Dominican Republic—the President had written and asked his countrymen to be excluded from employer sanctions. Within a week, a delegation of 10 members of the Guatemalan Parliament came to visit Senator Simpson. They said that if even as few as 10,000 immigrants came back, it could cause problems. It was interesting how everyone expected these large-scale deportations.

Did Congress alleviate the impact on the labor market? Apparently we did. We have agreed today that there is no labor shortage, and we have also heard evidence that the cost of labor has not increased in the United States. Has the law caused employment discrimination? Apparently there is some employment discrimination, according to the GAO. They tell us that 1 in 6 employers have either begun a practice of refusing to hire noncitizens or they have begun a practice of checking the documents of only those who look or sound like they need to be checked. Of course, the law prohibits both. Employment discrimination is no longer permitted against aliens; the bill is very specific about this and includes stiff penalties for failing to check the documents of every employee, whether it is the employer's mother or somebody completely unknown.

We believe, at least in the Senate Subcommittee, that what we need is more employer education. Employers have to understand that they will not get in trouble for hiring an alien and that they do have to check everybody. We think that the INS has not sufficiently disseminated that information. We also believe that the first GAO survey asked questions in an ambiguous way, so that it might have appeared to the employers being surveyed that the right answer to the question, "Are you hiring noncitizens?" would be, "No I am not," and that the right answer to the question, "Are you checking people who look like they need to be checked?" would be, "Yes I am." I understand that the GAO has taken a look at these questions for its next survey and is trying to avoid that effect.

Has the law become an unreasonable burden on employers? We do not think so. The Chamber of Commerce, the National Association of Manufacturers, and the Business Roundtable tell us that employers have pretty much taken these new requirements in stride. Whether it has become a burden on the small employer, the "ma and pa" operation, I do not know; they do not have the same kind of bookkeeping systems the larger ones do. But we still do not think the law has become an unreasonable burden.

Has there been voluntary compliance? I said we expected a compliance of 75 percent or more. The INS conducted computer-generated random surveys of employers, and the results tell us that more than 80 percent are complying with the law.

Most important, did the law reduce the pull factor? I believe it has, and I think Congress believes it has. But to what extent, we do not know. We credit employer sanctions for a lot of the recent incidents of Latin Americans claiming asylum in South Texas. Before employer sanctions these immigrants would have come into South Texas and gone on to the interior to look for jobs. Now they stop and ask for asylum because that means they get work authority. As you know, as soon as work authority is withheld and immigrants are told, "If you want to pursue an asylum claim beyond the first stage and appeal, you are going to be detained until your appeal is heard," those with frivolous claims stop coming into the United States.

If indeed the law has reduced the flow of unauthorized workers into the United States by 30 percent, I presume that the sponsors of the bill would be satisfied. We actually never thought about percentages because we were not thinking of the law in terms of stopping illegal migration into the United States; we just thought that there was no way to have rational or reasonable border control without having a law that prohibited employers from knowingly hiring people who slipped by that border control.

What might Congress do if the law proves to be ineffective? I think first they would try to more strongly enforce employer sanctions. They would try to move more people into the work place to enforce the law among America's employers. They might also increase the fines and other penalties. If those avenues did not work, then I suppose there would be increased pressure for more drastic measures. I am sure there would be calls for more fences, ditches, or whatever and certainly for more Border Patrolmen. The result would probably be the stern immigration controls referred to this afternoon.

Bilateral negotiations with Mexico? I have never really understood what would be negotiated. Fair labor standards for Mexican workers in the United States, perhaps. That is something reasonable and something that the Mexicans always raise as an issue with us—that their workers be treated like American workers. A temporary worker program? If we were going to have one that dealt only with Mexican workers, that should probably be negotiated. But neither country really seems to want that. We are having bilateral negotiations of a sort through Diego Asencio's commission.[2] The kind of conference we are having here today I suppose could be called some kind of bilateral meeting.

How do you talk to your neighbor about whether or not you should have controls over who enters your country? I think you should talk about the effect this might have on your neighbor and how the effect might be alleviated while still achieving the goal you are trying to accomplish. That is what Senator Simpson did. He decided to go to Mexico and tell them what we were up to and get their response to it. If we were doing something they really did not like, perhaps involving an effect we had not thought of, he wanted to hear about it. As Diego Asencio said, the Senator went to Mexico and met with everyone from the President, President-elect, and most of the Cabinet to their immigration director. However, he did not really succeed. I think the key thing is what President López Portillo said to Senator Simpson, along the lines of: "You have a sovereign right to do what you want with your borders. But I am glad a man as sensitive as you appears to be in charge of immigration up there because I want you to look after our workers. They should be treated just like your workers because they're doing you a lot of good or they would not get work within two weeks after they

<hr>

[2]Diego Asencio is Executive Director of the Commission for the Study of International Migration and Cooperative Economic Development. This Commission was established by IRCA.

arrived." And Senator Simpson asked how we could do that if the Mexican workers were illegal and hiding. López Portillo replied that *that* was the problem.

I spoke this afternoon a little about the legal-immigration reform legislation that is now before the Congress. In a sentence, it is designed to reduce somewhat the dominance of family-connected immigration, but not by much. We are allotting three-fourths of the visas for that and setting one-fourth of the visas aside for more independent immigration. This is designed to create diversity, to give an opportunity to nationals of other countries who now have almost no way to immigrate here. Most of our immigration now comes from about seven or eight countries. They get the lion's share of the visas. Other countries are shut out. And is it any more racist to try to open up our borders a little to these other countries than it was in 1965 to change immigration from those European countries that had a lock on the immigrant visas? Is it a good thing to have diversity or is it a good thing to have 85 percent of the immigrants coming from just two areas of the world? That is the debate in Congress, and not many people in Congress are speaking out against the desirability of having more diversity.

I believe that no matter what we do with legal immigration reform, we will eventually evolve a point system designed to try to select immigrants that will be more in the national interest rather than selecting them through a family connection. Since the law changed in 1965, the skill and education levels of immigrants to the United States have dropped. If we have a point system where points are given for age, education, English language ability, occupations needed in the United States, and experience in those occupations, that should give us a greater likelihood of receiving an immigrant that will be more in the national interest than one who only has a relative in the United States. But even with a point system, most immigrants will continue to come from those countries where the push factors are the strongest.

A VIEW FROM CANADA
Flora MacDonald

One of the real benefits of being at this conference is to see how different the situation is in Canada from how it is in the United States. In many ways, we share experiences. But I think that in the field of immigration and refugee policy, we have quite different challenges to meet and goals to achieve.

I want to situate Canada for you in this sense. We do, in fact, have a common border of 5,000 miles with the United States. We have a common border as well with the Soviet Union. We are the only country in the world that geographically lies between the two superpowers, and we in Canada think of that quite frequently. We do not have much movement from either side. We have some concerns about what goes on under our arctic ice cap; we are not sure whose nuclear-powered submarines are lurking there and we do not have any means of finding out. But we do not have mass migrations of people from countries on either side of us. So in that sense, our situation with regard to immigration and refugee policy is quite different from that of the United States.

I also want to mention something about Canada's continuing history. We, like the United States, are a country of immigrants. We have all come from somewhere, except for our native people, who receive a lot of attention and time in Canada. It is important to us that we continue the process of integration and that Canadians who have been in the country for both longer and shorter periods of time respect the integrity of the immigration system.

Our immigration has been as high as 400,000 some years and as low as 80,000 in the midst of the recession of the early 1980s. It is on a climb again. It is back up to 160,000 this year, and the goal is to increase it substantially in the years ahead. We do not have any limits.

The figure of 160,000 this year is a forecast. We try to forecast because family reunification is the major basis of our immigration policy and family reunification depends on the efforts of those within the country to ensure that their relatives come to Canada. Now we know, approximately, what that number will be in any given year, but it often exceeds the forecast; last year, for example, it exceeded by some 10,000. So we can only approximate what the immigration level will be for any given year.

I mentioned that the immigration levels this year are 160,000. Family reunification is 60,000. Refugees account for about 40,000, half of whom are government-sponsored. The people coming because of job-related reasons or because of the labor market are about 30,000 and their dependents about another 30,000. So the forecast of 160,000 really accounts for 40,000 refugees, 60,000 for family reunification, and 60,000 for job-related reasons and dependents.

The nature of our immigration has been changing drastically over recent years. In the last few years, over 50 percent of our immigration has come from Asia, primarily from India and Pakistan but as well from other countries in Southeast Asia. That, of course, and I will come back to that, is creating its own tensions within Canada. However, the moment that people come into the country as landed immigrants, they are extended all social benefits in Canada. We have a very open system regarding immigration policy. It is tremendously important to us that that continue, and I will give you one of the reasons why. Our population in Canada is 25 million. If you were to forecast ahead the population of Canada, based on the present birth rate, our population in the year 2020 would be 18 million. We probably have one of the lowest birth rates in the world, and we have a real concern that that population drop does not take place. That is very much on the minds of people in Canada.

The fact is that something has been occurring in recent years which is undermining the integrity of our immigration system. I want to move now from immigration to refugee matters. In the past, Canada was not a country of first asylum. People did come to Canada from refugee camps that had been established in other parts of the world, and we had and have been very open throughout our history to refugees. I think of movements where people have come into Canada from Hungary, from Uganda, from Czechoslovakia, and so forth, and probably the most recent effort in this regard was the movement from Vietnam.

All of these things have created a good impression in Canada. The Vietnamese boat people, for instance, were a remarkable experience. I was Foreign Minister at the time and overnight I moved the levels of refugee intake from Vietnam from 5,000 to 50,000. That is a fairly sizable increase from the perspective of asking people to accept it. I knew the increase would not go down easily in the country, so I went on national television and challenged the Canadian people to accept the sponsorship of families from Vietnam. I said the government would match costs for every family that you or your organization, church, or City Council accepts. And in fact, in the first year, we took in something like 70,000 refugees from Vietnam, all of whom had the costs of their first year totally provided by either the Canadian people directly or the Canadian government. That brought about a very good feeling of the Canadian people toward the individuals who were coming in as refugees. The ties and the links between them continue to this day.

As I mentioned, we have a very open refugee policy, probably the most open in the world. And this meant that while the government sponsored a great many refugees, we also had a policy where anybody who landed in Canada and who claimed to be a refugee could stay until all of the judicial reviews were completed, either through the refugee system or through the immigration appeals system.

The word seemed to get about the world that Canada was something of an easy touch if you wanted to jump the immigration queue and get in. What we have seen happening in the last three or four years was a massive number of people coming in, primarily by plane and some by ship. Within two or three years, we had a backlog of 85,000 refugees waiting to go through the review processes, which at this point were taking four to six years. We knew we had a problem and we knew we had to do something about it.

As Canadians saw the abuses that were taking place, they began to turn off to immigration in a major way, and that threatened our whole immigration policy. Now I am talking about abuses that in many ways were quite funny. For instance, we had large numbers of people coming from Portugal who claimed, while they were wearing crucifixes, that they were subjected to religious persecution in their country because they were Jehovah's Witnesses. They could not explain what Jehovah's Witnesses were, but they had been told to plead religious persecution. We had people coming for a variety of reasons. When I was Immigration Minister, I was very concerned with the coup d'état in Haiti and that Duvalier would come to Canada and claim to be a refugee. I wondered what I would do if that happened as it was a very real possibility.

One of the things I realized was that we had to develop legislation to begin to control the abuses. Seventy percent of the people coming in and claiming to be refugees were people who landed immediately, either by ship or by plane. Thirty percent were people who had actually come as visitors but who wanted to apply as landed immigrants; they were turned down from applying from within the country and they then claimed to be refugees because that would keep them from being sent back. It became very difficult to contemplate sending thousands of people back because, at this point, they would probably have Canadian children and the children could claim their parents. It became very complicated. Forty percent of the 85,000 claimants we found in 1988 had been in the country less than six months, so you can see the upward escalation that was taking place. Last year we finally put into effect legislation that we had been trying to get through the House in one way or another for two years. I thought we were pretty slow until I heard about the processes that have taken place in the U.S. Congress!

Legislation is not the only way that we have tried to control this major influx into Canada. Another method was limited visa applications. We do not have visas that apply to many countries in the world, but when the Portuguese situation developed that I mentioned, we did put visas on applications from Portugal as well as from Turkey. Also, seeking at the outset to prevent embarkation of improperly documented migrants, we went into major educational programs with the airlines to have the training of airline personnel more carefully carried out.

Let me tell you a bit about the legislation so that you can compare it with what has been done in the United States, keeping in mind, of course, that it is designed to deal with two quite different situations. We decided that, to really turn this situation around, we had to instigate high-level reviews, right at the outset, as quickly as possible. What we now do is to have an initial screening by immigration officials, probably within two weeks of the arrival of people claiming to be refugees. This initial immigration screening determines whether or not there is any legitimacy to the case. For example, the people coming from Portugal that I talked about earlier did not have any kind of legitimate claim to be refugees. Nor do we believe that people coming secondarily from, say, West Germany—though they may have been there from India— have a right to jump their refugee status in West Germany and come to Canada and ask for another refugee status. These types of things are caught in the initial screening.

Furthermore, we understood that the only way that we could get the support of refugee advocacy groups and others who were concerned would be if we made the system absolutely as water tight as possible so we would not be turning away any legitimate refugees. Therefore, within anywhere from 8 to 10 weeks after the initial screening, the individual goes before a high-level review panel. This panel consists of an adjudicator and an independent agent, who has been selected on the basis of work done in the refugee field over the years. I am talking about people who are lawyers, professors, teachers, and so on. We have set up a great number of these panels; there are probably now about 250 of them operating across the country. They hear two cases a day, and they go into the case background in great detail. The head of the Immigration Refugee Board is our former Chairman of the Canadian-Cuban Human Rights Commission, who is recognized worldwide as one of the great workers in the field of human rights. When a case comes before the two-member panel, if only one of the two members agrees there is any legitimacy to the refugee claim, the person is allowed to become a landed immigrant. Both panel members would have to refuse to hear a case before a person could be turned back.

This new legislation and practice came into effect the first of January 1989. It has already shown that legitimate refugees are going to be admitted to Canada. There have been very few refusals in the hearings so far, but when one does take place, the person is sent back; this has sent the word out around the world that we resolve refugee status within three months. This means people cannot wait three or five years to establish themselves in Canada before their case is heard. The fact is that Canada is a long way to come for most people to spend three months and go back again.

In December of 1988, there were 6,700 applications for refugee status. In the first three months of 1989, there were 3,300. That is a tremendous drop, but as I say, people are now aware that the initial screening and the Immigration Refugee Board hearings are all completed within a three-month period.

At the same time that this is going on, we have duplicate boards that are hearing the 85,000 cases in the backlog that has been creating such a political problem in Canada. The intake has greatly decreased, and what we see is that integrity is being restored to the system—and that is the goal. Once integrity is gradually restored, Canadians will believe in the refugee and immigration processes once again, particularly the refugee process. David Martin, whom some of you will know, describes our process as a pilot process for the whole world. It is critical for us to restore confidence in immigration. We have a massive problem ahead of us if we do not.

Over 50 percent of our immigration is now coming from Asia. That is creating new problems, problems that we have to adjust to. We have had over the years large quantities of immigrants from Europe, from the West Indies, and so on. But now the greater part of our immigration comes from entirely different cultures, and there will no doubt be a lot of adjustment difficulty along the way.

One thing I might say in closing is that we have a sizable number of people coming from Central America, but we have very few immigrating from Mexico. We have much stronger ties in this way with the countries of Central America—Guatemala, El Salvador, and so on—than we have with Mexico. We have very good relations with Mexico in the area of guest agricultural workers and I think that can be said by both Canada and the United States. But as far as permanent immigration from Mexico is concerned, Canada's situation is very different from that of the United States.

PART II

SUMMARY OF SESSIONS AND CLOSING REMARKS

SESSION 1: EFFECTS OF IRCA ON ILLEGAL IMMIGRATION

The overall goal of the 1986 Immigration Reform and Control Act (IRCA) is to legalize and regulate immigration to the United States. Given this goal, one of its primary objectives is to curb, if not eliminate, the flow of undocumented workers into the country. The success or failure of IRCA will be judged largely by how well it meets this objective.

To meet this objective, the law contains several provisions that are intended to discourage employers from hiring undocumented workers. Often referred to as "employer sanctions," these provisions

- prohibit all employers in the nation from hiring undocumented workers,
- require that all employers complete an employment eligibility verification form (I-9) for each new employee,
- establish graduated civil and criminal penalties for employers who hire undocumented workers.

In addition to these measures, the law aims to curb undocumented immigration through enhanced border interdiction. For that purpose, Congress authorized a 50 percent increase in the 3,600 Border Patrol personnel for FY87 and FY88.

The first session of the conference explored the extent to which IRCA is affecting the flow of undocumented immigrants across the U.S.-Mexican border.

SUMMARY OF PRESENTATIONS

This session included three presentations of ongoing empirical work. The first was made by Michael White of The Urban Institute, the second by Jorge Bustamante of the Colegio de la Frontera Norte, and the third by Beth Asch and Keith Crane of The RAND Corporation.

Several key provisions of IRCA are still being implemented, and the enforcement of "employer sanctions" is in its initial phase. Consequently, the presenters stressed that their findings were necessarily tentative and that they planned to continue studying this question into 1990. As the summary makes clear, there is some disparity in findings among the studies, which may reflect differences in data, analytical approaches, and/or the preliminary nature of these findings. The first study concluded that IRCA's employer sanctions have decreased the flow of undocumented workers, while the other two found no firm evidence to support that conclusion.

The Effects of IRCA on the Pattern of Apprehensions at the Border
by Michael J. White, Frank D. Bean, and Thomas J. Espenshade[1]

Michael White gave this presentation that described a time-series analysis of "linewatch apprehensions"—that is, apprehensions of undocumented immigrants made by the U.S. Immigration and Naturalization Service (INS) at the U.S.-Mexican border.

---

[1]A revised version of this paper was subsequently released as *The U.S. Immigration Reform and Control Act and Undocumented Immigration to the United States* by Michael J. White, Frank D. Bean, and Thomas J. Espenshade, The Urban Institute, PRIP-UI-5, July 1989.

Linewatch apprehensions are considered an indicator of the flow of undocumented immigrants across the border. If they are a reliable indicator, differences in apprehensions before and after IRCA's passage could be used to measure IRCA's effect on the flow. However, other factors could also affect the flow, and those effects could be confounded with IRCA's. Such factors include seasonal fluctuations, labor market conditions in the United States and Mexico, and the level of enforcement activities by the INS Border Patrol (linewatch hours).

Linewatch apprehensions did, in fact, drop by 50 percent between November 1986 (when IRCA was enacted) and May 1988. Press reports have attributed that drop to IRCA's implementation. However, White cautioned against such a "naive" interpretation because of several confounding factors. First, the magnitude of the post-IRCA drop is extremely sensitive to the time periods being compared. A comparison over a longer period of time—i.e., between average apprehensions in years 1983 to 1986 and average apprehensions in post-IRCA years 1987 and 1988—shows a decline of only 6 percent.

Second, a longer-term examination of linewatch apprehensions shows that they display a strong seasonal pattern: Apprehensions peak nearly every year in the spring (March, April, and May) and reach their lowest point in the month of December. Third, the post-IRCA drop in linewatch apprehensions occurred during the same time (second half of 1987 and 1988) that linewatch hours were also steadily declining.

To control for these confounding factors and isolate the effects of various IRCA provisions, the study developed a statistical time-series model that (1) uses the entire time-series of linewatch apprehensions since 1977; (2) controls for other push-pull factors that may influence emigration decisions; and (3) accounts for changes in INS linewatch hours, INS enforcement expenditures, and the IRCA legalization program for special agricultural workers (SAW). The push-pull factors include wages and unemployment rates in the United States, and income levels, unemployment rates, and size increases of the prime migration population in Mexico.

Estimates derived from the model suggest that IRCA has had multifaceted effects. Such effects include a decline in apprehensions due to (1) the legalization program for agricultural workers, which has removed people from the pools of "would be" undocumented crossers, and (2) a decline in linewatch hours throughout 1987 and into 1988. The latter was caused by personnel being redirected from Border Patrol activities to IRCA-mandated employer-education efforts. The model also estimates a 30 percent residual reduction in number of apprehensions that was attributed to other IRCA influences, including deterrence and implementation of employer sanctions.

Undocumented Mexican-U.S. Migration: Preliminary Trends from the Project Canyon Zapata by Jorge A. Bustamante

Dr. Jorge Bustamante described an analysis based on an innovative, unique approach to establishing trends in undocumented migration—actually counting the number, and interviewing some, of the would-be immigrants gathered at two major crossing locations on the Mexican-U.S. border. He also offered some observations on the intent of IRCA.

He noted that an estimated 83 percent of all crossings over that 3,000-kilometer border take place at six locations: Tijuana, Mexicali, Nogales, Ciudad Juarez, Matamoros, and Nuevo Laredo. A 1985 CONAPO (Consejo Nacional de Población) study of apprehended undocumented migrants shows that half of them crossed through the city of Tijuana, mostly (85 percent) at two specific locations: "El Bordo" and "Canyon Zapata." The latter was the single most active crossing point along the border until the summer of 1988, when Border Patrol enforcement was intensified there. Responding to this recent pressure, undocumented immigrants have increasingly used "El Bordo," which has now supplanted Canyon Zapata as the busiest crossing point.

Beginning in August 1986, Dr. Bustamante's research team has taken a daily count of those who gather at Canyon Zapata waiting for sunset before they begin the journey north. This count is based on three photographs taken daily at two hours, one hour, and 10 minutes before sunset. Because of the increased activity at El Bordo, the team has also been counting there since September 1988.

Beginning in April 1987, the counts have been complemented by interviews with a sample of would-be crossers at all six crossing locations. At each site, about 75 individuals are interviewed over the course of three days each week. To date, more than 10,000 interviews have been completed covering histories of immigration, places of origin and destination, sociodemographic characteristics, and work experience in the United States.

So far the data suggest some important trends:

(1) There seems to be an increase in the proportion of women waiting to cross at Canyon Zapata, from one in four at the beginning of the study to one in three more recently.

(2) Would-be crossers have an average of 3 to 4 years more schooling than the Mexican population average, and the women are somewhat more educated than the men.

(3) Socioeconomic characteristics of would-be immigrants differ by crossing location. Compared with people crossing from Tijuana into California, would-be crossers into Texas are poorer, less educated, and more likely to be men, and they pay less for their journey north. These differences may be partly explained by differences in labor market opportunities between California (primarily in the service and construction sectors) and Texas (primarily in agriculture). The lower cost of migration probably reflects the typically shorter distance into Texas.

(4) While costs of migration—including payments to "coyotes"—have increased since the passage of IRCA, they have generally not exceeded Mexico's national inflation rate.

Analysis of the data led Bustamante to tentatively conclude that (a) IRCA has not stopped undocumented immigration into the United States and (b) it is too soon to establish whether IRCA has led to a decline in migration flows. Bustamante argued that these conclusions are supported by "the declining trend data for men, but [the] increase in 1987 for women" and that "one should wait for 1989 data for a more definite answer."

Bustamante ended his presentation with some comments on the intent of IRCA. In his view, IRCA was designed less to stop undocumented immigration than to satisfy ideological and political pressures in the United States. He observed that "a country that is preoccupied with regaining control of its borders would be preoccupied with marking its borders. . . ." However, there are no such markings at Canyon Zapata, and would-be crossers actually gather on U.S. soil.

Further, he characterized the legalization provisions of IRCA as "racist." His rationale was that by requiring continuous residence in the United States since 1982, IRCA is prejudicial against Mexican immigrants who typically travel back and forth between the two countries. He also suggested that IRCA may have been designed as a precautionary measure against a recession and as an alternative to bilateral negotiations to resolve the undocumented immigration problem—since the latter would have resulted in increased labor costs for U.S. employers.

The Effect of Employer Sanctions on the Flow of Undocumented Immigrants to the United States by Beth J. Asch and Keith W. Crane[2]

Beth Asch and Keith Crane described and presented preliminary results from their study of changes in immigration flows since IRCA. No single indicator directly measures the flow of all undocumented immigrant groups. Further, all currently available indicators have other limitations, as well. Consequently, Asch and Crane are analyzing changes in several indicators to assess whether the prohibition against hiring undocumented workers, and its enforcement to date, have affected flows of undocumented immigrants. The study examines indicators of two types: (1) indicators of active entry into the United States, including total INS Border Patrol apprehensions and requests for tourist visas and asylum applications; and (2) economic indicators, including changes in wages in occupations with a large number of immigrants and in employers' applications for guest workers. At the time of the conference, their work focused primarily on analyzing changes in INS apprehensions and in wages.

Their approach to analyzing apprehensions differs somewhat from White, Bean, and Espenshade's (see above). Their focus is on total border patrol apprehensions, that is, the sum of linewatch apprehensions and apprehensions made at airports, bus stops, highway checkpoints, and other sites in the immediate interior. Their estimations use a predictive residual method. That method estimates the number of apprehensions that would have otherwise taken place in 1987 and 1988, after accounting for three major changes: (1) a decline in enforcement at the border, i.e., in linewatch hours allocated; (2) a decline in enforcement in the immediate interior;[3] and (3) the legalization applications of more than 3 million previously undocumented immigrants, who are awaiting or were granted temporary residence and can now cross the border legally.[4] The effect of employer sanctions and/or implementation is then measured by the difference between "predicted" and "actual" apprehensions.

Predicted apprehensions exceeded actual apprehensions in 1987, but were not significantly different in 1988, suggesting that IRCA's employer sanctions had had an effect in 1987, but not in 1988. Further, Asch and Crane reported that they found no changes attributable to IRCA between 1987 and 1988 in wages of entry-level occupations. These findings were based on an eight-city survey of wages in two occupations, dish washing and car washing, which past studies have shown to employ a high proportion of undocumented workers. Although there was a post-IRCA increase of 20 percent in applications for guest workers under the H-2 and H-2A programs, the increase in actual number (4,000) was too small to mean very much relative to the size of the U.S. labor market.

SUMMARY OF DISCUSSION

The discussion following these presentations centered on (1) issues affecting the interpretations of these preliminary findings and (2) the question of IRCA's intent. Overall, the participants' sense seemed to be that IRCA had decreased the *circulation* of undocumented immigrants across the U.S.-Mexican border through its provisions that allow for legalization of

---

[2]Complete findings from this study are contained in Keith W. Crane, Beth J. Asch, Joanna Zorn Heilbrunn, and Danielle Cullinane, *The Effect of Employer Sanctions on the Flow of Undocumented Immigrants to the United States,* The RAND Corporation and The Urban Institute, JRI-03, April 1990.

[3]This is suggested by a decline of 10 percentage points in the share of non-linewatch apprehensions relative to total apprehensions.

[4]Asch and Crane estimated that this population would have accounted for 135,000 to 400,000 additional apprehensions, with the most likely figure placed at the midpoint of this range.

some 3 million undocumented immigrants already in the United States. However, there was a prevailing skepticism about IRCA's deterrent effect on first-time undocumented immigrants and, hence, about the effectiveness, so far, of employer sanctions. Highlights of the discussion are summarized below.

Problems of Measurement

The discussion gave considerable attention to the weaknesses in indirect measures, especially apprehensions statistics, used to estimate changes in the undocumented immigration flow. One criticism was that they reflect an essentially administrative process whose relationship to the flow is unclear. An individual may be apprehended several times before crossing successfully, but with each interception, he/she will appear in the statistics as a *new* apprehension. Hence, apprehensions may be an unreliable proxy for the number of undocumented immigrants crossing successfully into the United States.

Douglas Massey illustrated the problem vividly. In interviewing immigrants, he used to ask how many times they had tried crossing into the United States and how many times they had been apprehended while trying. Nearly always, the number of tries exceeded the number of apprehensions by one. It was noted that this problem similarly affects the daily counts of would-be crossers at Canyon Zapata and El Bordo: Those apprehended might show up the next day at the same location to attempt another crossing.

A second problem with INS apprehensions is that they are sensitive to fluctuations in level of enforcement. There was skepticism that the measures of Border Patrol linewatch hours used in the modeling fully accounted for variations in enforcement effectiveness. The technology used to detect crossers has continuously improved. Thus, a linewatch hour in 1980 may not have been as productive as a linewatch hour in 1988—as two of the studies assumed. Also, linewatch hours include time spent on activities other than the interdiction of undocumented immigration. They also include activities directed at drug traffic interdiction. The share of time devoted to one or the other has varied over time, and this variation is not captured by the INS linewatch-hours statistics.

Despite these problems, several participants thought all the efforts were worthwhile because they have begun to tease out, carefully and systematically, the influences of different factors that affect apprehensions statistics. Moreover, rather than being cause for alarm, the disparities between the presentations underline one of the great strengths of interactive scientific discourse. Initial disparities and apparent contradictions may be more beneficial than coming up with the "definitive" answer on the first try. Attempts to understand and resolve these disparities are more likely to go beyond naive interpretations and "canned" methodologies and lead to genuine breakthroughs—for both science and policy. This is particularly important in the controversial climate and context that surrounded IRCA's formulation and now surround its implementation.

Two additional comments were made regarding data and measurements. One participant noted that the data show only a small increase in the number of H-2 and H-2A guest worker applications since the passage of IRCA. He suggested that this may reflect a surplus of agricultural workers due to the unexpectedly large number of SAW program applications (in excess of 1.3 million). Hence, one would not expect agricultural and other employers to need and apply for H-2 or H-2A licenses.

Another participant suggested that two other sources of possibly firmer data are available to assess IRCA's effects on the flow of undocumented immigrants. Increases in both sources

32

would indicate a belief by would-be immigrants that IRCA's increase of the Border Patrol is discouraging illegal border crossing.

The first is data on the number and characteristics of applicants for nonimmigrant visas (NIV) who have been denied such a visa (95 percent of NIV applications are for tourist visas). NIV applications from Mexico have increased steadily from 620,000 in 1986 to 667,000 in 1987 and 819,000 in 1988; they are expected to reach more than 1 million in 1989. The data on these applications are available from the Department of State and include the applicants' age, economic status, origin in the home country, destination in the United States, and reasons for visiting.[5] The nature of these applications and the applicants' reasons for visiting may indicate that some people are using this avenue instead of crossing illegally.

A second potential source is data on the results of secondary inspections. In these INS inspections, a legitimate visa holder may be identified as entering with illegal intentions: That is, his demeanor, number of dependents, and possessions may belie his stated intention of touring or visiting temporarily. An examination of pre- versus post-IRCA trends in numbers and characteristics of the individuals denied entry at this inspection might help to understand further the effects of IRCA on undocumented immigration.

Distinguishing IRCA's Effects on Different Populations

The three studies used data that, at best, measure the gross flow of immigrants into the United States. However, this flow comprises three different subgroups of immigrants, and IRCA may affect each differently. These subgroups are:

1. *First-time crossers*, i.e., undocumented immigrants leaving Mexico to come to the United States for the first time.
2. *Undocumented repeat immigrants* who move back and forth across the border. This subgroup has been affected by IRCA's legalization programs, which granted temporary residence to more than 3 million undocumented immigrants. Obviously, those who are now "legalized" no longer contribute to this type of undocumented flow.
3. *Grandfathered and other undocumented immigrants remaining in the United States.* This subgroup also used to cross back and forth, but IRCA's effects may well have increased its propensity to stay put. Inhibition of its movement would also diminish the revolving flow of undocumented workers.

It will be difficult to separate the effects of IRCA on the first subgroup (the primary group targeted by "employer sanctions") from effects on the other two. Two of the studies here attempt to account for the effects that the legalization programs had on the number of undocumented immigrant crossings (subgroup 2) but not for the effects on subgroup 3.

Net Effects of the Various IRCA Provisions

The discussion raised another issue analogous to distinguishing IRCA's effects on different subgroups: attributing measured effects to one or more of IRCA's many provisions. The comments reflected a strong belief that research terms should be used with greater clarity and specificity, and that semantic imprecision reflected current problems in sorting out effects. One participant observed that the presenters often talked about "IRCA's effects" when they were actually looking at the effects of employer sanctions.

---

[5]These data were subsequently analyzed and the findings reported in Crane, Asch, Heilbrunn, and Cullinane, *The Effect of Employer Sanctions.*

The effectiveness of employer sanctions is certainly a key policy issue and the main reason for attempting to separately estimate how legalization, border enforcement, and employer sanctions affect illegal immigration. However, the effectiveness of employer sanctions is inherently ambiguous because it depends on several mechanisms, ranging from deterrence to INS enforcement of employer requirements to voluntary employer compliance. It was pointed out that the INS is currently in more of an employer "education" mode than an "enforcement" mode and that enforcement and use of sanctions are just beginning. Hence, whatever effects that cannot be fully attributed to legalization must be attributed to voluntary compliance, deterrence of would-be immigrants, and/or a reduction in the revolving flow of the grandfathered and other undocumented immigrants already in the United States.

Asch and Crane's measurement of such a residual effect in 1987, but not in 1988, might be attributed to these other factors. There was some speculation that the 1987 effect reflected a "wait and see" attitude among would-be immigrants immediately following the passage of IRCA, possibly due to the well-publicized stories about forthcoming mass deportations to Mexico. The disappearance of the residual effect in 1988 could indicate that crossings resumed after it became clear that deportations and other feared IRCA effects were failing to materialize.

The Influence of Other Factors

Several participants suggested that, besides the non-IRCA factors accounted for by the studies, other factors are likely to affect the long-term potential for illegal immigration from Mexico into the United States. One is a reduced emigration potential in Mexico. A second is change in the U.S. political climate. And a third is a changing attitude in the established Mexican-American community.

Regarding the first point, Jesús Arroyo Alejandre said his studies indicate that potential migration from the rural areas of western Mexico to the United States is continuing to decrease. This decrease results partly from reduced fertility rates and partly from the redirection of migration toward small- and middle-sized Mexican cities where immigrants create their own "popular" economy. However, another participant noted that these factors may be counterbalanced by increased pressures for emigration from Mexico: the decline in opportunities for economic upward mobility and growing political dissatisfaction in Mexico.

It was noted that two other changes may encourage Mexican immigrants to stay in the United States, thus reducing the revolving flow. One change is in the political position of Mexican Americans. One participant stated that, as a group, Mexican Americans are now less vulnerable to "abuses by political and legal authorities," and this is making the United States a more attractive permanent residence. Another change is in the attitude of Mexican Americans toward Mexican immigrants. In the past, that attitude oscillated between hostility and indifference; now it oscillates between indifference and support. As a result, Mexican Americans are making efforts that are new in scope and intensity to assimilate Mexican immigrants. These developments, in turn, increase Mexican immigrants' propensity to stay.

Intent of IRCA

Another theme in the discussion was the intent of IRCA. This is a highly significant issue because people will assess IRCA's success or failure depending on how they view its intent. Conference participants differed on this issue. Some evidently assumed IRCA's intent was to "stop undocumented immigration altogether," and that if IRCA did not do this it would be considered a total failure. Others saw IRCA as one of several instruments for reducing, but not stopping, undocumented immigration. As one participant directly involved in the formulation of IRCA said, "If IRCA (i.e., employer sanctions) reduced undocumented immigration by 30 percent, we might have hoped for more, but we will take it."

Several participants took strong exception to Jorge Bustamante's statement that "racism" informed IRCA's concern with "control of the border." Diego Asencio, who was involved in formulating the legislation, commented that

> if any racist elements intruded, they sure got by me. This is not to say that racism does not exist, either in the United States or in the Congress of the United States, but certainly I would think that the people who worked on the legislation leaned over backwards to avoid, as much as possible, any discriminatory measures. And I would also say that I consider it entirely consistent with a perfectly proper posture to concern oneself with continuing violations of the border and in legalities without [having it] construed as racism.

SESSION 2: EFFECTS OF IRCA ON U.S.-MEXICO RELATIONS

Although undocumented immigrants to the United States come from nearly every country in the world, no one country is expected to be more affected by IRCA than Mexico. It has been estimated that more than half of the undocumented immigrants residing in the United States are Mexicans; and more than two out of three of the 3.1 million applicants to IRCA's legalization programs are Mexicans. Session 2 explored questions of how IRCA has affected (in the short run) and is anticipated to affect (in the longer run) U.S.-Mexico relations: Is it affecting the perceptions of Mexican elites about immigration and other important issues in U.S.-Mexican relations? What is the significance for Mexico, for the United States, and for the future of their bilateral relations of the legalization (and eventual naturalization) of nearly 2 million Mexicans residing in the United States? Are new institutional arrangements between the two countries desirable and feasible to help address issues of immigration?

SUMMARY OF PRESENTATIONS

The Anticipated Effects of IRCA on U.S. Relations with Mexico
by Diego C. Asencio

To establish the background for this presentation, Diego Asencio pointed out that before IRCA was enacted the U.S. Department of State attempted to consult with the Mexican government on Mexican-U.S. immigration issues. For several reasons, the Mexican government refused these overtures. However, since the enactment of IRCA, Mexican (and U.S.) attitudes have changed. These changes, according to Asencio, create "an historic opportunity to engage in a bilateral approach to the problem . . . and take into account some of the things that would tend to ameliorate immigration pressures."

Drafting and passage of IRCA were driven largely by domestic, internal, and political considerations. Precious few foreign policy implications entered into the debate. Still, efforts were made in 1981, 1982, and 1983 to place the Mexican government's views before Congress while IRCA was under consideration.

However, the Mexican government "stonewalled," according to Asencio, for very good reasons. First, Mexico considered that any change in U.S. immigration policy would work to Mexico's detriment. Second, Mexico expected that if it entered into such consultations, sooner or later it would be asked to "patrol its side of the border to help prevent illegal crossings." It was not, of course, prepared to do that. Third, Mexico was concerned that the United States might use immigration as a bargaining chip. Asencio believes that this was a misreading of how the U.S. Congress works: The reality of U.S. politics constrains Congress from making tradeoffs of that sort. The fourth reason was that engaging in such consultations would constitute an intrusion into the domestic political concerns of another nation. That would have meant breaking a principle of noninterference, a principle held very seriously in Mexico. Finally, like many people in the United States, the Mexican government did not expect IRCA to pass. Hence, why enter into consultations about it?

Experience in the post-IRCA period has been quite different, again for perfectly understandable reasons. IRCA had passed, it was being implemented, and the Mexican government had to deal with it. Asencio noted that one indication of Mexico's change is the welcome it has extended to the Commission for the Study of International Migration and Cooperative Economic Development (CSIMCED), which he chairs.

The creation of this Commission signals a new way of thinking for the United States. And it offers a second chance to take "into account some of the things that would tend to ameliorate immigration pressures." It is also a unique chance because it was mandated by Congress and is not simply an elaboration of an Executive Branch policy. Cynics believe the Commission was created to soften whatever "negative blows" Mexico and other countries may receive as a result of IRCA (i.e., a kind of carrot to accompany the big stick). Asencio asserted, in fact, that the architect of the provision creating the Commission

> distinctly felt that we had an obligation to do something other than react to the domestic political considerations driving IRCA, and to see what could be done with Mexico and other countries in the hemisphere to eliminate the so-called push factors and complement whatever the sanctions program would do to the pull factors.

Asencio then addressed the question of what role immigration would play in U.S.-Mexico relations over the next five years. He described two extreme scenarios. The first is predicated on (a) a strong economic recovery of the Mexican economy, (b) the legalization of 2 million Mexican workers in the United States, and (c) family reunification through legal means. This combination of elements would diminish pressures for undocumented emigration from Mexico, and Mexican migration into the United States would largely fade from public attention. A second, less favorable, scenario anticipates continued economic difficulties in Mexico and mounting pressures for undocumented emigration. In this event, the issue would return to center stage, which would increase pressure for extreme measures to control the border.

Nevertheless, the American perception and response to Mexican migration will depend largely on developments in the U.S. labor market. If, as some analysts forecast, the market demands higher skills than the traditional unskilled Mexican migrant has, pull factors will diminish. However, an unskilled-labor shortage might make room for the orderly immigration of seasonal or permanent workers in the service and agricultural sectors. In practice, if not design, the SAW (special agricultural worker) and RAW (replenishment agricultural worker) programs may become the de facto institutionalization of a guest-worker program for thousands of Mexican workers.

Asencio concluded his presentation by suggesting that the time may be ripe to strengthen formal mechanisms for bilateral consultations on immigration matters. The primary means would be the U.S.-Mexican consultative mechanism jointly chaired by the U.S. Secretary of State and the Mexican Foreign Ministry. A number of pressing issues could be fruitfully addressed, including problems faced by both countries with respect to undocumented Central American migration, victimization of civilians along the border, and the implementation and continuing operation of the RAW program.

The Immigration Reform and Control Act of 1986 and Mexican Perceptions of Bilateral Approaches to Immigration Issues by Carlos Rico F.

Carlos Rico returned to the issue of Mexico's ambivalence about consultation on immigration issues. He reviewed the historical reasons for the apparent contradiction between the Mexican government's insistence on the need for "bilateral solutions to a bilateral problem" and its limited response to U.S. calls for some kind of consultation during the pre-IRCA legislative debate.

According to Rico, ever since the unilateral termination of the Bracero program in 1965, Mexican actions have been guided by two policy objectives: (1) to keep the "safety valve" open for labor migration to the United States and (2) to protect the rights of Mexican migrants in that country. However, in pursuing these objectives, the Mexican government's views and actions varied during the post-Bracero/pre-IRCA period. Between 1965 and 1974, the Mexican government actively sought to negotiate a new agreement establishing a degree of bilateral participation in controlling the flow of migrants between Mexico and the United States. Such cooperation had previously existed under the Bracero program. At the time, a bilateral agreement seemed the best way to keep the flow open and protect the migrants.

By 1974, several events prompted Mexico to reassess this approach. In preparation for President Ford's first visit to Mexico, the United States sent signals suggesting a willingness to discuss "a new Bracero" type of agreement. These signals coincided with the energy crisis and the discovery of oil in Mexico's southeastern region. Thus, they were perceived as an attempt to link migration to other issues in the bilateral relation. Also, it had become clear that the termination of the Bracero program had not closed the "safety valve" but had merely changed the status of the Mexican migrants. A formal agreement was no longer perceived as necessary to keep the "valve" open or, for that matter, to assure protection of migrant workers' rights. Hence, demands for a formal agreement were dropped and protection of Mexican workers became the main focus of Mexican government attention.

Over the years, satisfaction with the status quo grew stronger, based on several *Mexican perceptions*:

- Migration was increasingly seen as primarily an economic issue of push-pull factors that benefited the U.S. economy and that would, at any rate, be difficult for the U.S. government to control.
- There was seemingly no common ground for negotiations: For Mexico, bilateral negotiations would be premised on "regulating an unavoidable flow," while the U.S. debate over IRCA seemed to be premised on "stopping the flow."
- A "positive" change seemed improbable because Mexican migration was in the economic interest of the United States, while a "negative" change seemed unlikely because U.S. authorities would neither want nor be able to stop the flows.

Rico then addressed the question of whether these perceptions had changed or would change as a result of IRCA's enactment and implementation. Mexican policy objectives remain the same: protecting Mexican workers in the United States and maintaining the flows. With respect to the latter, however, the option that best balances the tension between short- and long-term interests is temporary immigration. Over the last few years, concern over human capital flight has increased in Mexico. Temporary migration in the short term serves to ease labor-market pressures at home and in the long term keeps the door open for the return of these workers.

With this in mind, Mexican reactions to IRCA went through two phases. In the first phase, there were two different expectations: (1) The law would have no significant effect; and (2) significant numbers of Mexican workers would be repatriated (that is, massive expulsions were not ruled out in spite of U.S. assurances to the contrary).

In the second phase, as the likelihood of the latter scenario faded, the focus of attention was redirected to those provisions of IRCA designed to keep the door open: the RAW and the H-2A programs. There is now a nascent concern, not with the objectives of these programs, but with the possibility that these programs may be implemented unilaterally, including recruitment and selection of workers under their aegis.

In the broader context, however, the prospect for bilateral solutions to the immigration problem depends on changes in both Mexican and U.S. attitudes. Such changes, in turn, depend primarily on how successful IRCA is. If it is "too" successful in reducing undocumented immigration, unilateral action will be perceived as working, and the United States will have no incentive for bilateral negotiation. On the other hand, if IRCA "fails," Mexico will perceive no need for change. Hence, a precondition for changing attitudes in both countries will be that IRCA is neither too successful nor a complete failure. Its middle-range effectiveness may induce each country to seek the other's assistance to pursue its own interests through a bilateral approach. Such an approach might be encouraged by the work of CSIMCED and by the positive climate in overall government relations that has emerged since the simultaneous inaugurations of Carlos Salinas de Gortari and George Bush as presidents of their respective countries.

Other developments could also lead to changes in attitudes and offer new forms of bilateral approaches, including joint efforts directed at third-country migrants and joint actions in other areas, such as drug interdiction, that affect migratory flows. Even though there may be no direct connection between immigration and drug interdiction, border actions cannot be expected to discriminate between the two.

Mexican Immigration, U.S. Investment, and U.S.-Mexican Relations
by David F. Ronfeldt and Monica Ortíz de Oppermann

In his presentation, David Ronfeldt looked at the effects of Mexico's Foreign Investment Law (MFIL) of 1975 on U.S.-Mexico relations in an effort to anticipate the long-term effects of IRCA on U.S.-Mexico relations. MFIL and IRCA, Ronfeldt argued, have many similarities, including arguments in the policy dialogue that led to their enactment, their implementation, and the initial reactions and effects following their enactment.

He recognized that there are also, of course, dissimilarities. IRCA targets individual migrants who are politically and economically powerless, while MFIL targets large investors, many of them politically and economically influential. The United States has many alternative destinations for its investments, but Mexico has few, if any, alternative destinations for its emigrants. Finally, MFIL is already 15 years old, while IRCA was passed only two years ago. However, for the purpose at hand, Ronfeldt argued that the similarities are more important than the dissimilarities.

First, the stocks of foreign investments in Mexico and immigrants in the United States are quite similar in size and visibility: Foreign investments total 7 percent of the Mexican gross national product, and immigrants represent 6 percent of the U.S. population. Further, U.S. investments account for about the same percent of foreign investments as the percent of Mexican immigrants in the U.S. immigrant population.

Second, the arguments in support of the two laws were strikingly similar. The economic concerns regarding displacement of native-born workers or entrepreneurs were strong in both cases. Furthermore, arguments about sovereignty and cultural, political, and even security effects were strikingly similar. Even the range of arguments against the law were conceptually alike. In the end, both laws emerged from environments of rising nationalism, following years of low control and increasing flows into the country. In these contexts, a feeling spread that the country was too open, too accommodating, and at risk of being flooded, in one case by migrant workers and in the other by foreign investors.

Third, the laws themselves have significant similarities. Both focus on restricting the flows. In IRCA's case, the law tries to reduce the flow of undocumented workers by prohibiting the United States from hiring them. MFIL tries to restrict the influx of foreign capital by prohibiting investment in specified industries. Both laws establish penalties for nationals who violate the laws.

Hence, both look tough, restrictive, and protectionist, but both laws also represent pragmatic compromises reflecting the tensions in the policy debates. They also "leave the door open" through a range of exceptions. For example, MFIL allows foreign investment in the maquiladoras (in-bond assembly plants) and up to 49 percent in some industries, and it also set up a national foreign investment commission with flexibility to negotiate terms of foreign investments in Mexico's high-technology and export industries. IRCA allows slack in immigration "quotas" through the SAW, RAW, and H-2A programs.

Finally, the two laws are similar in the immediate reactions and expectations they evoked. In both cases, passage was followed by an outcry in the neighboring country that the law had targeted it "in an unfriendly and unilateral manner." In both cases, the legislating country rushed to reassure its neighbor about the law. Ronfeldt characterized the message thusly:

> [It] is not aimed at you (though of course it is); it is not meant to halt the flow, only to regulate it; the law is not as tough as it might have been; and implementation and enforcement will take time and be done in a friendly, pragmatic manner.

He speculated that in the long run, if IRCA follows the path of MFIL, the following outcomes are likely:

- The law slows the flow, but does not stop it.
- The share of migrants to the United States from Mexico declines and those who come are more likely to stay permanently.
- Regulations and enforcement will continue to be implemented in a gradual, pragmatic manner.
- Exceptions will become the rule, particularly if the United States faces a labor shortage in the future. If the shortage persists, alternative mechanisms will be sought to accommodate the flows needed.

In conclusion, Ronfeldt reflected that laws like MFIL and IRCA, which are few and far between, become the centerpieces of dialogue. Although designed to assert nationalism (or at least slow down the silent integration occurring between the two countries), they, by their very presence, transform the policy debate into something that is more pragmatic and more moderate. If they succeed (and that is a condition), they can become a vehicle of accommodation: The results imply that the legislation has allowed the country to regain control and that it is in no danger of being overrun by its neighbor. This process has been occurring in some parts of Mexico because of MFIL. IRCA might lead to a similar outcome in U.S. thinking about Mexico.

Mexico's Policy Issues After IRCA by Manuel García y Griego[1]

Manuel García y Griego's presentation explored Mexico's policy issues after IRCA. He described the present situation "as a tentative effort to modify the nature of migratory flows

---

[1]The revised resource paper by García y Griego that appears in Part III differs considerably in emphasis from the presentation summarized here. The revised paper focuses on the extent to which emigration is a "safety valve" for Mexico and how IRCA might affect it.

between Mexico and the United States, which should be expected to have only modest consequences." He identified three main areas of Mexican concerns for the short to medium term: (1) the consequences of the legalization of a large number of Mexican immigrants in the United States; (2) increased demand for consular protection of Mexican migrants in the United States; and (3) the demographic pressures and the expected "complementarity" between labor-force demands in the United States and Mexico.

The Consequences of Legalization. According to García y Griego, when IRCA was enacted, Mexico's concern centered on how to respond to (1) the expected closure of the "escape valve" and (2) the possible repatriation of a large number of undocumented immigrants. IRCA was perceived primarily as instituting new restrictive "police" measures, and these concerns dominated the public discourse in Mexico. However, by the end of 1988, repatriation did not materialize and it became clear that the United States was moving slowly in implementing employer sanctions. The Simpson-Rodino Act was perceived as the "bomb that did not explode."

By the same token, the size of the legalization program drew much attention, and policy concerns began to focus on that area. The questions are now (1) how to deal with the large population that has decided to stay in the United States (this was an unexpected development for some Mexican observers) and (2) how to deal with a potentially large number of temporary migrants who are citizens of Mexico but working legally in the United States. Those questions may become more pressing as the number of admitted migrants increases under the RAW program, which will be effective from 1990 to 1993.

In this new context, García y Griego argued that neither a passive policy of "doing nothing" nor an active policy seeking a bilateral agreement to manage the legal flow of Mexican workers appears attractive and/or feasible. "Doing nothing" carries risks for Mexico, both in relation to the formulation of U.S. policies contrary to Mexican government interests and with respect to Mexico's domestic considerations. Joint management of the flows would require Mexico to actively participate in controlling undocumented emigration—an unattractive prospect. Hence, a middle-of-the-road policy appears most likely.

Consular Protection of Mexican Immigrants. García y Griego noted that consular protection of the rights of migrants to and in the United States has been an ongoing, central concern for Mexico. A major aspect of this concern is how the United States has treated allegations of abuse and maltreatment of immigrants by INS Border Patrol agents. He claimed that in 90 percent of the cases, the State Department acknowledges receipt of the complaint but takes no further action. There is currently no effective official administrative channel to deal with such complaints. While this problem is not expected to change as a result of IRCA, legalization is likely to increase demands for support of Mexican consular affairs in the United States. The legalized population may also become more demanding and expect better treatment from Mexican customs officials when returning to Mexico.

Demographic Pressures on Immigration. Finally, García y Griego stated that the main political and economic problem in Mexico will be how to generate sufficient work opportunities for a labor force that is growing 3.5 percent annually. Solving this problem, which should help reduce emigration pressure, will require more attention to be directed toward external debt and foreign investments, this in the hopes of reactivating economic growth in Mexico. It might also be time to consider redirecting scarce public investment and development resources toward those regions of Mexico with a high rate of emigration.

The Domestic and Foreign Policy Consequences of Mexican and Central American Immigration: Mexican-American Perspectives
by Rodolfo O. de la Garza, Nestor Rodríguez, and Harry Pachon

This presentation by Rodolfo de la Garza centered primarily on two topics: (1) the social, economic, and cultural effects of Central American and Mexican immigrants on the Mexican-American community; and (2) the political implications of this recent wave of immigrants in general and of IRCA's legalized population in particular.

At the outset, de la Garza indicated that although Central American immigrants are still small in aggregate numbers, they are growing increasingly more important because of their concentration in some places (e.g., Houston and Miami). Interaction has increased between Central American and Mexican immigrants and between those two groups and the Mexican-American community. Because of the linguistic, ethnic, and racial diversity of Central Americans, the nature and frequency of interactions among them, other immigrant groups, and Mexican Americans may differ. These interactions have cultural, economic, and political dimensions, and they are mutually reinforcing.

At the cultural level, Mexican and Central American immigration helps to perpetuate the most traditional aspects of the Mexican-American subculture. For instance, it is creating a linguistic and cultural environment that supports the maintenance of Spanish heritage among Mexican Americans, although whether this will last is "open to real doubt." And, the growth of media and other institutional practices in the Spanish language directed at immigrants also reinforces this aspect.

Both immigrant groups are important clients and also a source of labor for Mexican-American ethnic and nonethnic businesses. Mexican immigrants have also become investors. However, Central American immigrants are displacing Mexican immigrants as the perceived "super worker." In South Texas, there are reports of Central Americans displacing Mexican immigrants in Mexican-American businesses in the service sector. This may in part be because Central American immigrants have higher skills. Although still small in number, Central American skilled immigrants are also beginning to hold jobs that, in the early 1980s, would have been held by Mexican Americans. It may be that Mexican Americans face greater competition for skilled labor with Central American immigrants than with Mexican immigrants.

Immigrants are not homogeneous and have a "business" as well as a "labor" component. With regard to capital investments in the Mexican-American communities, there are two kinds of Mexican immigrants. The first is an elite wealthy Mexican immigrant who retains financial and social ties to Mexico and who deals nearly exclusively with the Anglo community, investing primarily in nonethnic businesses. The second is a less affluent but upwardly mobile Mexican immigrant investor, who deals primarily with small Mexican-American businesses.

Finally, at the political level, Mexican Americans are increasingly aware of the political significance of immigrants as allies. De la Garza identified three ways that increased Mexican immigration has politically affected the Mexican-American community.

The first concerns the fact that electoral districts in the United States are population-based. The presence of Mexican immigrants, legal or undocumented, has increased Mexican-American political representation, and the Mexican-American community is actively campaigning against a resulting "two-pronged" backlash. One prong takes the form of a federal lawsuit to exclude undocumented immigrants from the count, and the other prong consists of similar actions that might take place at the state level.

The second political dimension concerns Mexican Americans' change in attitude toward the presence of Mexican immigrants. In the past, the attitude has ranged from ambivalence to hostility. This is no longer the case. Today, Mexican-American groups such as the Mexican American Legal Defense and Educational Fund (MALDEF) and the National Association of Latino Elected and Appointed Officials (NALEO) are actively supportive. Such support includes a drive to naturalize the population legalized under IRCA and actions—e.g., simplification and standardization of the application process and simplification of examinations—to remove institutional barriers that have traditionally impeded naturalization. The Mexican-American attitude to Central Americans remains divided. Some believe that Central American immigrants compete with Mexican immigrants and are treated better.

The third political dimension is the increased involvement of the Mexican-American community in foreign policy issues. This is an important new phenomenon for Mexican Americans. Some groups of Mexican Americans have been concerned and vocal about U.S. policy toward Central Americans.

Perhaps this most important change results from the increasing number of Mexican immigrants who have left Mexico in part for political reasons. They are acting out that political dimension in the United States in a variety of ways. In 1988, Mexican Americans responded in large numbers to the candidacy of Cuahtemoc Cárdenas for President of Mexico, including raising money in his support, an event without precedent. Further, the Mexican American Democratic Caucus of California officially requested that the Democratic Party ask the U.S. State Department to pressure the Mexican government to conduct honest elections in 1988. These examples suggest that the potential connection exists for Mexican Americans to actively influence Mexican politics and to actively influence U.S. policy toward Mexico and Central America.

SUMMARY OF DISCUSSION

Following the presentations, the discussion centered primarily on two topics: (1) what might happen if there were an open U.S.-Mexican border; and (2) the motivations behind IRCA and the current legal-immigration debate in the United States.

An Open U.S.-Mexican Border

Several participants returned to this issue, which had also been raised in the Session 1 discussion. They suggested that before IRCA, a "quasi-open border" existed between the two countries. Supposedly, this type of openness was implied by the fact that for any individual attempting to cross there "would always be one less apprehension than there were entries." In this context, the question was raised about what would happen if that border were formally open, assuming no Border Patrol enforcement and no employer sanctions.

There was no consensus regarding the numbers of immigrants that might result from such a measure, and estimates varied widely. At one extreme, a participant estimated that 6 to 8 million Mexicans might move into the United States legally within a two-year period. This immigration would be fueled by the increased disparity in wages between the two countries. In the past six to seven years, real wages in Mexico (and relative to the U.S. dollar) have declined by nearly 50 percent. Hence, the potential economic benefits of emigration have increased significantly over the past few years. However, the conjecture was that many of these emigrants would not necessarily reside permanently in the United States, a situation that would increase the revolving labor flow between the two countries.

At the other extreme, several participants opined that the change would have only a marginal effect on emigrant numbers because most Mexicans who wanted to emigrate had already done so. One participant suggested that the appropriate question is not how many more might go, but rather why haven't more people gone, given the overwhelming economic incentives to do so. To answer that question, it was remarked, one must go beyond the issue of relative wages between the two countries and identify the cultural and other motivational determinants of emigration.

Although there was no consensus on emigration numbers, there did appear to be a consensus that, given an open border, an increasing percentage of the Mexican middle class, particularly Mexican professionals, would emigrate. One participant raised the subject of an open border broadened into some form of North American integration (including Canada, the United States, and Mexico). He suggested that the result of such a border, it is generally believed, would be a concentration of capital and labor, including the "best workers, administrators, and technologists," into the United States. Consequently, "both Mexico and Canada would be drained and impoverished." Yet it was noted that this scenario did not deter Canada from recently signing a free-trade agreement with the United States.

Madam Flora MacDonald addressed this question, recalling that for much of its history Canada had been preoccupied with that possibility. It was generally feared that Canada's resources and "best people" would be attracted to the better economy and living standard in the United States, leaving Canada "bankrupt in a number of areas." However, as Canada's industrial base has matured, "brain drain" to the United States has lessened considerably. Further, foreign investment no longer dominates the Canadian economy. Indeed, currently more Canadian investment goes into the United States than vice versa.

Hence, she stated, Canada is now more self-assured that it can compete with the United States and in the world. These changes led to a drastic overhaul of the basic trading patterns between the two countries—a trade arrangement that removed trade barriers but also included a dispute settlement mechanism "which may well prove to be a key item for the General Agreement on Tariffs and Trade [GATT] as it looks for the structures for new trading arrangements in the world."

At the same time, Canada is ensuring the protection of those institutions it considers vital to the country, including banking, broadcasting, and telecommunications, by keeping their control in Canadian hands:

> There are areas where Canadian culture differs from that of the United States, and we want to make sure that it be the way we want it and not just dominated by that south of the border.

MacDonald's remarks notwithstanding, participants expected that if an open border did result in a Canadian brain drain into the United States, it could provoke a negative political reaction, even a backlash, in Canada. That reaction could be generated by the prospect of increased competition in the skilled labor market and in part by cultural and related reasons. Another comment was that it might also reduce the perceived imperative for educating Chicanos, blacks, and other disadvantaged minorities; one participant paraphrased this response as "Why educate our own when we can bring in replacements?" Should such an attitude develop in the majority electorate, reaction against the open-border policy would be quite strong among those minority groups.

From a purely economic perspective, it was argued that an open U.S.-Mexico border would, in the long run, be beneficial to both Mexico and the United States. Although it would involve negative externalities, even pockets of unemployment in the United States, the process of labor supply and demand would clear fairly rapidly (i.e., over about a 20-year period). The cost of living in the United States would decline, and Mexico would benefit from higher levels of remittances to assist in its local and regional development.

IRCA, Legal Immigration, and Discrimination

In the discussion, the participants returned to the question of the motivations behind IRCA and behind the current efforts in the U.S. Congress to decrease the relative importance of "family reunification" in determining who can enter the country legally for permanent residence.[2]

It was pointed out that if there was any discriminatory purpose in IRCA, it was not against Mexican immigrants. Mexico has benefited from IRCA's legalization programs more than any other country of origin. About 55 percent of undocumented immigrants counted in the 1980 census were from Mexico, whereas more than 70 percent of the current legalized population under IRCA are Mexicans.

Concerning present efforts to change legal immigration laws, some participants believed that the motivation behind that debate was antipathy toward the character of current immigration to the United States—that is, "too many Asians and too many Latins." In the current debate, the term "discrimination" has been used to characterize contemporary legal immigration policy. However, it refers to discrimination against Europeans. Recently, 20,000 legal immigrant visas were allocated, primarily to Europeans, in a lottery. And the whole attempt to increase the number of independent immigrants can be seen as an effort to restore some sort of "balance," i.e., as a way to bring more Europeans into the United States.

The debate that followed these "statements" became heated and at times emotional. Some participants clearly viewed the current efforts to reform legal immigration law as driven primarily by nativist, and even racist, motives. As one participant put it:

> Given a long history of systematic discrimination (that is today attenuated for sure), one should not be surprised that Mexican Americans would say there is reason to believe that many of the people who are advocating such changes do so because they do not like me. . . .

Opposition to the proposed changes, besides coming from the Hispanic community which "does not like the English language points,"[3] comes even stronger from the Asian community. After being shut out for so many years from immigrating to the United States, Asians are only now catching up in number with other immigrant groups; they perceive the proposed changes (i.e., establishing a ceiling on immigration of immediate relatives and lowering the ceiling on the number of other relatives) as an attempt to retract these new opportunities.

Other participants felt that the motivations behind the current debate partly reflect a perceived need to build political support for a continued "liberal" immigration policy in the United States:

---

[2]Both the Senate and House are considering legislation (S.358 and H.R.672) to make U.S. legal immigration policy more responsive to labor market needs by increasing the number of independent legal immigrants admitted under labor market criteria.

[3]At the time of the conference, the Senate's legislative proposal would have allocated 150,000 visas (up from 54,000) annually to immigrants chosen on the basis of a point system. Labor market needs were to drive the allocation of points. In addition, fifteen points would be given for applicants who "spoke English." The final Senate bill (S.358) eventually dropped the points for "English language."

> [A]s long as immigration policy in the United States is perceived by the broad public . . . as serving the interests of primarily one or two minority groups, it will not have broad public support. So part of the purpose of the proponents of these reforms is to broaden the public support for a liberal immigration regime rather than what seems to be a pretty broad public opposition to the current immigration regime.

Or these participants felt that the motivations were directed at serving a broader "national interest" by increasing the number of legal immigrants admitted for labor-market consideration:

> [T]he idea is to get an immigrant that will be more in the national interest than one who happens to come because he/she has got a family member in the United States. Is it more in the national interest to get a nurse, if we have a nursing shortage, from the Philippines than it is to have a person come just because he happens to have a brother in the United States to petition for him?

Finally, other participants recast the debate, recognizing that discrimination will exist in any country where there are incoming movements of people who are different culturally and linguistically, a reaction that some participants thought was inherent in human nature. Fear that the immigrants constitute an economic or political threat may reinforce these attitudes. This was graphically illustrated by one participant who recounted a meeting he had with an influential group of people who had direct experience with Mexico and interest in foreign affairs:

> They said directly that their fear is there will be nothing left for their children with the contemporary immigration. That the Asians were going to take over the country in terms of economics and the Latins were going to take over politically.

In this context, it was observed that the question is not "why there are conflicts between natives and immigrants in the United States," but rather "why there are so few." A partial answer that was given is that the immigrants themselves understand what it takes to settle without conflict. For instance, one of the things they understand is that they need to and should learn English. That partly explains why such large numbers of Hispanics, both in Florida and in California, voted for the English-only proposition.

The discussion reflected a number of very real issues about culture and the nature of society that permeate the contemporary immigration debate. These issues range from English-only laws to what kind of assistance, if any, should be provided to immigrants to facilitate their adjustments to a new society. There was consensus that these issues cannot be ignored, should be openly discussed in the debate, and should be accommodated and met directly. The importance of such action is underscored by the large numbers of immigrants who will continue to come from Asia and Latin America. Despite perceived efforts to encourage West Europeans to immigrate, that area is presently an unlikely source (except perhaps for Ireland): The economy in Western Europe is strong and optimism for its economic future surpasses anything that may be encountered in the United States or Canada.

Other Issues

In addition to the above, other topics were briefly discussed.

First was the analogy between IRCA and MFIL, used by Ronfeldt in his presentation. One participant pointed out that the two laws were not strictly comparable: IRCA was directed at *illegal* immigration and MFIL was directed at *legal* investment. Ronfeldt responded that, on the surface, that is the case. However, he argued that at the time MFIL was enacted much investment in Mexico was perceived as operating at the margin of the law through the use of "presta nombres" or "fronts" to disguise actual ownership of capital.

While this and other limitations of the analogy were granted, other participants argued that the analogy is important because it emphasizes the need for the receiving nation to control exchanges of capital or labor through an "orderly process." Otherwise, political backlash is likely. A recent manifestation of this phenomenon is the debate in the U.S. Congress over the need for "orderly capital markets" for investments in the United States. That debate is being fueled by large, visible Japanese investments. The point was made that those investments are not necessarily matters for real concern. However, they take on large symbolic and political dimensions through shock effect. Such shock effects are generated when, for example, the Japanese buy the Riviera Tennis Club in Los Angeles, own 60 percent of the buildings in downtown Los Angeles, and purchase a number of major banks.

A final issue in the discussion was U.S. responsibility to compensate Mexican communities if IRCA actually "closed the door." That closure would decrease the flow of immigrant remittances to Mexican communities of origin, causing, in turn, a decrease in their capital accumulation. It was argued that as a result of our labor needs, the United States created a certain amount of dependency and affected the behavior of Mexican sending communities over a long period.

SESSION 3: EFFECTS OF IRCA ON MEXICO

Immediately after IRCA's passage, governments and the press in several countries of origin predicted two dire consequences: first, mass involuntary and voluntary return of migrants from the United States; second, the consequent exacerbation of any economic, political, and social difficulties in the countries of origin. Economic concerns were fueled by the prospect that these countries would suffer significant losses in foreign exchange and other benefits accruing from remittances sent home by migrants. Session 3 explored this and other questions: For example, how do emigrants and would-be emigrants think that IRCA has affected and/or will affect them? How has IRCA affected their ability to cross the border illegally? Have their job opportunities in the United States declined? How have communities of origin been affected?

SUMMARY OF PRESENTATIONS

Jesús Arroyo Alejandre and Gustavo López Castro, of Mexico, presented preliminary findings from interviews with emigrants, residents, and elites in several Mexican rural areas that supply high migration to the United States. Both sought to assess the effects of IRCA on regional migratory and job behavior and/or expectations and to develop hypotheses about the effects IRCA has had or might have on places of origin.

Some Effects of IRCA on a Region of Jalisco with High Migration to the United States by Jesús Arroyo Alejandre

Inhabitants of the state of Jalisco have a long tradition of migrating to the United States. Consequently, Jalisco provides a prime location for studying IRCA's effects on emigration. Jesús Arroyo Alejandre presented the results of such a study.

Arroyo first briefly described the characteristics of Jalisco and of its emigration history. The state of Jalisco has 6 million people. Almost two-thirds of them now reside in the metropolitan area of Guadalajara. The remaining one-third live in less populated areas, about half in villages of 2,500 people or less.

Over the years, Jalisco has contributed an estimated 10 to 20 percent of all legal and illegal Mexican migrants to the United States. To date, the places of origin are distributed throughout the state, including 42 of its 124 municipalities. Relative to other municipalities, those with high migration to the United States are primarily rural and characterized by low socioeconomic development. Most emigrants from Jalisco go to California; most are males between the ages of 16 and 30; about half are married; and most are responsible for the economic support of four or more dependents.

The study was based on interviews of 67 emigrants in 19 high-emigration municipalities of Jalisco, who had returned to their homes for Christmas of 1988. The analysts complemented these interviews with interviews of local elite residents, including teachers, officials, and priests. Analysis of the interviews led to the following conclusions.

Concerning IRCA's effects on individual emigrants, about 80 percent of those interviewed had been legalized, nearly all through the Special Agricultural Worker (SAW) program. One in five had gone north specifically to take advantage of this program. Sixty percent of those legalized under SAW were currently (December 1988) employed in agriculture, with the balance fairly evenly divided between the service and construction sectors.

Labor-market expectations differed depending on the immigration status of the respondents. In one group of those legalized under IRCA, most believed that their opportunities for better jobs, higher earnings, and/or higher fringe benefits would increase. In another group of legal immigrants, nearly half believed there would be more competition and thus reduced job and earnings opportunities, but the other half believed there would be no change. Most of those who were still undocumented perceived no change in their job opportunities and their ability to cross the border illegally.

The study also explored the immigrants' intentions with respect to the United States. Seventy-five percent of those legalized indicated they would stay in the United States permanently, and 50 percent intended to seek citizenship.

Concerning IRCA's effects on places of origin, Arroyo made the following key observations.

First, contrary to early expectations, IRCA has not been followed by a massive return by such migrants to their places of origin. However, legalization may increase the number and frequency of such visits. In fact, the interviews suggest that many more migrants had returned in 1988 than in previous years. Such an increase might positively affect the economic development and well-being of nonmigrating inhabitants.

Second, IRCA might lead to more, rather than less, migration from the places of origin surveyed, principally to reunify families. If legalized immigrants realize greater job and earnings stability, they may find it easier and more desirable to support relatives and/or friends in the United States.

Third, interviews with key local officials suggest that migrants to the United States were more and more likely to consist of professionals and the well-educated. This trend was reported in several of the municipalities visited for the study. For example, in Guadalajara 200 teachers had reportedly received temporary visas to go to the United States.

The Simpson-Rodino Act: The Viewpoint of Sending Villages
by Gustavo López Castro

Gustavo López Castro reported findings from a household survey conducted in the summer and fall of 1988 in three villages in the states of Jalisco and Michoacán. The villages were selected because they have a tradition of high migration to the United States but vary in their socioeconomic characteristics. About 120 respondents were interviewed to assess (a) their knowledge of the provisions and intent of IRCA and (b) how they perceive IRCA's potential effects on migratory behavior and job opportunities in the United States.

More than 80 percent of the respondents had heard of IRCA either from the media or from relatives and friends. As might be expected, perceptions of the law's principal intent depended on a respondent's prospects for legalization. Eligible respondents saw the main intent to be legalization of undocumented workers. Ineligible respondents tended to focus on the restrictive intent of the law: About 45 percent of the respondents stressed this aspect. About the same proportion also indicated they would try to cross the border illegally in the coming year. Many indicated that they expected few changes in the United States resulting from the law.

SUMMARY OF DISCUSSION

Following the two presentations, discussion focused primarily on two issues: (1) changes in migration patterns due to IRCA; (2) problems of methodology.

Changes in Migration Patterns

Participants identified three potential changes in migration patterns from Mexico to the United States that were unintended but might be induced by IRCA: (1) In the short term, undocumented immigration might increase; (2) undocumented immigrants might stay in the United States longer; (3) legal travel between the two countries might rise.

Why Undocumented Immigration Might Increase. It was suggested that undocumented immigration might increase for two reasons—desire to take advantage of U.S. legalization programs, and desire for family reunification. The SAW legalization program was seen as especially alluring because it has minimum eligibility requirements and can be applied for in Mexico. The legalization-programs argument was supported by the experience of analysts in the summer and winter of 1987. They were unable to interview households in three villages of Michoacán and Jalisco because members of three in five households had emigrated. Six years earlier, the pattern had been two out of five households. However, it was believed that this "induced" emigration was a short-term effect of IRCA.

It was also suggested that family reunification might cause an increase in undocumented immigration. More than 3 million previously undocumented immigrants applied for legalization. Legalization has given immigrants greater feelings of security and stability and less fear of the U.S. Immigration and Naturalization Service (INS). Before legalization, the only contact these people had with the INS was through illegal border crossings. For many, the legalization process brought them in contact with a different, "kinder" INS. Their changed image of the INS, together with their greater personal security, may lead many to risk bringing undocumented family members and friends across the border. This tendency might be reinforced by hopes of another amnesty for these family members. Furthermore, it would be consistent with a practice that goes back a hundred years. In some areas of Mexico, like Jalisco, the migratory networks are so well established that nearly 95 percent of Jaliscans have relatives or friends in the United States.

This discussion raised the issue that "legalization" might have set in motion a self-perpetuating and progressively more encompassing cycle of immigration. Each wave of immigrants would draw another wave behind it. However, some discussants pointed out that this effect was likely to be short-lived because of differences among the relevant subgroups—that is, Mexican immigrants, first-generation Mexican Americans, second-generation Mexican Americans, and beyond. Even though these subgroups are not neatly divided into distinguishable communities, there is evidence that they behave differently.

First-generation Mexican Americans are less likely than Mexican immigrants to have close family ties across the border and to feel the imperative for family reunification. Consequently, "induced" immigration is likely to have a 15-year impetus and then die down—barring another, unrelated event. Such was the case after the Mexican revolution when a large number of Mexicans settled in the United States. For a limited time, they pulled over some of their relatives. After that, the next wave of immigrants came for economic, rather than family-reunification, purposes.

Effects on Illegal Immigrants' Length of Stay. The discussants disagreed about IRCA's effects on length of stay in the United States and the subsequent pattern of revolving illegal immigration. One group pointed out that stays vary according to type of immigrant. Some analysts of Mexico-U.S. migration flows distinguish among three types:

(1) *Commuters.* They come in, stay for a short period, go home, and then return, repeating the pattern again and again over the years.
(2) *Sojourners.* They stay in the United States temporarily, then return to Mexico for good.
(3) *Settlers.* They come intending to stay in the United States.

Several participants argued that they expected IRCA to increase the proportion of "settlers," certainly among the legalized population. In turn, they expected that the length of stay for "commuters" and "sojourners" would increase. Evidence from some emigrant surveys suggests that the latter trend is already under way. In rural places of Michoacán and Jalisco, the length of stay in the United States was 6½ months in 1983 compared with 11½ months to 12 months in 1988.

These expectations were not shared by everyone. Indeed, some argued equally strongly that IRCA will decrease the tendency for immigrants to settle in the United States:

Immigrants go to the United States for economic reasons exclusively, they do not go to stay. . . .

According to some participants, another important factor inducing legalized immigrants to leave the United States is the discrimination they continue to experience there. One person stated that:

[discrimination] is one of the most important reasons cited by immigrants for their return to their place of origin. . . .

Like similar comments in other sessions, this one generated strong reactions from other participants:

[T]he Mexicans, for their own reasons, overstate the role of racism and Mexican Americans. . . .

Opponents of the discrimination argument went on to ask why, if discrimination against them is rampant, so many Mexicans stay in the United States. They also pointed out that discrimination must have gotten worse if it is now strong enough to drive Mexican nationals out. However, there is no evidence of that. Indeed, indicators of integration, acceptability, and government outreach all suggest that there is less discrimination today than there was in the 1950s, 1960s, and 1970s. One discussant opined that one reason Mexicans cling to the "older [racist] view of the United States" has to do with a "romanticism," making it unbelievable that a Mexican might want to go to the United States and stay there.

Why Travel Between Countries Might Increase. There were few differences of opinion regarding the third and last expected effect of IRCA, an increase in the frequency of travel between Mexico and the United States. Several participants contributed anecdotes that were consistent with the observations made by the presenters. They recounted meeting with recently legalized immigrants now spending regular weekends in Tijuana. IRCA is expected to significantly increase (1) this form of travel across the southern U.S. border, (2) the frequency of visits by legalized immigrants to the interior of Mexico, and (3) travel of relatives from Mexico to the United States. Overall, these developments were viewed as positive for Mexico and its economy, a far cry from the view that prevailed immediately following the passage of IRCA and that conjured images of massive returns of impoverished emigrants.

Other Issues Related to Migration Patterns. The participants raised two other important questions, but lack of information precluded discussing them in the way they merited. The first was whether one might expect the changes in patterns to vary between men and women migrants. No one knew of any study or work that addressed that question directly. The second question was how undocumented immigrants were adjusting to IRCA in general, and what they may be doing to obtain employment. Here, too, no one had much information to offer. The data from the interviews suggest a division of opinion among respondents: Some expect no change, and some believe it will be more difficult to obtain work and stay in the United States.

Methodological Issues

Three methodological issues were raised during the discussion.

First, the two presentations in Session 3 were based on a relatively small number of interviews in an even more limited number of places. Hence, the findings do not necessarily represent the full range of responses and perceptions. At best, the results indicate that the hypotheses should be tested using larger, more representative samples.

Second, several participants noted the contrast in kinds and levels of analysis between the studies presented in this session and those in Session 1. Both types seek to answer the same kind of question, i.e., what effects IRCA is having. This session's studies observed or interviewed individual migrants. The Session 1 studies analyzed aggregate national and/or regional data. These two types of analyses were seen as complementary. The first sheds light on the qualitative complexities of incentives and disincentives that determine whether a person will migrate: For example, if economic conditions are the primary reason to migrate, why hasn't everyone migrated? The second sheds light on the law's quantitative effects: For example, has undocumented immigration decreased, and by how much? Both are essential to understanding the migratory flows, but the bridge between these two types of analysis must be developed.

A third methodological issue was the need to recognize and study the regional, rather than national, process of Mexican migration to the United States. Immigrants to the United States do not come equally from all regions of Mexico. Similarly, once here, they concentrate in a few regions, even subareas, of states and in specific industries. Thus, participants argued, it is critical to pay more attention to the regional context. Further, it is important to consider the psychosocial context that often affects individual decisions. For example, why is it that given two people of identical age and education in the same locality, one emigrates and the other does not? They may be responding to different sets of perceptions and attitudes. But to understand this, analysts must deal with these questions at the psychological and social levels.

SESSION 4: IRCA AND INTER-AMERICAN RELATIONS

The final session moved the focus of attention away from Mexico. It dealt with how IRCA is affecting U.S. relations with the other nations in the Caribbean Basin, including Central America and the West Indies. The main questions addressed in this session were: How do countries in the Caribbean (other than Mexico) believe IRCA will affect them? How important is emigration politically and economically for these countries? How significant is migration to U.S. relations with the countries in the Caribbean Basin?

SUMMARY OF PRESENTATIONS

United States–Caribbean Immigration Relations
by Anthony P. Maingot

Anthony Maingot began by stressing the importance emigration has played and will continue to play in the history of the West Indies.[1] Over time, a value system and "culture" of West Indian emigration has developed, which, in turn, has given these migrants a favorable image in the United States. Most migration from the West Indies is legal. Hence, IRCA's significance to the West Indies lies not so much in its "control" apparatus but in its potential to change the climate for West Indian emigrants in the United States.

The Caribbean Basin's population has increased at a 3 percent annual rate since 1940; that is, it has increased from 55 million in that year to 166 million in 1980. Much of this increase results from declining mortality rates due to improved health standards. Relative to the populations of Mexico and Central America, however, the West Indies' population has decreased and is expected to grow more slowly. Its overall population share in the region will decline from 4.1 percent today to 3.3 percent by the year 2000. One reason is the increased use of birth control. Another is that emigration is included in population projections. In the West Indies, as in other parts of the Caribbean, emigration is an integral part of economic and political planning.

In terms of immigration numbers and issues, the West Indies has not been nearly as significant as Mexico. However, the West Indies cannot and should not be overlooked, for several reasons. First, it has provided an increasing share of legal immigrants to the United States. While the European share of total legal immigrants fell from 59 percent in 1951–1960 to 19 percent in 1979–1980, the West Indian share climbed from 5 to 18 percent. The second reason is the composition of these immigrants: In the 1970s 70 percent of West Indian immigrants to the United States were professionals, managers, and skilled workers.

At the same time, West Indian immigrants have assimilated well and projected a positive image, for various reasons. West Indians speak English and have a well-established network of social-cultural enclaves in the United States. These things have combined with the family reunification bent of U.S. immigration policy to make possible a disproportionate, but primarily legal, immigration.

---

[1]The West Indies had a 1985 population of 5.5 million people distributed among Jamaica, Trinidad/Tobago, Guyana, the Bahamas, Barbados, Grenada, and St. Vincent/Grenadines.

This ease of entry is very important for the West Indies: Without emigration, it is difficult to conceive that the economies of these countries could generate the number of jobs necessary to absorb the expected growth in population. For instance, the Jamaican labor force is expected to double between 1965 and 2000; however, there is no conceivable development scheme for Jamaica to double the number of jobs during that period. This job dearth seems particularly probable because of fast-growing urbanization, with its capital-intensive development.

Given the vital role emigration plays in their economies, countries like those of the West Indies should be vitally concerned that the conditions making legal immigration possible do not change. Even though West Indians, like Mexicans, claim a historical right to migrate to the United States, continuation of this process cannot be taken for granted. Maingot pointed this out:

> There is nothing in world history that provides anybody any historical right to go anywhere where there is a sovereign government. Now . . . we assume that because we have always migrated, we have that right. No sir. We are going to have to develop some other arguments and that is part of the challenge to the West Indian intellectual community.

In this respect, IRCA is significant not so much because of its legal controls, but because it signals a change in the immigration policy context. This new context places the favorable image of West Indian immigrants at risk in two ways. The first relates to ethnicity. West Indian blacks have benefited a great deal by taking advantage of the gains made through the U.S. civil rights movement. They have benefited primarily because they were highly educated and politically savvy. However, over time, the resulting advantages and competition with American blacks might create conflicts.

The second problem—and potentially the most damaging—is the increase in criminality among these immigrants. This is a relatively recent phenomenon involving (1) Jamaican and Haitian gangs and syndicates in the drug trade and (2) an increase in the number of illegal immigration schemes revealing themselves throughout the Caribbean, particularly through fraudulent visas and passports. This increase in illegal activities has led to calls in the United States for a tightening of the visa-granting process. An immigration atmosphere charged with suspicion might lead to a situation where the illegal minority threatens the traditional good relations that generations of Caribbeans have shared.

Despite the population pressure that makes immigration to the United States vital, Caribbean governments are concerned about one drawback—"brain drain." Although this is not a new phenomenon, the increasing loss of talent presents problems to their development plans and may become a source of friction with the U.S. government.

Changing the Rules: The Impact of the Simpson/Rodino Act on Inter-American Diplomacy by Christopher Mitchell

Christopher Mitchell discussed how IRCA has affected international relations, primarily in the Hispanic Caribbean and in Central America, including the Dominican Republic, El Salvador, Nicaragua, Guatemala, and Honduras. According to Mitchell, the source states responded to IRCA differently during two periods: (1) from late 1986, when IRCA enactment into law became all but assured, to early 1988; and (2) from early 1988 to the present (spring 1989).

In the first period, the sending-nation governments accorded migration a priority it had seldom, if ever, enjoyed in the past. They responded with "professed alarm, a good deal of lobbying in Washington, and even some hint of joint diplomatic action."

As noted in earlier sessions, initial press reports in those countries tended to alarmism, for example, speculation that several million migrants might be expelled back to Mexico or that 700,000 migrants might be expelled back to Santo Domingo. Governmental sources (at the presidential or foreign minister level) estimated that millions, if not billions, of dollars in remittances would be lost to their respective countries (including Mexico, El Salvador, and Santo Domingo). In El Salvador, resistance to IRCA ran the entire political gamut from the Farabundo Martí National Liberation Front (FMLN) to the Arena. Fear of losing traditional access to a long-standing labor market was a primary reason for this reaction. Mitchell noted that there was also:

> a certain motivation on the part of the sending-country governments to find somewhere to offload the blame for contemporary economic privation, which has been particularly sharp in Central America.

Through letters, diplomatic communications, statements, and/or visits to the United States, sending-nation governments sought special treatment and/or delays in enforcement of the new law. They were also motivated to join in action. In May 1987, all five Central American labor ministers signed a declaration in Guatemala City appealing to the United States.

These lobbying efforts had virtually no effect for two reasons. First, the drafters of IRCA were not inclined to make ad hoc concessions without giving the matter a great deal of thought. Second, the lobbying efforts were not very well conceived: They were directed at the executive branch, rather than Congress, and made no use of established lobbying avenues. One concession was made in July 1987, when the U.S. Attorney General instituted a policy of leniency in granting political asylum to Nicaraguan applicants.

The second period began in early 1988, marked by receding fears as mass deportations failed to materialize. Indeed, the actual number of deportations and involuntary departures did not increase in the post-IRCA period and remained relatively low (e.g., in 1988 4,500 to El Salvador and 2,800, 1500, and 200 to Guatemala, Honduras, and Nicaragua, respectively). As a result, the volume of lobbying activities dropped, and inter-country attempts at joint actions were superseded by country-specific migration concerns. For instance, Mexico began to cooperate officially with the U.S. Justice Department's efforts to slow undocumented migration from Central America. El Salvador continued to lobby more subtly for Congressional rather than Administrative action (i.e., in support of the Moakley-DeConcini bill) to assure "temporary safe haven" of Salvadoran immigrants in the United States.

Equally important, this period witnessed a blending of immigration issues with other political issues; for example, Honduran concerns about the Contras—where will they go? Will they be repatriated?

These two periods of political responses have resulted in two changes that will endure. First, IRCA has helped to put migration on the foreign policy agenda as it has never been before. This effect will persist and may intensify if employer sanctions operate as intended. Countries of origin will be intensely concerned if they begin to see traditional levels of access to the U.S. labor market erode and traditional levels of remittances decline. For some countries, such as the Dominican Republic, remittances are the largest source of foreign exchange, outstripping sugar and tourism.

The second enduring change is that migration is no longer an isolated issue. It is connected with other political and security issues, a phenomenon of "issue-interpenetration." This is particularly the case with Central America.

Mitchell concluded with a brief discussion of the prospects for bilateral negotiations on the conditions, terms, and rates of migration. The door remains open for such negotiations.

He reminded the audience of the Cuban and Haitian migration agreements, which have helped to isolate those countries from the current debate. Under those accords, the country of origin restrains emigration in return for concessions that may include economic aid and political toleration (as in the Haitian case).

He described four prerequisites for successful bilateral negotiations:

- The issue must be perceived as a problem by both the sending and receiving countries.
- Both countries must believe that there is something to negotiate.
- Both countries must have some capacity to do something about the problem and this capacity must be mutually perceived.
- Any agreement must be seen as supplementing, rather than contravening, IRCA.

SUMMARY OF DISCUSSION

The discussion centered on two issues: (1) the desirability and potential for bilateral negotiations regarding migration; and (2) the desirability of formulating an immigrant policy and its relation to affirmative-action legislation.

Bilateral Negotiations

There was considerable agreement among the participants on the four prerequisites for bilateral negotiations outlined by Christopher Mitchell. However, the question was raised concerning the "capacity" of some countries of origin to do anything about emigration. One response was that even relatively weak governments may have unsuspected abilities to exercise control over exits—if they have the political will to do it. For example, the existence of so-called "travel agencies" in both Nicaragua and El Salvador, which openly advertise and facilitate undocumented immigration (often via Guatemala), is within the range of potential governmental actions. Similarly, it may be within the range of Guatemala's government to impose visa requirements for Central American citizens using Guatemala as a way station to the United States. Indeed, the U.S. and Guatemalan governments have discussed imposing such a requirement.

Some participants felt that migration has enlarged from a binational to a multinational problem. This is nowhere more apparent than when dealing with Mexico. There it has become difficult to separate Mexican immigration issues from the issues raised by Central American or other third-country immigrants who use Mexico as channel of entry into the United States. The discussion raised the possibility that it may become impossible to limit the problem to the binational level, as international migration is growing ever more multifaceted and involving more and more interested parties with increasingly higher stakes.

Immigrant Policy and Affirmative Action

Several participants underlined the importance of both differentiating between and linking immigration and immigrant policy. In his presentation, Anthony Maingot distinguished between immigration policy, which deals with who is allowed to enter and who is kept out, and immigrant policy, which aims to support and assimilate those who are admitted.

With respect to the latter, there was intense debate about the desirability, if not the need, to separate affirmative action and immigrant policies. One participant suggested that there is:

now among Mexican Americans and Puerto Ricans a serious debate about the lack of attention to immigrant policy associated with changes in immigration policy . . . and with Civil Rights efforts, and much of the affirmative-action programs that were developed to address historic discriminatory practices.

The discussion addressed the concern of some groups that people who have never been discriminated against are realizing the benefits of the changes and increased access brought about by civil rights legislation and affirmative action. For instance, Mexican Americans and Puerto Ricans have waged and won a fight that limits the bestowal of university fellowships on U.S.-born citizens only. Some universities have made this policy public (e.g., Michigan), and some have not because they cannot politically do so. The principle involved was simply illustrated.

> It is hard for somebody from Guadalajara to get to the United States tomorrow and say, I have a right to be hired because I have been discriminated against historically.

This discussion prompted some in the audience to reexamine affirmative-action legislation and to characterize it as "politically divisive in the United States." One participant attributed the recent difficulties of the Democratic Party, a "peculiar coalition of conflicting interest groups put together by Franklin Roosevelt in the 1930s," in part to the divisive character of affirmative-action policies.

To other participants, the principles and issues raised in one area of this debate were labeled as "thoroughly un-American." For example, one participant stated that the United States is:

> the one country that has separated the notion of citizenship from nationality . . . and the notion that only U.S.-born minorities rather than immigrant groups can share in the benefits of certain policies, I find most extraordinary.

In wrapping up this discussion, it was pointed out that Canada was seeking to address these very issues through two major pieces of legislation recently introduced. One centers on the issue of the diversity now emerging in Canada as a result of its immigration policy; although Canada has had a policy of multiculturalism in the past, that policy is not grounded in legislation or supported by the Constitution. The second piece of legislation deals with "equity in employment," which differs from affirmative-action legislation in the United States. It is:

> based upon public disclosure of hirings, promotions, firings, wage increases, and so on, in all federally regulated companies, so that you know whether or not women, disabled, visible minorities, and native Canadians are being advanced through the whole labor structure in a manner consistent with their participation or their numbers in the population.

In short, both of these pieces of legislation have been defined to address what is happening to Canadian society as a result of immigration policies.

PALABRAS DE CLAUSURA
Mario Ojeda Gomez

Fuí invitado a hablar en esta reunión que tiene por objeto examiner los efectos de la legislación norteamericana de 1986, sobre reforma y control de la immigración, en base a mi experiencia como miembro de la Comisión Bilateral sobre el futoro de las relaciones México–Estados Unidos. En consecuencia, mi intervención se orientará más bien a ubicar el tema de la migración dentro del marco más amplio de las relaciones México–Estados Unidos.

Quisiera, con el permiso de ustedes, iniciar mi intervención con un anécdota histórico. Richard Nixon, en uno de su primeros actos como Presidente de los Estados Unidos, recibó en visita oficial al Primer Ministro del Japón. En su discurso de bienvenida, Nixon dijo que se sentía muy honrado de recibir al mandatario del principal socio comercial de los Estados Unidos.

Estas palabras, que constituían una declaración oficial del gobierno norteamericano, por provenir de su propio presidente, irritaron profundamente a los canadienses. Debemos recordar que en aquel entonces—y todavía en la actualidad—era el Canadá y no el Japón el principal socio comercial de los Estados Unidos, tanto como importador como exportador.

En consecuencia este incidente produjo una reacción negativa de parte de los medios de información canadienses. Los periódicos dieron por publicar numerosas notas y artículos quejándose de que los norteamericanos no sabían siquiera de la existencia del Canadá como país independiente o de que los norteamericanos tomaban al Canadá por su patio trasero.

La ola de indignación que este incidente produjo en la opinión pública canadiense fue tan grande, que John Holmes, fallecido recientemente, y en aquel entonces Director del Instituto Canadiense de Asuntos Externos, se sintió obligado a escribir un artículo para calmar los ánimos. En dicho artículo Holmes hacía un llamado a los canadienses a olvidarse del asunto, ya que de lo contrario—decía—correremos el riesgo de que los norteamericanos nos descubran, de que nos descubran los medio de información, de que nos descubra el Congreso y de que nos descubran las universidades. Añadía Holmes que este descubrimiento del Canadá por parte de los Estados Unidos seguramente desembocaría en la creación de algún o algunos programas de estudios sobre el Canadá, de los que surgiría un proyecto de política especial de Washington hacia su vecino del norte y que eso habría de gustar aún menos a los canadienses.

Creo, por mi parte, que hoy día nos encontramos ante un caso similar respecto a México: Hemos sido descubiertos en los Estados Unidos. Nos han descubierto los medios de información, nos han descubierto las universidades, y nos ha descubierto el Congreso. Somos parte ya del debate interno de los Estados Unidos y somos parte ya de ese peligroso juego que allí se practica bajo el nombre de *Constituency Politics*. La única diferencia es que para México ya no es posible dar marcha atrás, como sugería Holmes a los canadienses. México ha sido descubierto por los Estados Unidos y los mexicanos tenemos que aprender a vivir con esa nueva realidad. Tenemos que aprender a defendernos de las consecuencias negativas de esa nueva realidad y tenemos que aprender también a sacar provecho de lo positivo que ello tiene.

Desafortunadamente para nosotros los mexicanos, el descubrimiento de México por parte de los Estados Unidos ha sido más bien por causas negativas que positivas. México ha sido descubierto debido a su enorme deuda externa; a la creciente migración de indocumentados; al tráfico de drogas; a la corrupción interna y a otras cosas negativas. Esto nos genera, por principio de cuentas, mala voluntad de parte de la opinión pública norteamericana y nos coloca a la defensiva. Debemos recordar que para enfrentar los problemas que suscita nuestra intensa relación bilateral, es indispensable ante todo una atmósfera de buena voluntad.

Mucho de lo que ahora digo lo aprendí por la vía de la experencia, sobre todo en lo que se refiere a la atmósfera de buena voluntad como requisito previo para enfrentar bilateralmente los problemas de la relación. Digo enfrentar y no resolver deliberadamente, pues la mayor parte de los problemas que suscita nuestra relación son de orden estructural y, en consecuencia, no es a base de mera buena voluntad que se van a resolver o a atenuar estos problemas.

Hablo fundamentalmente a partir de la experiencia que me ha tocado vivir durante dos años de trabajo como miembro de la Comisión Bilateral sobre el futoro de las relaciones México–Estados Unidos. Esta Comisión no es oficial, sino que tiene un carácter privado, ajeno a los cargos que desempeñan o a las profesiones y artes que practican sus miembros. La Comisión, por ser bilateral, tiene dos presidentes: uno por México que es el ex-Senador Hugo Margáin y otro por los Estados Unidos que es William Rogers, quien fue Secretario de Estado para Asuntos Inter-Americanos. La Comisión está compuesta por un grupo de hombres y mujeres, ciudadanos de ambos países, con actividades profesionales distintas y con orientaciones políticas diferentes. Se trata, en consecuencia, de un grupo en alto grado heterogéneo.

La idea de crear la Comisión Bilateral surgío precisamente en momentos en que la atmosféra de la relación bilateral entre los dos países se había deteriorado profundamente. Los años de 1985 y 1986 fueron especialmente difíciles y de gran tirantez. Las causas de esta tirantez fueron varias. Una de ellas fue el creciente consumo de drogas en los Estados Unidos que originó que ciertos sectores de ese país empezaran a acusar al gobierno mexicano de negligencia en el combate del tráfico de estupefacientes. Más tarde, el asesinato ocurrido en México de un agente de la Oficina Norteamericana Antinarcóticos (DEA), elevó el tono de las acusaciones, al grado de que llegaron a presentarse imputaciones a funcionarios mexicanos de colusión con mafias y traficantes. La presentación de estas imputaciones, sin aportación de pruebas, irritó profundamente al gobierno federal mexicano. Conforme al punto de vista oficial mexicano estos sectores norteamericanos de opinión, lejos de reconocer el esfuerzo del gobierno de México en la lucha las drogas, acusaban a varios de sus funcionarios de colusión con los traficantes.

Durante este periodo, el gobierno mexicano fue acusado también, por ciertos sectores políticos de los Estados Unidos, de cometer fraude electoral en varios Estados de la República. Estas acusaciones fueron interpretadas en los círculos oficiales de México como actos de intervención en los asuntos internos del país.

Coincidiendo con estas acusaciones, se produjo durante este periodo un crecimiento significativo de inmigrantes mexicanos indocumentados hacia los Estados Unidos. Esto fue consecuencia en gran parte de la crisis económica de México. Fue así que empezo a difundirse la idea en los Estados Unidos de que a consecuencia de estas oleadas migratorias estaban perdiendo el control de su frontera sur.

1985 y 1986 fueron años también en los que las discrepancias en materia de política exterior entre México y los Estados Unidos se acentuaron. Este fue el caso de las diferencias en cuanto al patrón de voto de cada uno de los dos países en las Naciones Unidas y este fue el caso tambíen de las discrepancias con relaíon a los conflictos en Centroamérica. Al menos un sector influyente en Washington dio por interpretar el voto de México como una provocación a los Estados Unidos y acusó al gobierno mexicano de consentir, con su política hacia Nicaragua, la entronización del comunismo en Centroamérica tal y como con anterioridad lo había hecho respecto a Cuba.

Todas estas percepciones y discrepancias reales, sumadas a declaraciones poco escrupulosas de algunos diplomáticos, envenenaron la atmósfera de la relación y por lo tanto impidieron que ambos gobiernos concertaran medidas tendientes a subsanar los verdaderos puntos neurálgicos de esa relación. Fue entonces—como se dice arriba—cuando surgió la idea de crear una Comisión Bilateral, independiente de ambos gobiernos, que se echara a cuestas la tarea de analizar objetivamente los asuntos de la relación y de presentar sugerencias a ambos gobiernos. La coyuntura era propicia, pues en poco tiempo nuevos presidentes habrían de ascender al poder en ambos países y esto daba la oportunidad de superar los agravios pasados y enfrentar los asuntos de la relación con nuevos enfoques.

La Comisión Bilateral trabajó con entusiasmo durante dos años seguidos y culmino su esfuerzo con un informe que hizo público en noviembre de 1988. El informe está basado en el análisis de 48 monografías preparadas por destacados especialistas de los distintos asuntos que conforman la relación. Sin embargo, la Comisión no se limitó únicamente a analizar estos trabajos, sino que solicitó también a otros expertos que presentaran verbalmente sus puntos de vista, y sostuvo por otra parte entrevistas con funcionarios de ambos gobiernos y con autoridades de nivel intermedio, como fue el caso de autoridades migratorias de la frontera. En un momento dado, la Comisión se dividió en subcomisiones a fin de poder conocer opiniones más allá del círculo de los expertos y los funcionarios.

El informe lleva por título, *México y los Estados Unidos: el Desafío de la Interdependencia*. Con este título se quieren significar dos cosas: primera, que México y los Estados Unidos están ligados aún a su pesar, por la geografia y por una dependencia mutua que se ha ensanchado en la medida en que ha crecido la intensidad de la relación; y segunda, que si bien esta interdependencia genera problemas, también crea oportunidades para lograr muchas cosas positivas, mediante acciones conjuntas que no hemos sabido aprovechar. De aquí entonces el desafío que se nos presenta hacia el futuro: desarrollar el enorme potencial de la cooperación bilateral.

Este es, a grandes rasgos, el mensaje principal de informe. Por lo demás no presenta nada que sea espectacularmente nuevo, ni sugiere fórmulas mágicas para la solución de los problemas entre México y Estados Unidos. Esto se debe, en primer lugar, a que ninguno de los comisionados cree que existan soluciones plenas para los problemas: lo que hay que buscar son salidas para subsanarlos o fórmulas para atenuarlos o para regularlos.

La segunda razón de que no haya nada espectacular en el informe—y esto es tal vez lo más importante—es que no se trata de un libro de un solo autor, de una visión única, o de las preferencias voluntaristas de una sola persona. Se trata del resultado de un análisis conjunto de un grupo de personas altamente heterogéneo. Un grupo diferente en cuanto a nacionalidad, distinto en cuanto a actividad profesional y opuesto en cuanto a orientación política. El informe es el resultado de la convergencia de conclusiones a las que se fue llegando en forma gradual, a través del análisis y la discusión conjunta. Esta es, sin duda, la mayor aportación del informe, la más rica experiencia, experiencia que puede ser de utilidad práctica.

La primera convergencia de ideas se dio en cuanto a una conclusión que puede parecer simplista a primera vista, pero a la que no es fácil arribar en la práctica cuando se trata de un grupo heterogéneo. Esta conclusión es la siguiente: las causas de los problemas que suscita la relación entre México y los Estados Unidos tienen su origen en ambos lados de la frontera. Esta conclusión, que parece verdad de perogrullo, es algo difícil de aceptar en México, en donde existen amplios sectores de opinión cuya percepción de las relaciones bilaterales es la del "pobre México tan lejos de Dios y tan cerca de los Estados Unidos." Pero si esta es una conclusión difícil de aceptar en amplios sectores de la opinión pública de México, lo es todavía más en los Estados Unidos, en donde prevalece la percepción mayoritaria de que los problemas que suscita nuestra relación provienen exclusivamente de México.

A partir de esta primera conclusión, la Comisión Bilateral arribó a una segunda. Esta es en el sentido de que si las causas de los problemas que suscita la relación bilateral tienen su origen en ambos lados de la frontera, luego entonces, existe una corresponsabilidad en cuanto a éstos. De aquí, a su vez, se concluyó lo más importante: los problemas suscitados por las relaciones entre México y Estados Unidos no se pueden enfrentar con éxito basándose en medidas unilaterales, sino en base a una cooperación bilateral. A esta última conclusión habría que añdir un corolario: no es con medidas legalistas como se pueden enfrentar con éxito problemas que tienen un evidente trasfondo socioeconómico.

Tomemos como ejemplo el caso de las drogas, uno de los problemas que mayor irritación ha causado últimamente. Para nosotros los comisionados, ha quedado claro, despues de examinar un número amplio de testimonios, que el problema tiene sus causas en ambos lados de la frontera: este es un problema de oferta y demanda. En consecuencia no puede ser atacado con éxito a base de medidas unilaterales y menos aún si éstas son de carácter meramente legalista y polícíco. Tal es el caso, por ejemplo de la llamada "certificación" de parte de Washington de la buena conducta en materia de cooperación de los distintos países en la lucha norteamericana en contra de las drogas. En el caso de México, país que recibe ayuda económica bilateral de los Estados Unidos única y precisamente para el combate a las drogas, la negativa de certificación tiene un efecto contrario. Esta significa la reducción de la capacidad de México para combatir el narcotráfico.

Otro punto a destacar con relación a las drogas es que lejos de lo que muchos piensan, la sociedad mexicana sufre también las consecuencias de este problema. No me refiero necesariamente al consumo interno—problema que puede agudizarse al futuro—sino a consecuencias de tipo indirecto. Por ejemplo el hecho de que resulte más rentable sembrar mariguana que alimentos básicos, ha conducido a que muchos campesinos mexicanos desvíen el uso de sus tierras para cultivarla o que las abandonen para ir a la sierra a producirla. Otro impacto negativo de las drogas en México es el de la creciente inseguridad que se ha generado en algunas regiones. El problema, a decir verdad, no es nuevo, pero no cabe duda que ha crecido en la medida en que ha aumentado la demanda de estupefacientes y con ello las mafias que se disputan el control del mercado.

Esto me lleva a mi último comentario que será muy breve. El fenómeno de la emigración de indocumentados obedece también a una doble causa: los factores de expulsión del lugar de origen acrecentados por la crisis económica que padece México y los factores de atracción, generados por la demanda de mano de obra barata en los Estados Unidos.

Este fenómeno no se va a poder detener ni aun controlar a base de medidas unilaterales o legalistas. Este fenómeno se va a tener que enfrentar a la larga en bien de ambos países, a base de medidas de cooperación bilateral que ataquen su trasfondo socioeconómico. Cuando digo en beneficio de ambos países lo hago consciente de que para muchos la migración resulta una válvula de escape al desempleo en México. Es probable que a corto plazo así lo sea, pero no cabe duda de que a largo plazo, México es quien más sufre, pues pierde lo mejor de su fuerza de trabajo.

CLOSING REMARKS
(English Summary)
Mario Ojeda Gomez

President Richard Nixon, in one of his welcome speeches, professed that he was honored to receive a member of the government of Japan, the *principal* trade partner of the United States. Canadians were irritated by this remark because it was Canada, not Japan, that was the principal trade partner of the United States. The negative reaction in Canada was so strong that John Holmes, then Director of the Canadian Institute for Affairs, felt he had to write an article calling on Canadians to forget the incident, because otherwise the country ran the risk of being discovered by the United States, and the consequences of that would displease Canadians even more.

Today Mexico is in a similar situation: It has been "discovered" in the United States—by the media, the universities, and even Congress—and for that reason it is now part of the internal political debate and part, too, of what is called "constituency politics." The only difference with the Canadian case is that this trend is irreversible. Mexicans must learn to live with this new reality, to defend themselves from its negative consequences, and to benefit, too, from its positive effects.

Unfortunately, such a discovery took place for negative reasons—Mexico's enormous debt, increasing undocumented migration, drug trafficking, domestic corruption—which generate ill will among Americans toward Mexico and place Mexico on the defensive. We should keep in mind that an atmosphere of good will is indispensable and is a prerequisite for confronting the problems within our intense bilateral relationship.

This is what I learned as a member of the Bi-Lateral Commission on the Future of United States–Mexico Relations. This Commission, independent from the U.S. and Mexican governments, was created (1) in response to the deterioration of the relations between the two countries in the years 1985 and 1986 and (2) to analyze objectively the nature of the relationship and present suggestions for both governments. In 1988 the Commission released "Mexico and the United States: The Challenge of Interdependence." This title sought to communicate two major points: (1) the two countries are linked (even though reluctantly) by geography and a mutual dependence that has increased over time, and (2) although this interdependence creates problems, it also offers opportunities that have not yet been fully exercised. Hence, the challenge before us is to develop the enormous potential for bilateral cooperation.

The Commission reached the conclusion that the causes of the problems in the relationship between the two countries are to be found in *both* countries. This may seem simplistic, but it is something that is difficult to accept in Mexico and may be even more difficult to accept in the United States. It also leads to another important conclusion: Problems in the two countries' relations can be addressed effectively only through bilateral cooperation.

An example of the necessity for bilateralism is the drug problem. This is a problem of demand and supply that has causes on both sides of the border and, consequently, it cannot be confronted by unilateral measures and even less so by measures of character purely legalistic or political. Such is the case of the so-called "certification" by Washington in matters related to combating the traffic of drugs. For Mexico, a negative "certification" means a reduction in economic aid from the United States and hence a reduction in Mexico's ability to address the problem. And, as is the case with the United States, Mexico feels strongly the undesirable effects of drug trafficking on its people, for example in the form of increased insecurity in some parts of the country.

As with the problem of narcotics, undocumented migration derives from two causes: (1) expulsion factors, increased by Mexico's economic crisis, and (2) attraction factors, generated by the demand for cheap labor in the United States. This, too, is a phenomenon that cannot be halted or controlled by unilateral or legalistic measures. It is a phenomenon that both countries should attack bilaterally at its socioeconomic bases. In some people's view, migration is an escape valve for Mexico's unemployment problems. Certainly this assertion is true for the short term, but in the long term, Mexico suffers the most because it loses the best of its labor force.

CLOSING REMARKS
Flora MacDonald

It has been very satisfying for me to be able to come here, listen, and be associated with what I think is an ongoing, healthy effort to take a look at immigration policy and where it is leading in the United States and its neighboring countries.

The most unexpected comment that I have heard during the conference was when Diego Asencio said that there were those who were surprised by the passage of the legislation. Coming from a parliamentary system, I find failure of passage almost impossible to conceive. When you go through the genesis of policy coming from the parties, being passed by caucus, introduced into a cabinet, introduced into parliament, then introduced into committee, you know that once legislation starts on the road, it is eventually going to pass. So I enjoy the idea that you might unexpectedly pass legislation—there are some things I would like to be able to do in Canada.

We came here to discuss the international effects of the Immigration Reform and Control Act (IRCA) of 1986, and the discussion has been lively. Has the legislation had an impact? My assessment is a resounding "maybe." But at this stage, surely this is not the most important point. The most important point is that during IRCA's implementation, its ongoing impact is being actively monitored, analyzed, and annotated.

We cannot expect to have a very clear picture of the results of the legislation which, as Georges Vernez told us at the outset, has 50 provisions being phased in over a five-year period with some of the most critical and tough measures yet to be implemented.

I was impressed by the studies done to date. The data, while soft, showed clearly that employer sanctions are not the only, perhaps not even the major, factor in altering the rate of apprehensions and flows: amnesty, grandfathering, psychological pressures, and other factors have had an up-front influence.

It is critical, as Jorge Bustamante's presentation showed, to quantify the human dimensions which can so easily be overlooked, such as the question of gender. Is there selectivity and if so on what is it based? Is there harassment through different corridors? Are there family and dependency pressures? All of these, although very localized, can then be translated into the larger picture, which also allows for an interpretation of other groups coming from other countries. Are they the same? Do they demand different measures? Does new immigrant policy have to be adopted to address these localized issues that are emerging from the studies discussed during the last two days?

Equally important is the analysis of change to the internal U.S. political scene. New political imperatives are emerging: The growing electoral clout of the Mexican American community, emerging conflicts between Mexican Americans and Central Americans, and the function of a different language and culture in what is predominantly an English-only country. All of these internal political factors will have a broad influence on how U.S. public opinion is formed in the future, and that must be continually measured from the outset.

There is a factor that I did not hear discussed, that I would have liked to have heard more about, and that I hope will emerge in future gatherings of this kind; that is the changing role of work. It seemed to me that much of the discussion was predicated on the kind of work that migrant workers coming into the country have done in the past. In an age that is rapidly creating an information society, the nature of work is changing. Therefore, the nature of the contribution of workers is changing and, perhaps most important in that context, the role of women in society and the role of women in the labor force is changing. That is going to have quite an impact on migration in the future. This is an area that I think cries out for study.

Illegal immigration creates an exploited underclass; IRCA tries to address and correct this. Some of its detractors say it is too tough, others, too soft. In the long run, IRCA will probably satisfy some domestic concerns, but it is not designed to address the large issues regarding movement of peoples from third-world countries to the more developed nations. As someone pointed out, flows are governed by economics, not by law. To the extent possible, the law must be seen to be working, but migration, legal or illegal, is a permanent feature of Mexican-U.S. relations.

So, we come back to the larger questions raised by Diego Asencio and Madam Gomez Maganda, which place immigration concerns in a global context. Industrialized countries are reacting to domestic pressures and introducing restrictive measures to stem flows of peoples from third-world countries. That may become very explosive. You cannot continue to do this and expect that the flows of people, given economic situations elsewhere in the world, are going to cease.

If the creative energies being devoted to these pursuits could be persuaded to forget turf wars for the moment and collectively try to address more effectively the problems that generate the flows in the first place—third-world debt, economic disparities, environmental dangers—we will have taken a great step forward. That may sound a bit idealistic, but I was interested in hearing Christopher Mitchell comment about how this idea has to be added to foreign policy agendas. As long as I have heard these discussions, they have been at the agenda level of ministers of immigration, such as we have in Canada, or people who are dealing with immigration commissions; they are seldom raised to the level of foreign ministers and heads of government.

Just recently, I was at a conference in Brussels, the Quadrangular Forum, where the discussion was about the agenda of the economic summit coming up in July of 1989. For the first time, I heard the subject of illegal immigration introduced as a destabilizing factor in security matters. This may not be the best way to combat it, but nevertheless, illegal immigration is, for the first time, being discussed at the level of the seven economic leaders. It will be on their agenda as a matter of security. It should be moved from the broad security issues and looked at from the perspective of how, if it were to become a security threat, it could be alleviated and what the leaders of the industrialized countries could do in a major way to resolve the problems that generate the flows.

I do not have the solutions. None of us does. But those issues will have to be tackled in a much broader way than they have been in the past.

PART III

RESOURCE PAPERS

THE EFFECTS OF IRCA ON THE PATTERN OF APPREHENSIONS AT THE BORDER

Michael J. White, Frank D. Bean, and Thomas J. Espenshade
The Urban Institute

Considerable discussion has taken place in the media in recent months about whether the new immigration law in the United States, the Immigration Reform and Control Act (IRCA) of 1986, has had an effect on illegal immigration, particularly whether it has reduced the stock and flow of undocumented workers to the United States. This paper presents some research results that may help shed light on whether IRCA has influenced the immigrant flow across the U.S.-Mexican border. The discussion focuses on analyses of monthly apprehensions data, that is, on statistics on the apprehensions of individuals at the U.S.-Mexican border by the U.S. Immigration and Naturalization Service (INS), as a rough indicator of changes in illegal flows. The research approach is to build a statistical model of migration and then use it to analyze the apprehensions data. The paper first presents the basic outlines of the model and then some of the initial results obtained to this point in the analysis.

Figure 1 gives some indication of the difficulties in interpreting changes over time in apprehensions data. The U.S. media often interpret the effect of IRCA on illegal flows by quoting figures on apprehensions. For example, the recent 40 percent decline in apprehensions

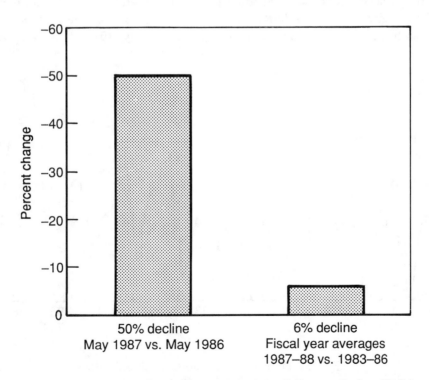

Fig. 1—Change in number of apprehensions before and after IRCA, using only time as a variable

from fall 1986 to fall 1987 was used as indicating a reduction in the flow.[1] It is important to emphasize, however, that the selected time period influences how much reduction in apprehensions has occurred. For example, the left-hand portion of Fig. 1 compares the number of apprehensions at the border in May 1987, after IRCA, with May 1986, prior to IRCA, when apprehensions were at their peak. A comparison of only these two months indicates about a 50 percent decline in apprehensions. However, if one compares averages for certain fiscal years before and after IRCA, in this case 1983 to 1986 with 1987 to 1988, one finds only a 6 percent decline in apprehensions. Thus, different answers can be obtained depending on the period of comparison. The model we use will introduce still more factors that need to be taken into account before conclusions are drawn about the extent to which apprehensions have changed over time.

Figure 2 illustrates the time trends of the apprehensions. These are monthly data on apprehensions made by Border Patrol officers at the U.S.-Mexican border for 1977 to 1988. Over this period a gradual increase in the average annual number of apprehensions occurs, reaching a peak in early 1986. We also observe a very strong monthly pattern. Within most of the annual observation periods, apprehensions reach their peak in March, April, or May and then decline throughout the rest of the year to a low in December.

The far right portion of Fig. 2 represents the period after IRCA. Since 1986, apprehensions have declined, but considerable fluctuation remains. *But* apprehensions were not the only thing that changed over this period. Figure 3 graphs the number of linewatch hours registered by Border Patrol agents at the U.S.-Mexican border for 1977–1987. The time on linewatch actually observing or apprehending aliens, as logged by the officers, is at first fairly stable but then begins to increase fairly substantially beginning in the mid-1980s. It reaches high values with some fluctuation in 1986 and into early 1987; however, we observe a

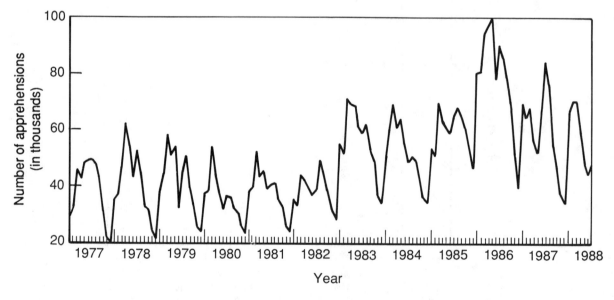

Fig. 2—Total apprehensions on linewatch
at the U.S.-Mexican border

---

[1]*New York Times*, June 18, 1989.

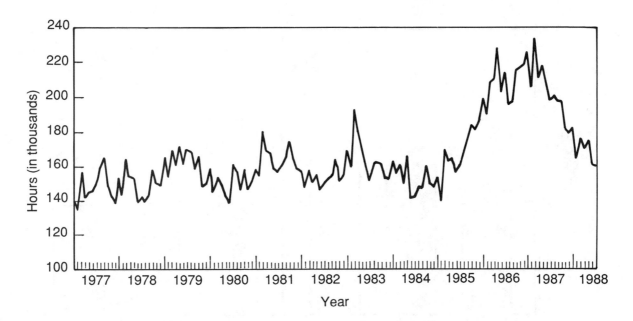

Fig. 3—Officer hours on linewatch at the U.S.-Mexican border

substantial decline in hours throughout 1987 and into 1988. This decline would probably contribute to a decline in apprehensions, irrespective of any deterrent effects of IRCA.

To take into account these and other factors that may influence the total number of apprehensions, we elected to develop a multivariate statistical model. This model makes use of a long time series of information; it includes both measures of incentives to migrate to the United States from Mexico and measures of the INS resources put into Border Patrol activity.

The factors influencing the pool of potential migrants to the United States include economic conditions, that is, wages and unemployment rates in the United States and in Mexico, and a demographic effect measuring the size of the Mexican population in the prime migration ages. We also include a measure (dummy variable) for each month of the year to control for the strong monthly pattern visible in Fig. 2. We include the following measures of INS effort: officer hours at linewatch, and capital expenditures. We measure the effects of IRCA through changes in these INS efforts; through changes in the number of applications to the legalization program for Special Agricultural Workers (SAWs); and through a measure of any additional IRCA effects such as deterrents, sanctions, and the absence of new starts, as captured by the dummy variables for the post-IRCA period.

Our model predicts variation in this time series very well. Demographic, monthly, and seasonal factors explain a considerable amount of variation in the time trend of apprehension data. Push and pull effects and population size effects are important. Some additional explanatory power is associated with INS effort and the other IRCA-related variables. Our model is designed to measure the actual magnitude of these influences.

Figure 4 presents selected results from this time trend analysis. Examining first the results for early fiscal year 1987, we see in the bar labeled "A" a measure of the effect of IRCA, that is the proportionate reduction in apprehensions that occurred, without controlling for INS resources of the legalization program. In bar "B," we control for the changes in INS resources

70

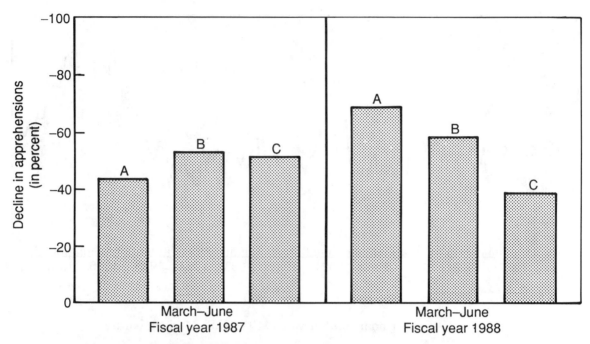

NOTES: A = without INS resources controlled;
B = with INS resources controlled (capital budget and linewatch hours);
C = with INS resources and SAWs controlled.

Fig. 4—Post-IRCA time trends of apprehension reductions,
two time periods

throughout the time period, that is, for shifts in budgetary expenditures and linewatch hours. And in bar "C," we control for INS resources and enrollment in the SAW program. The effect of the SAW legalization program is that upon legalization SAWs are removed from the pool of undocumented workers because they either remain in the United States or obtain documentation that allows them to move back and forth legally. Therefore, more SAW applications should mean fewer apprehensions.

Comparing bars "A" and "B" for 1987, we note that, upon controlling for INS effort, apprehensions are estimated in bar "B" to have been down even a little more than they actually were. This is because, in this earlier period, linewatch hours and budgetary expenditures were actually increasing. Bars "B" and "C" are nearly equal in this period because almost no legalization had yet begun for the SAW program. It is interesting to contrast these results with those for March through June of 1988. Again, "A," "B," and "C" represent the effects of IRCA, or the proportionate reduction in apprehensions, first without controlling for INS effort, then controlling for INS effort, and finally controlling for INS effort and the SAW legalization program. As we compare bars "A" and "B," we see that the effect of IRCA is somewhat reduced (in proportionate terms) from what one would otherwise expect because INS resources, particularly linewatch hours by Border Patrol officers, were reduced during this period. Comparing "B" and "C," we see a further proportionate reduction in IRCA effectiveness due to the SAW legalization program.

In Fig. 5 we examine these sorts of comparisons between "A," "B," and "C" for six successive periods, approximately four months each, following the initiation of IRCA. Across the entire post-IRCA period, particularly as one moves toward fiscal year 1988, bar "C" is particularly shortened compared with bar "A" or "B," suggesting that SAW legalization removed people from the pool of eligibles. Controlling for this factor, then, makes the most difference later in time. Another interesting feature of this particular graph is that apprehensions are down an extra amount in the spring periods, March through June 1987 and 1988. Bar "C" for the March–June periods is a bit longer than the corresponding "C" bars for November through February and July through October, suggesting that the reduction in apprehensions attributable to IRCA seems to be stronger in the spring.

Our statistical model indicates the following preliminary conclusions: First, the demographic, economic, and seasonal or monthly variables are quite influential in determining the pattern of apprehensions observed at the U.S.-Mexican border. A one percentage point decline, say from 6 percent to 5 percent, in the unemployment rate in the United States predicts a 3 percent increase in apprehensions at the border. The growth of the young Mexican population, likely to be of a migratory propensity, is also particularly strong in predicting apprehensions. Even in this model, the seasonal pattern persists. The differentiation across months is quite large.

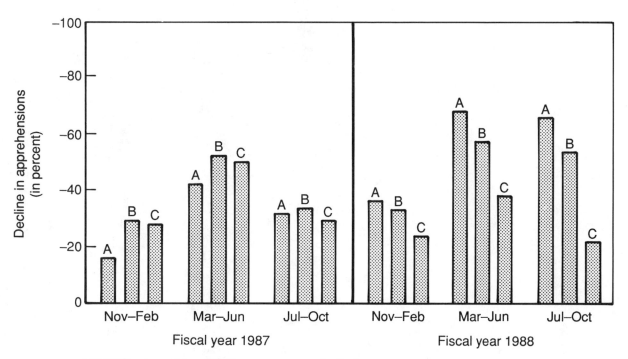

NOTES: A = without INS resources controlled;
B = with INS resources controlled (capital budget and linewatch hours);
C = with INS resources and SAWs controlled.

Fig. 5—Post-IRCA time trends of apprehension reductions,
six time periods

With respect to IRCA itself, our results seem to indicate that IRCA has had an impact and that that impact is multifacted. When one talks about *the* effect of IRCA, one has to be quite specific about what is meant by the term. In this discussion, the effect of IRCA includes a decline in linewatch hours throughout 1987 and into 1988, which would tend to reduce the number of apprehensions, and the effect of the legalization program for special agricultural workers, which tends to remove people from the pool of eligibles and thereby reduce apprehensions at the border. Supplementing both of those influences, we find that there is an additional apprehension reduction of about 30 percent, a rough average as estimated by our statistical model. We also find that there seems to be a seasonal pattern to apprehension reduction, with the largest relative reductions occurring in the spring. Finally, our results do not cover a long enough time period to enable conclusions about a post-IRCA time trend. As more time passes, further research will be required to clarify more precisely the nature and magnitude of IRCA's effects on undocumented flows.

MIGRACIÓN INDOCUMENTADA MÉXICO–ESTADOS UNIDOS; HALLAZGOS PRELIMINARES DEL PROYECTO CAÑÓN ZAPATA

Jorge A. Bustamante
El Colegio de la Frontera Norte

INTRODUCCIÓN

Este es un segundo informe de investigación del Proyecto Cañón Zapata. El primero fue publicado hace poco más de un año en un número especial, sobre la frontera norte, de la revista *El Cotidiano* de la Universidad Autónoma Metropolitana, Unidad Azcapotzalco.[1] El propósito de este trabajo es ofrecer nuevos datos que permitan hacer una evaluación sobre los efectos de las reformas a las leyes de inmigración de Estados Unidos, después de que han terminado los plazos para solicitar la legalización que se ofreció a los indocumentados y después de que han entrado en vigor cabalmente las sanciones a los patrones que contraten indocumentados. La primera sección de este trabajo explica algunas de las medidas principales de dicha legislación. La segunda explica la paradoja de una ley orientada hacia la restricción de la inmigración al mismo tiempo que ocurren patrones demográficos que apuntan hacia una mayor demanda de mano de obra extranjera en Estados Unidos. La tercera sección explica de manera resumida en qué consiste la medición de los flujos migratorios que se hace en el llamado "Proyecto Cañón Zapata." La cuarta parte consiste de dicho proyecto. La quinta y última sección se dedica a algunas interpretaciónes a manera de conclusiones, derivadas de los datos presentos.

LAS REFORMAS A LAS LEYES DE INMIGRACIÓN DE ESTADOS UNIDOS

La aprobación de las reformas a las leyes de inmigración de Estados Unidos (Immigration Reform and Control Act of 1986—IRCA), conocidas popularmente como Ley Simpson-Rodino, el 6 de noviembre de 1986, fue impulsada principalmente por la percepción de que el país había "perdido el control sobre sus fronteras."[2] Diversos factores ideológicos propiciaron un temor muy extendido en la opinión pública estadounidense de que había un "serio peligro" en la presencia de los migrantes indocumentados.[3] La fuerza de esos factores ideológicos hizo que no se escucharan voces autorizadas que sostuvieron que la inmigración indocumentada hacía más

---

[1]Bustamante, Jorge A., "La Migración de los Indocumentados," *El Cotidiano*, Número especial 1, México D.F.: UAM-Azcapotzalco, 1987, pp. 13–29.

[2]La frase, "We have lost control of our borders," que resultó ser el resumen más elocuente para justificar la necesidad del proyecto de Ley Simpson-Mazzoli y luego Simpson-Rodino, se acuñó en el calor de las vísperas de la contienda electoral Reagan vs. Carter, cuando los republicanos trataban de demostrar la debilidad del presidente Carter frente a los más de 200 mil cubanos que se desbordaban sobre las costas de Florida en imagenes dramaticas proyectadas por las cadenas nacionales de la television estradounidense. Cuando paso el furor de la llamada "invasión del Mariel," la frase, que ya habia capturado la imaginación de los televidentes, fue trasladada por los propugnadores del proyecto de Ley Simpson-Mazzoli a la frontera con México.

[3]El 87 por ciento de los entrevistados en una encuesta de opinión realizada en California en 1985, respondió que la inmigración indocumentada desde México era en ese tiempo "algo seria" o "muy seria." Véase uno de los raros libros que ponian en duda la creencia en la negatividad total de la inmigración indocumentada en vísperas de la aprobación de IRCA: Muller, Thomas, y Thomas J. Espanshade, *The Fourth Wave: California's Newest Immigrants,* Washington, D.C., 1985, p. 201.

bien que mal a la economia estadounidense.[4] El hecho es que el objectivo principal de las nuevas reforms fue el de reducir hasta eliminar la entrada ilegal de extranjeros.[5] Para este efecto, la nueva legislación (IRCA) estableció varias medidas. La más notoria, por la controversia que provocó en el proceso legislativo, fué la de imponer sanciónes a los patrones que emplearan extranjeros indocumentados. Esta medida derogaba lo establecido en las reformas de 1952 conocidas como Ley Walter-McArran, en virtud de la cual, mediante la "enmienda texana" (Texas proviso), Estados Unidos se convirtió en el único país que autorizaba expresamente a los patrones a contratar a los extranjeros que hubieran entrado al país en violación de sus propias leyes migratorias.[6]

Otra medida fue la de regularizar la situación migratoria de los indocumentados, conocida en Estados Unidos como "amnistía." La nueva legislación ofreció básicamante dos vías para obtener la legalización. Una fue la que so podría llamar "legalización regular," que se abrió para los indocumentados que pudieran probar una residencia continua en Estados Unidos desde antes del 10 de enero de 1982. Al terminar el período para presentar solicitudes, que fué del 5 de mayo de 1987 al 4 de mayo de 1988, el Servicio de Inmigración y Naturalización (SIN) del gobierno de Estados Unidos informó que se recibieron un millón setecientas mil solicitudes, de las cuales se calcula que seria aprobadas más del 90 por ciento.[7] Esta cifra resultó por abajo del cálculo de 2 millones de solicitudes que había hecho el SIN al inciarse el programa de legalización.

La otra vía fué para lo que se llamó "trabajadores agrícolas especiales." Esta se abrió para los extranjeros que pudieran probar que trabajaron en los Estados Unidos en labores agrícolas de productos perecederos, por un mínimo de 90 dias durante los tres años previos a la aprobación de la nueva legislación (6 de noviembre de 1986), siempre y cuando trabajaran un mínimo de 90 dias en labores agrícolas el primer año de su estancia legalizada. Para esta categoría se estableció un tope de 350 mil legalizaciones. Aun dentro de esta vía, se abrió otra subcategoría para otorgar permiso temporal para trabajar por un año, con opción a la legalización definitiva, siempre y cuando fuera para trabajar exclusivamente en labores agrícolas. Después de lo cual podrían optar por la legalización como "trabajadores agrícolas especiales." Para esta subcategoría no se estableció ningún tope numérico. Al terminar la última extensión del período de más de un año para la presentación de solicitudes, que fue al 30 de noviembre de 1988, el SIN informó que había recibido algo más de un millón de solicitudes. Dado que la "legalización regular" no admitía a los indocumentados con una residencia posterior al lo de enero de 1982, la mayor parte de los indocumentados mexicanos no pudieron calificar pues su patrón migratorio ha sido siempre un flujo de entrada y retorno a México para visitar a los familiares. Esto hizo que esa mayor parte tratara de calificar en la vía de "trabajadores agrícolas especiales." Dado que en esta categoría se estableció un tope numérico de 350 mil, era de esperarse que hubiera un exceso de solicitudes en dicha categoría. El SIN ha estado informando que muchos de los solicitantes en esta última categoría han estado presentando documentación apócrifa, por lo que se espera que, en contraste con el caso de la "legalización

---

[4]Véase le nota 7 del artículo citado del autor, publicado en *El Cotidiano* donde se cita al *Economic Report of the President (1986)* en apoyo a la misma afirmación.

[5](Citar alguna frase alusiva de Simpson.)

[6]Véase la nota 9 del artículo del autor publicado en *El Cotidiano*, antes citado, donde se transcribe el texto de la "enmienda texana."

[7]Espenshade, Thomas J., Frank D. Bean, Tracy Ann Goodis, y Michael J. White, "Immigration Policy in the United States: Future Prospects for the Immigration Reform and Control Act of 1986," Program for Research and Immigration Policy, The Urban Institute, Washington, D.C., 1988, p. 13.

regular," habra un alto porcentaje de solicitudes rechazadas en la categoría de "trabajadores agrícolas especiales."[8]

En teoria, los indocumentados que no hubieran obtenido su legalización por alguna de las vías abiertas por la nueva legislación, tendrían que regresar a sus países de origen. En la práctica esto no parece estar ocurriendo. La razón principal es que los patrones estadouidenses no han dejado de contratar extranjeros indocumentados.[9] Esto ha provocado, no solo que los indocumentados que no pudieron obtener su legalización se queden en Estados Unidos, sino que continúe con creces la entrada de nuevos indocumentados, sobre lo cual se ofrecerán datos más adelante.

LA PARADOJA DEL LIMOSNERO Y CON GARROTE

Resulta paradójico que una legislación tan restrictiva como la IRCA se hubiera aprobado el mismo año en que se iniciaría un notable incremento de la demanda de mano de obra extranjera a causa de cambios en los patrones demográficos estadounidenses. En efecto, en 1986, año en que se aprobó la legislación IRCA, ocurrió lo que se podría ver como un parteaguas en la dinámica de población de Estados Unidos. En ese año se inició un défict en la entrada al mercado de trabajo de personas del sexo masculino en el grupo de edades más jóvenes. En el Departamento del Trabajo del gobierno federal de Estados Unidos se calcula que para el año 2000 habrá un decremento del 6 por ciento en el número de jóvenes varones de 16 a 24 años de edad y un decremento del 15 por ciento en el grupo de edad de 24 a 34 años. La proporción del mercado de trabajo ocupada por los jóvenes varones en 1972 era del 23 por ciento, en tanto que en 1986 decendió al 20 por ciento; calculándose que para el año 2000 decenderá al 16 por ciento. Para entonces, la proporción de trabajadores en el grupo de edades mayores de 35 años se incrementará del 51 por ciento en 1986 al 61 por ciento.[10]

Si con los datos citados no fuera aún convincente la relación entre esos cambios demográficos y un incremento en la demanda de trabajadores inmigrantes indocumentados, se podrían agregar las proyecciones más recientes sobre la composición de la fuerza de trabajo en Estados Unidos.[11] Silvestri y Lukasiewics de la Oficina de Estadísticas Laborales del Departamento del Trabajo del gobierno de Estados Unidos han encontrado que, dentro de las 12 ocupaciones que tendrán una mayor demanda, de 1986 al año 2000, se encuentran las siguientes: meseros y mesaras, despachadores en tiendas de alimentos, aseadores de casas, oficinas y lugares públicos, afanadores y afanadoras, ayudantes de cocinero y cocineros de restaurant, depachadores de bares, mozos y ayudantes de clubes privados y personal de vigilancia. Como se puede inferir, estas son ocupaciones donde se encuentra más de la mitad de los inmigrantes indocumentados, como se mostrará más adelante. Los autores citados añaden que el sector de

---

[8]Véanse los cálculos desarrollados por: Martin, Philip, y J. Edward Taylor, "SAWs, RAWs and California's Farm Labor Market," Departamento de Economía Agrícola de la Universidad de California, Davis, 1988.

[9]El Sr. Ned Sullivan, Director de la zona de Los Angeles del Departamento del Trabajo del gobierno federal de Estados Unidos, aparce citado en una nota publicada en el diario *Los Angeles Times*, escrita por Henry Weinstein, del 16 de enero de 1989, titulada, "Illegal Immigrants Vulnerable," donde se afirma que el número de casos de patrones que pagan por debajo del salario mínimo ha aumentado desde que se aprobó la ley IRCA. En la misma nota aparece el abogado Anthony Mischel de la Oficina de Ayuda Legal de Los Angeles diciendo que "el número de casos (de violación a la ley de salarios mínimos) abiertos formalmente por nuestra oficina, se ha triplicado de 1986 a 1988." Según esta nota, la mayor parte de estos casos son en perjuicio de extranjeros indocumentados, sobre lo cual da datos de casos especificos.

[10]Fullerton, Howard N., Jr., "Labor Force Projections: 1986 to 2000," *Monthly Labor Review*, No. 110 (9), 1987, pp. 19–21.

[11]Véase: Silvestri, George T., y John M. Lukasiewics, "A Look at Occupational Employment Trends to the Year 2000," *Monthly Labor Review*, Vol. 110 (9), 1987, pp. 46–63.

servicios, donde se encuentran las ocupaciones mencionadas, será el que crezca más rapidamente de aquí a que termine el siglo. Este crecimiento será de 17 millones y medio en 1986 a casi 30 millones en el año 2000. Dados los patrones de crecimiento de los grupos de edad que estarán trabajado de aquí al final del siglo, no hay manera de que la población dispuesta a trabajar en Estados Unidos cubra la demanda de más de 5 millones de vacantes que se abrirán en las ocupaciones de salarios y requerimientos de calificación de niveles más bajos. A menos de que en los próximos años se invente un robot que haga las tareas de las ocupaciones antes mencionadas, por el precio al que se consigue un trabajador o trabajadora indocumentados, la economia de Estados Unidos se verá amenazada con disminuir su ritmo de crecimiento económico, social y políticamente aceptable, si no "importan" de alguna manera a la mano de obra extranjera que cubra los déficits producidos por el ritmo de envejecimiento de su población trabajadora.

Los datos anteriores apuntan hacia una mayor dependencia de Estados Unidos de la mano de obra extranjera, precisamente a partir de 1986 en que se aprobó una ley cuyo propósito explícito es restringir drásticamente la inmigración indocumentada.

LA MEDICIÓN DE LOS FLUJOS MIGRATORIOS TRANSFRONTERIZOS

Todo lo anterior sugiere la necesidad de responder con fundamento científico a la pregunta sobre si las reformas a las leyes de inmigración de Estados Unidos (IRCA), han producido el efecto que se propusieron sus propugnadores. En El Colegio de la Frontera Norte nos propusimos responder a esa pregunta mediante dos procedimientos se supervisión de los flujos hacia el norte de inmigrantes indocumentados. Uno, basado en la administración de un cuestionario corto a una muestra seleccionada al azar de 25 personas cada día, durante tres dias de cada semana, en ciudades donde El Colegio de la Frontera Norte cuenta con oficinas permanentes a lo largo de la frontera (Tijuana, Mexicali, Nogales, Ciudad Juárez, Nuevo Laredo, y Matamoros). Estos cuestionarios fueron diseñados para administrarse en menos de tres minutos a inmigrantes indocumentados en los sitios de cada ciudad por donde tiene lugar el cruce o los cruces más intensos de inmigrantes indocumentados hacia Estados Unidos. Los cuestionarios se administran interrumpidamente desde el mes de septiembre de 1987. El otro procedimiento se hace a base de fotografías tomadas sistemáticamente en tiempos y espacios, enfocando zonas aledañas a la frontera, en territorio de Estados Unidos, entre Tijuana y San Diego, en donde tiene lugar el cruce más intenso de inmigrantes indocumentados de toda la frontera entre los dos paises. Se han tomado tres fotografías diarias, con una hora de intervalo, tomando como tiempo de referencia la puesta de sol. La última de las fotografías se toma 10 minutos antes de la puesta de sol. La segunda, una hora antes de la tercera y la primera, dos horas antes que la última. En el período exploratorio previo al diseño definitivo, se encontró que en el lapso de dos horas anteriores a la puesta de sol alcanza habitualmente el número máximo de inmigrantes indocumentados que cruza durante el dia en el espacio cubierto por la fotografía. Las fotografías que se anexan son un ejemplo de las tres tomas que se hacen diariamente en uno de los dos lugares. En ellas se puede aperciar la variación en el número de personas que aparecen en cada fotografía. El espacio corresponde a lo que se conoce en Tijuana con el "Cañón Zapata." La frontera internacional se encuentra en el accidente de terreno que se apercia diagonalmente en la parte baja de la fotografía. De ahí para arriba es Estados Unidos. El otro espacio fotografiado sistemáticamente es el conocido en Tijuana como "el bordo." Este es un lugar paralelamente aledaño a la frontera, en territorio de Estados Unidos, que se encuentra a lo largo de un tramo de la calzada que lleva a la carretera escénica de Tijuana a

Ensenada. Ahí se marcan los cuatro espacios de "el bordo" que son enfocados sistematicamente en dos tomas fotográficas diarias, con una hora de intervalo, antes de la puesta de sol. Del lado sur de la calzada se encuentra la parte vieja de Tijuana conocida como "zona norte." La cercanía de "el bordo" a los lugares de reunión de donde parten los indocumentados a la jornada subrepticia hacia Estados Unidos, hace que permanezcan menos tiempo en ese lugar esperando que oscurezca, que los que cruzan por el Cañón Zapata. Por esta razón, el intervalo cubierto por las fotografías en el primer lugar, es de sólo una hora entre las dos tomas que se hacen diariamente ahí.

Juntando los espacios enfocados por las fotografías que se toman diariamente tanto en el Cañón Zapata como en "el bordo," se cubre el 90 por ciento del total de espacios por donde cruzan los indocumentados de Tijuana a San Diego. Este dato es importante a la luz del hecho de que por Tijuana cruza aproximadamente el 50 por ciento del total de inmigrantes indocumentados que cruza la frontera hacia Estados Unidos, según los hallazgos de las encuestas realizadas por el Consejo Nacional de Población.[12] Los registros fotográficos se proyectan al revés en el formato de transparencia sobre una pantalla translúcida. Del otro lado de la pantalla se ve la imagen al derecho sobre una cuadrícula que facilita el conteo de la gente que aparece en la transparencia y su registro electrónico en terminos de espacios entre coordenadas. Cada mes se producen tres tipos de gráficas, una para totales, otra para hombres y otra para mujeras, del número mayor de indocumentados de las tres tomas diarias en el Cañón Zapata y de las dos tomas en "el bordo."

Ambos procedimientos constituyen lo que en El Colegio de la Frontera Norte llamamos el Proyecto Cañon Zapata, en honor del lugar donde empezaron nuestras mediciones sitemáticas, que ahora cubren cinco ciudades fronterizas por donde cruza a Estados Unidos el 93 por ciento del total de los inmigrantes indocumentados. Algunos de los hallazgos más importantes de este proyecto se publican bimestralmente desde finales de 1987, en *El Correo Fronterizo*, que es el órgano oficial de información de El Colegio de la Frontera Norte.

ALGUNOS HALLAZGOS PRELIMINARES

Las gráficas 1 y 2 permiten una comparación del número más alto de indocumentados encontrado diariamente al comparar las tres fotografías que se toman cada día en el Cañón Zapata, correspondiente a mujeres y hombres, en los meses de diciembre de los años de 1986, 1987 y 1988. Aquí tambien, los picos corresponden a los fines de semana y los volúmenes del flujo a los niveles más bajos de los respectivos años. Cabe hacer notar la diferencia en los volúmenes diarios del flujo de hombres, comparado con el de mujeres, en una proporción que varía entre un tercio y un quinto de mujeres en el flujo total. Estas proporciones son de las más altas que se observan a lo largo de la frontera, debido al mayor mercado para mujeres en los campos de servicios e industria textil en el estado de California. Tan importante como los datos sobre las proporciones son los de las diferencias en los quiebres de las lineas de las gráficas respectivas a cada sexo, indicando una cierta independencia en los patrones migratorios de las mujeres respecto del de los hombres, corrrespondientes a mercados de trabajo diferentes para cada sexo.

Las gráficas 3 y 4 permiten una comparación más amplia de las diferencias en los patrones migratorios de los dos sexos, sugiriendo la necesidad de estudiar separadamente la

[12]Consejo Nacional de Población, *Encuesta en la Frontera Norte entre Trabajadores Indocumentados Devueltos por las Autoridades de Estados Unidos de América; diciembre de 1984 (ETIDEU); Resultados Estadísticos*, México, D.F.: CONAPO, 1986.

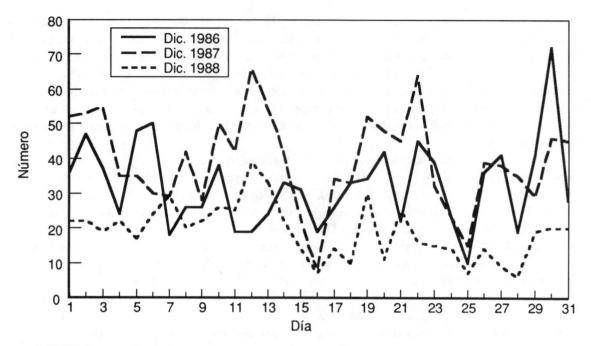

FUENTE: Proyecto Cañón Zapata, El Colegio de la Frontera Norte.

Gráfica 1—Proyecto Cañón Zapata: Número mayor de indocumentados por día,
valores comparativos de diciembre 1986–1988 (Mujeres)

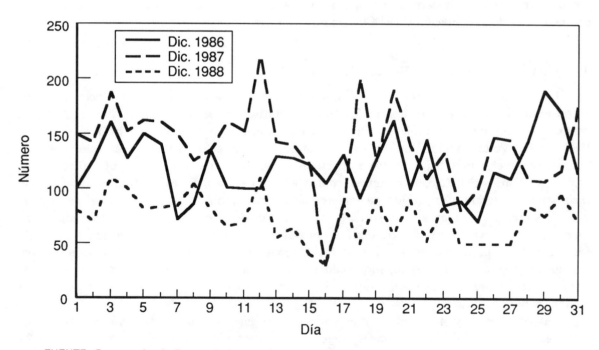

FUENTE: Proyecto Cañón Zapata, El Colegio de la Frontera Norte.

Gráfica 2—Proyecto Cañón Zapata: Número mayor de indocumentados por día,
valores comparativos de diciembre 1986–1988 (Hombres)

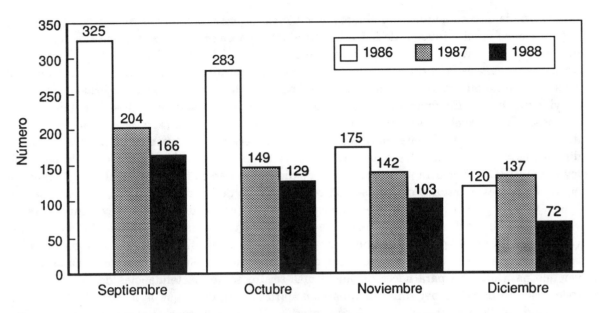

FUENTE: Proyecto Cañón Zapata, El Colegio de la Frontera Norte.

Gráfica 3—Promedios mensuales del número mayor de indocumentados de
cada día en el Cañón Zapata (Hombres)

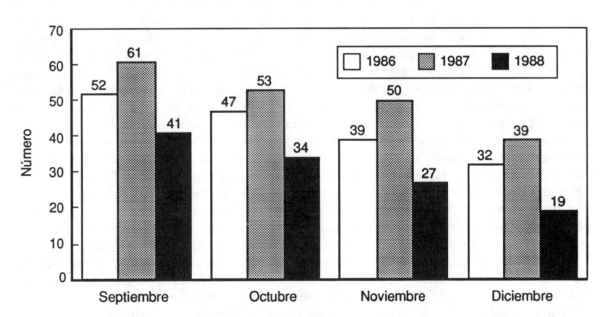

FUENTE: Proyecto Cañón Zapata, El Colegio de la Frontera Norte.

Gráfica 4—Promedios mensuales del número mayor de indocumentados de
cada día en el Cañón Zapata (Mujeres)

migración de indocumentados, hombres y mujeres. En estas gráficas se puede apreciar el patrón cíclico de disminución de los volúmenes del flujo migratorio hacia al mes de diciembre, no obstante las diferencias entre los meses de los años registrados. Estos 4 meses representan un período demasiado corto para concluir de manera definitiva si hay un decremento en los niveles del flujo migratorio de indocumentados posterior a la aprobación de la legislación IRCA (noviembre 1986). En favor de tal interpretación parecerían estar los datos de hombres para los meses de septiembre, octubre y noviembre. Sin embargo, en el caso de las mujeres, el año de 1987 aparece con volúmenes mayores que el año anterior en los mismos meses y las mayores diferencias aparecen entre los años de 1986 y 1987 en meses en que aún no se aprobaba la legislación IRCA. Por otra parte, en el mes de diciembre parece haber un cambio en la tendencia de los meses anteriores cuando se observan los datos de hombres en 1986, comparados con 1987. Contamos con los datos que demuestran que el patrón de diciembre continúa durante varios meses de 1988; sin embargo vuelve a ser menor en los meses del último año a partir del verano. El hecho de que las diferencias no sean muy grandes en el mes de diciembre para los tres años registrados, tanto para hombres como para mujeres, sugiere que conviene esperar a ver que pasa en 1989 para hacer un juicio más seguro sobre las tendencias de los flujos. En todo caso, no parece haber suficientes bases empíricas para decir que la legislación IRCA está reduciendo el flujo migratorio de indocumentados. Sobre todo cuando sabemos que hay otros factores ajenos a la legislación estadounidense que pudieran estar produciendo, desde México, efectos inhibitorios en la conducta migratoria hacia Estados Unidos, como son los ligados al costo de la migración, desde que sale el emigrante de su lugar de origen hasta que llega a la frontera norte.

Las gráficas 5, 6 y 7 dan una idea de la importancia de considerar el factor del costo de la migración en la explicación de los flujos migratorios hacia el norte. Los datos de estas gráficas corresponden a la suma de los conceptos de gastos principales (alimentos, pasajes, habitación, coyote o pollero y extorsiones policiacas o asaltos) reportados por los emigrantes entrevistados. Las regiones de origen que aparecen en las gráficas son las que mostraron un número de casos mayor a 4 por mes, con excepción de las gráficas 6 y 7, donde las lineas correspondientes a las regiones noroeste en la de Tijuana y sur en la de Ciudad Juárez, no llegaron los casos a ese limite. El número de entrevistados por mes en las ciudades de cada gráfica varió entre ciudad y ciudad. El promedio mensual fue de 230 casos para Tijuana, 75 para Ciudad Juárez, 320 para el agregado de las ciudades de Nuevo Laredo y Matamoros. Las regiones de origen mencionadas en las gráficas incluyen las siguientes entidades federativas: "Sur" = Oaxaca, Chiapas, Quintana Roo. "Golfo" = Veracruz, Tabasco y Tamaulipas de Tampico hacia el sur. "Norte" = Estados fronterizos. "Centro-norte" = Zacatecas, Durango, San Luis Potosi, Aguascalientes, Querétaro. "Nor-oeste" = Sinaloa, Baja California Sur, Nayarit. "Centro-oeste" = Colima, Jalisco, Michoacán, Guanajuato, Guerrero, Distrito Federal, Hidalgo, Tlaxcala, y Puebla.

Como era de esperarse, el costo de llegar hasta Tijuana es el más alto de las ciudades incluidas en las tres gráficas. El promedio de inflación en los datos de la gráfica 5 fue menor (43 por ciento) que el oficial para el país en 1988 (55 por ciento). En el caso de los datos de la gráfica 6, el promedio de inflación fue mayor (74 por ciento) que el nacional para el mismo período y en el caso de los datos de la gráfica 7, fue mucho menor (22 por ciento) que el nacional. Mi hipótesis es que las diferencias se deben a la proporción en que los gastos de la migración se estén financiando parcial o totalmente en dólares enviados por parientes o amigos desde Estados Unidos. En todo case, los costos de la migración subieron en 1988 bastante menos que en los dos años anteriores.

81

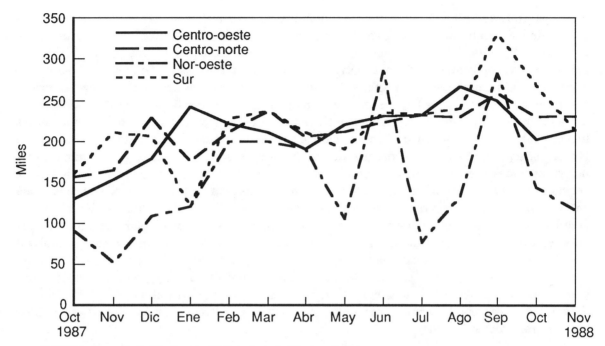

FUENTE: Proyecto Cañón Zapata, El Colegio de la Frontera Norte.

Gráfica 5—Gastos totales de los inmigrantes desde sus regiones de origen hasta la frontera norte (Tijuana)

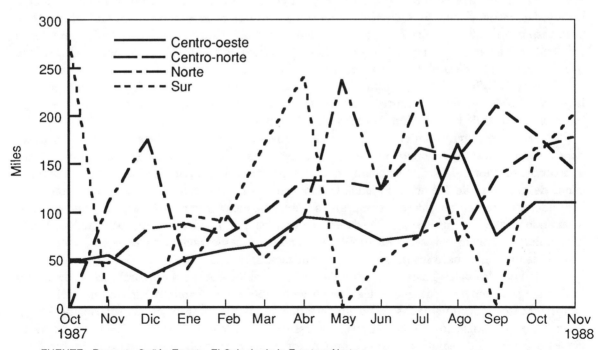

FUENTE: Proyecto Cañón Zapata, El Colegio de la Frontera Norte.

Gráfica 6—Gastos totales de los inmigrantes desde sus regiones de origen hasta la frontera norte
(Ciudad Juarez)

Las gráficas 8, 9 y 10 muestran la dinámica de los niveles de escolaridad de los inmigrantes indocumentados. El hallazgo más importante es el del mayor nivel de escolaridad de la mujeres inmigrantes indocumentadas que el de los hombres, como se puede apreciar en las gráficas correspondientes a Tijuana. Otro hallazgo importante es la diferencia notable en los niveles de los inmigrantes a Tijuana, en comparación con los que llegaron a Nuevo Laredo y Matamoros. Parecería, que hay una relación entre nivel de escolaridad e ingreso y probabilidad de llegar hasta Tijuana, que es obviamente el punto de la frontera norte más lejano de los lugares habituales de origen de la migración de indocumentados hacia Estados Unidos. En todo caso, aquí encontramos evidencias de que los niveles socioeconómicos de los inmigrantes indocumentados varían en relación con el lugar de la frontera norte donde cruzan hacia el país vecino. Llama la atención tambien la tendencia que se observa en los niveles de educación baja en la gráfica 10, en comparación con los datos del mismo nivel en la gráfica 9. En el primer caso hay un claro incremento de la proporción en el nivel más bajo de escolaridad, en tanto que en el caso de Tijuana la tendencia parece ser la opuesta, tanto en hombres como en mujeres inmigrantes. De ser asi, la sangria de capital humano por vía de la emigración parecería ser mayor por Tijuana que por el noroeste. Ciertamente, no estamos en presencia de los emigrantes del pasado, caracterizados por su predominancia en origen rural, pobres y analfabetas. Estamos en presencia de personas con promedios de tres a cuatro años más altos de escolaridad que los promedios nacionales.

CONCLUSIONES

1. A juzgar por la persistencia de los flujos migratorios hacia Estados Unidos, se puede afirmar que la legislación IRCA esta muy distante de haber alcanzado su objetivo principal de acabar con la entrada de inmigrantes indocumentados. Se podria adelantar la hipótesis de que tal legislación no se hizo para eliminar la entrada de inmigrantes indocumentados, tanto como para responder políticamente a las razones ideológicas que estuvieron detrás de las propuestas más restrictivas, como las resumidas en la frase "We have lost control of our borders." Un país que deveras ha perdido el control sobre sus fronteras se preocuparía por lo menos de colocar una indicación oficial de dónde está la frontera en el punto de cruce de indocumentados más intenso de toda la frontera norte, como es el Cañón Zapata. En ese lugar no hay ninguna indicación oficial de la ubicación de la frontera internacional.

2. Hasta este punto en el tiempo pareceria que los programas de legalización se diseñaron para favorecer desproporcionadamente a los inmigrantes indocumentados no mexicanos, al fijar una condición de residencia permanente que es contraria a la práctica de los inmigrantes mexicanos de ir y venir de México a Estados Unidos cada año. Por otro lado, parecería como si los legisladores hubieran querido a los migrantes mexicanos exclusivamente para labores agrícolas, diseñando requisitos más probables de ser complidos por mexicanos que por cualquier otra nacionalidad. De ser asi, sería inevitable pensar en un sesgo racista en la selectividad de las categorías diseñadas para los programas de legalización.

3. Vistos los datos hasta diciembre de 1988, a más de dos años de aprobada la legislación IRCA, surge la hipótesis de que la legislación se diseñó de tal forma que mantuviera el influjo de inmigrantes indocumentados de tal manera que se mantuvieran bajos los salarios de los que obtuvieran la legalización. Esta hipótesis se refuerza con los datos que indican que las violaciones a las leyes de salarios mínimos en California se han triplicado desde que se aprobó la legislación IRCA, según la información citada en la nota 9.

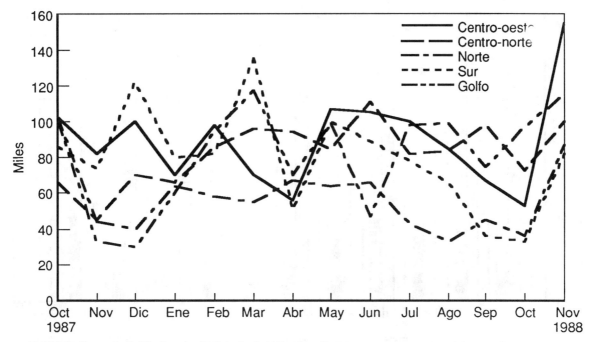

FUENTE: Proyecto Cañón Zapata, El Colegio de la Frontera Norte.

Gráfica 7—Gastos totales de los inmigrantes desde sus regiones de origen hasta la frontera norte
(Nuevo Laredo y Matamoros)

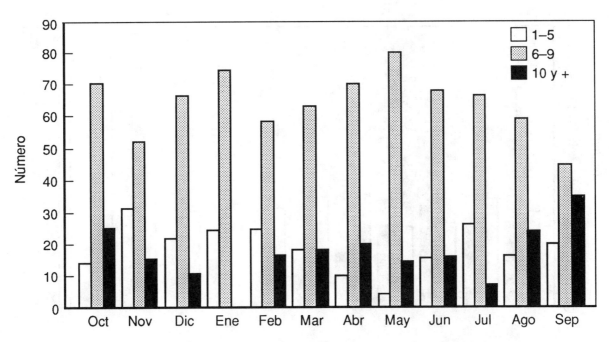

FUENTE: Proyecto Cañón Zapata, El Colegio de la Frontera Norte.

Gráfica 8—Escolaridad de indocumentados que cruzaron por Tijuana, de octubre de 1987
a septiembre de 1988 (Mujeres)

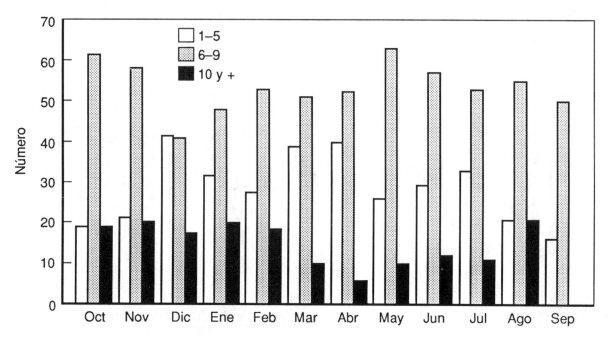

FUENTE: Proyecto Cañón Zapata, El Colegio de la Frontera Norte.

Gráfica 9—Escolaridad de indocumentados que cruzaron por Tijuana, de octubre de 1987 a septiembre de 1988 (Hombres)

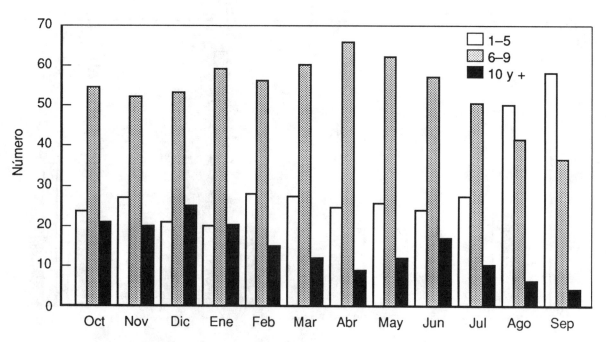

FUENTE: Proyecto Cañón Zapata, El Colegio de la Frontera Norte.

Gráfica 10—Escolaridad de indocumentados que cruzaron por Matamoros y Nvo. Laredo, de octubre de 1987 a septiembre de 1988 (Hombres)

4. Los datos recabados hasta el presente parecen reforzar la hipótesis de que la legislación IRCA se diseñó como un instumento precautorio para casos de recesión económica en los que fuera necesario tomar medidas drásticas para deshacerse masivamente de los inmigrantes indocumentados y, para que en períodos de expansión económica, la ley pudiera funcionar con un máximo de flexibilidad cercana a la nulidad.

5. Por último, se adelanta la hipótesis de que la legislación IRCA constituyó en realidad una alternativa más conveniente que la negociación bilateral o multilatera. Estas últimas opciones hubieran encarecido la mano de obra extranjera. En tanto que una medida unilateral, como lo es por definición una legislación, permite un mayor control sobre los flujos y sobre el mercado de mano de obra en el que participan los inmigrantes indocumentados.

En la sección de conclusiones se hará una interpretación del por qué ha fracasado la ley Simpson-Rodino separando las siguientes razones: (a) esta ley no se hizo para detener el flujo de indocumentados sino para aplacar una presión política que la demandaba basándose en factores ideológicos; (b) se diseñó para favorecer a indocumentados no mexicanos que son los que inmigraron de manera definitiva; (c) se diseñó para canalizar a los indocumentados mexicanos hacia la agricultura por razones racistas; (d) se diseñó para que funcionara en la práctica como un programa de aprovisionamiento de mano de obra barata en el que la continuidad de la presencia de los indocumentados es un elemento necesario para abaratar la mano de obra de los inmigrantes legalizados; (e) se diseñó para deshacerse fácilmente de los indocumentados en caso de una recesión económica; (f) se diseñó como alternativa a la negociación bilateral que acabaría encareciendo la mano de obra y podría propiciar la organización de los trabajardores migratorios.

THE ANTICIPATED EFFECTS OF IRCA ON
U.S. RELATIONS WITH MEXICO

Diego C. Asencio
Commission for the Study of International Migration
and Cooperative Economic Development

In assessing the likely impact of the implementation of the Immigration Reform and Control Act (IRCA) of 1986 on U.S.-Mexican relations, it is instructive to begin by reviewing the Department of State's experience in its dealings with Mexico during the years the legislation was being debated in Congress. At that time, the Department proposed to the Mexican authorities the formation of a consultative mechanism within which to discuss Mexican-U.S. immigration issues in a bilateral context. The Mexican government declined the U.S. invitation, saying that controlling immigration is the sovereign prerogative of states and that it hoped only that the rights of its immigrating citizens would be respected. There were other, unstated reasons for the Mexican position; some of them appeared to be:

1. For Mexico, the status quo ante represented the best of all possible worlds. Any changes related to immigration would work to the detriment of Mexico.

2. By agreeing to enter into bilateral discussions, the Mexican government feared that it would be assuming joint responsibility for results that might well be unfavorable to its citizens and to itself.

3. The Mexican government had the erroneous impression, evidently, that the United States wanted to use the immigration issue as a bargaining chip for other questions of major concern to Mexico.

4. Underlying the above was the stated Mexican view—premised on a strongly held philosophical position—that immigration control is the sovereign right of the receiving nation. Hence, U.S. immigration issues were beyond Mexico's direct policy purview. By agreeing to engage in dialogue on such issues, the impression could have been created that Mexico was interfering in U.S. domestic affairs. This would have conflicted with Mexico's adamant stance that no nation should interfere in the internal concerns of any other, and could have established a precedent for the United States to meddle in Mexico's own domestic affairs.

The passage of IRCA surprised the Mexican government. It had long been assumed that the U.S. Congress would never agree on an acceptable immigration reform package. IRCA was all the more shocking because its passage coincided with a severe economic crisis in Mexico (the foreign debt problem, currency devaluations, declines in oil prices, opening of the domestic market to international competition, major structural reforms), which played back on Mexico's social and political institutions. For the first time, the Institutional Revolutionary Party (PRI) faced a major political challenge in the 1988 presidential elections. This was but the most obvious manifestation of these tensions.

MEXICO'S RESPONSE TO IRCA

Once IRCA was adopted, Mexico could not reasonably maintain the same posture. The sensible and politically wise course of action was to adjust to the new situation. The welcome mat extended to the Commission for the Study of International Migration and Cooperative Economic Development, which this author chairs, was consistent with this policy change. The Commission itself, a creation of IRCA, represented a new way of thinking for the United States. Many on our side of the border had felt that we had not paid sufficient attention to Mexico's preoccupations. The Commission can be regarded as an attempt to redress past neglect and to break new ground in the bilateral relationship. From the Mexican perspective, the Commission's mandate signaled that the United States was at last willing to listen to what Mexico had been saying all along: that undocumented migration is a concomitant of economic development and can only be resolved if Mexico's development needs are addressed. This acknowledgment by the United States led to the ongoing joint research program being conducted by the Commission and the Mexican government through the Consejo Nacional de Poblacíon (CONAPO), the Mexican counterpart organization designated by former President Miguel de la Madrid, and more recently ratified by the government of President Carlos Salinas de Gortari.

FOREIGN POLICY ASPECTS OF UNDOCUMENTED MIGRATION

This is an area in which evidently many academic analysts, in Mexico as well as the United States, have erroneously assumed that immigration has occupied a preeminent place on the U.S. foreign policy plate. In fact, it never has.

Things may change in the future, but it is likely that immigration issues will only resume center stage if they are accompanied by a foreign policy debacle, such as the 1980 Mariel boatlift. The lesson to remember from that experience is that immigration only attracts major foreign policy attention when there are considerable domestic ramifications. Part of the problem, of course, is that the U.S. government functions in a highly compartmentalized fashion. It is very difficult to bridge different policy areas even when there is a strong commitment to advance the national interest, particularly when this includes ventures involving overseas actors. The Caribbean Basin Initiative (CBI) is a good example. The political stability and economic prosperity of some of our most vulnerable and strategically important southern neighbors are key to the U.S. national interest. Yet, the different domestic interests negatively affected by some of the provisions first proposed under the CBI had sufficient clout to considerably water down these provisions. As a result, much of the anticipated effectiveness of the CBI was lost.

THE NEXT FIVE YEARS AND BEYOND

What would the role of immigration be in the U.S.-Mexican bilateral relationship over the next five years? As the two countries continue to be drawn closer together by geography, history, immigration, trade, and a host of other common interests, it is anticipated that the role of immigration in the relationship could take one of two roads.

The more optimistic scenario foresees that a strong economic recovery will contribute to an increase in the capacity of the Mexican economy to generate productive jobs. A more robust economy, together with the legalization of over 2 million formerly undocumented Mexican migrants under IRCA, should result in diminished illegal migration pressures over the short to medium term. Countless seasonal workers formerly crossing the frontier illegally will from now on be able to do so legally. Further, the family reunification provisions of U.S. immigration law will permit relatives of newly legalized migrants to take advantage of the legal entry option. To some degree, however, these forces will be counterbalanced by continued high population and labor force growth rates in Mexico over the next several decades. Powerful social networks will likewise continue to pull migratory flows, but mostly of authorized migrants. Under these circumstances, Mexican migration to the United States would largely fade from public attention.

A less favorable scenario visualizes continued economic difficulties in Mexico with sluggish economic growth and the consequent inability to satisfy the labor demands of a growing and frustrated population. Mounting migration pressures could result in a U.S. legal or administrative backlash capable of souring the bilateral relationship. Some voices in the U.S. polity might call for extreme measures to "control the border," and the migration issue might once again come to occupy center stage in the political rhetoric of interest groups on both sides of the border. Mexican and U.S. nationalistic and political sensitivities might again be roused, emotion again clouding the fundamental underlying issues. Whether this rhetoric would pave or hinder the way for a continued and fruitful dialogue is anyone's guess. But if past experience teaches anything, it is that nothing is gained and much is lost by the use of inflammatory language. Issues tangentially related to migration, such as Mexico's foreign debt, trade concerns, and drug trafficking, might further sour the bilateral relationship.

The American perception and response to Mexican migration will largely depend on developments in the U.S. labor market. Despite current localized shortages of unskilled workers, a consensus is emerging as to the nature of worker demand by the turn of the century. Some analysts forecast that most new entry jobs will require skill levels well above those the traditional unskilled Mexican migrant has been able to provide. The speed with which labor market adjustments occur as technological innovations and labor-saving devices are introduced, as well as how well the economy performs, will help determine the type and amount of labor demand in decades to come.

In the event these forecasts are proven wrong and the American economy experiences future unskilled labor shortages, there might be room for the orderly importation of seasonal or permanent service and agricultural workers. What the nature of these arrangements will be is uncertain, as are the institutional mechanisms to bring them about, but there is the precedent of the Bracero agreements and, more recently, the H-2 and H-2A programs. Novel approaches, often the result of tough political compromises, should not be discontinued either.

In practice, if not by design, the Special Agricultural Worker (SAW) and Replenishment Agricultural Worker (RAW) programs of the IRCA legislation will amount to the de facto institutionalization of a guest-worker program for hundreds of thousands of Mexican workers. Mounting evidence suggests that many of the Mexican migrants regularizing their status under the SAW program have no intention of permanently residing in the United States. Rather, they intend to use their legal residence permits to work intermittently in the United States, while maintaining their permanent homes in Mexico. Whether or not these migrants will continue working in agriculture is another matter altogether. Other voices have clamored for the institutionalization of modified H-2A programs for nonagricultural workers to regularize the outflow of badly needed skilled workers in countries (e.g., some of the smaller English-speaking Caribbean island nations) experiencing the detrimental effects of excessive skilled emigration.

There is and will continue to be strong opposition to any programs along those lines among many influential constituencies in the United States, however.

INSTITUTIONAL ARRANGEMENTS: ARE THEY DESIRABLE?

The time may be ripe for strengthening existing formal institutional mechanisms that could be used for ongoing consultations on immigration matters. The most obvious channel is the U.S.-Mexican Consultative Mechanism jointly chaired by the U.S. Secretary of State and the Mexican Foreign Minister. The precedent established by the Commission for the Study of International Migration and Cooperative Economic Development in its dealings with the Mexican government through CONAPO offers a model that can easily be adapted within the broader context of the U.S.-Mexican Consultative Mechanism. The working relationship between these two bodies has provided an open and effective channel for the exchange of views on issues of mutual concern, and for the exploration of ideas for politically and economically feasible solutions to deal with immigration-related problems.

Once the work of the Commission is completed in July 1990, it might be desirable for both governments to agree to continue with regularly scheduled formal consultations under the sponsorship of each country's top foreign affairs official. A number of pressing issues could be fruitfully addressed. These include the common problems both countries face with respect to undocumented Central American migration, the victimization of civilians along the border, and the continued regularization of seasonal agricultural workers under the RAW program.

Mechanisms of this nature could serve as models for future consultations with governments of other Western Hemisphere nations from which originate significant numbers of undocumented migrants to the United States. Such an approach will be particularly appealing to the more than 20 million Americans of Hispanic origin the United States will have by the dawn of the new century. These and other Americans, many of whom are first generation Americans themselves or descendants of recent migrants, will look with favor at such a consultative process.

THE IMMIGRATION REFORM AND CONTROL ACT OF 1986 AND MEXICAN PERCEPTIONS OF BILATERAL APPROACHES TO IMMIGRATION ISSUES

Carlos Rico F.
El Colegio de México

During the decade and a half that led to the passing of the Immigration Reform and Control Act (IRCA) in 1986, countless meetings were held in both Mexico and the United States regarding the sources, scope, and characteristics of migratory flows between the two countries. In those discussions one of the themes frequently stressed by Mexican scholars and officials was the need for "bilateral solutions to a bilateral problem." At the same time, however, Mexican participation was very limited in parallel *domestic* U.S. debates related to congressional action on this issue. Mexico showed a clear lack of initiative and active lobbying on Capitol Hill during the process that led to IRCA. In fact, it made no systematic effort on this particular occasion to translate its interest in bilateralism into actions that might have injected some concern for Mexican views into the bill.

Such an attitude was frequently perceived by North American observers as contradictory. This related particularly to the limited response of Mexican authorities to U.S. initiatives directed at establishing some kind of consultation. There is still disagreement on both sides of the border regarding whether such initiatives represented genuine exercises in consultation.[1] The basic point, however, remains: Mexican authorities insisted on having migration included in the agenda of almost any meeting that took place between officials or legislators of both countries, emphasized the need for "bilateral solutions" to the problem, but refused to be involved in limited consultations about legislative reform.

This paper analyzes this seeming inconsistency. The hypothesis here suggests that its roots are found in Mexican attitudes—dominant during the period—regarding the nature of the migration flows, the likelihood of different U.S. responses toward them, and the specific content of a relevant bilateral approach to immigration issues between the two countries. After summarizing the evolution of Mexican attitudes from the end of the Bracero program (in the mid-1960s) to the mid-1980s, the paper describes the effect those dominant perceptions had on Mexico's preferences regarding a bilateral approach to the management of migratory flows. The third section evaluates what impact, if any, the Immigration Reform and Control Act could have on those perceptions. Mexican attitudes, it is argued here, may change in response to the new context created by the passing of IRCA and also in response to new developments such as the emergence of significant flows of "third-country" migration to Mexico and to the United States through Mexican territory.

---

[1]Conflicting claims have been made about the extent to which Mexico was in fact consulted in the course of the legislative reform. While Mexicans frequently complain about the lack of such consultation, U.S. officials also frequently complain that whenever they attempted to discuss the issue with Mexican authorities, the latter avoided actually talking about solutions to the problem before Congress—frequently limiting themselves to presenting proposals directed at furthering the study and scientific knowledge of the migration flows. These claims and counterclaims are not new. An early example took place in August 1977, when the Carter Plan was presented to Congress. Diego Asencio, chairman of the Commission for the Study of International Migration and Cooperative Economic Development and one of the U.S. officials who participated in consultations with the López Portillo administration, and Richard Day, Minority Chief Counsel of the U.S. Senate Committee on the Judiciary, have both expressed similar complaints. See their participation in these Proceedings.

Even if such a change in Mexican perceptions were to take place, however, it could not—in and of itself—lead to more bilateralism in the management of migratory flows. For a shared perception of the need for bilateral solutions, changes must also take place in the assumptions that have dominated North American debate on this issue for the last decade and a half. This author believes that the circumstance most likely to encourage these necessary parallel changes would be some middle level of success of IRCA. This possibility is explored in the concluding section.

MEXICAN ATTITUDES TOWARD UNDOCUMENTED LABOR MIGRATION, 1966–1986

Two basic policy objectives guide Mexican concerns in this field throughout the two decades covered in this paper. The first and, in this author's opinion, most important is the need to preserve the flows—to keep the "safety valve" open. The second is the protection of the rights of the migrants.

Mexican assumptions about the best ways to achieve these two objectives can vary even during the same period, in part as a result of changes in Mexican perceptions of migratory flows and in part as a result of the kinds of relevant policy options open to governments.[2] Two pertinent subperiods may be identified since the end of the Bracero agreement. The first one covers 1966–1974 and the second runs until the mid-1980s. Migration is defined as a bilateral issue in both of these subperiods, but the specific policy approach that would take the bilateral nature of the phenomenon into account changes from one to the other.

A Decade in Search of a Formal Agreement

Mexican preferences during the first subperiod clearly derive from the unilateral termination of the Bracero agreement by the United States. An important precedent was established at that time regarding Mexican influence on ostensibly internal U.S. decisionmaking processes. Although U.S. domestic interests and concerns defined the debate that led to the termination of the program,[3] Mexican authorities openly and repeatedly expressed their opposition. They were deeply concerned about the possible consequences of what they saw as the tightening—if not complete closing—of the safety valve. That concern may be seen in the measures Mexico implemented in anticipation of the program's termination. The Border Industrialization Program of 1965, for example, explicitly related to providing jobs for those Mexicans who could no longer be expected to work in the United States.[4] It is, in fact, hardly surprising that Mexican authorities tried to influence decisions related to the future of the Bracero program. Their success, however, was not commensurate to either their interest or their expectations. Although Mexican actions contributed to the extension of the Bracero program for one year,[5] the program's termination was not avoided.

[2]To talk about "the Mexican perception" is of course a simplification. There is not one Mexican view on these issues. The ideas identified in this section, however, are in this author's opinion clearly dominant ones south of the border during each of the subperiods identified.

[3]Richard B. Craig, *The Bracero Program: Interest Groups and Foreign Policy* (Austin: University of Texas Press), 1971.

[4]Donald W. Baerresen, *The Border Industrialization Program of Mexico* (Lexington, Mass.: Lexington Books), 1971.

[5]Larry Manuel García y Griego, *The Bracero Policy Experiment: U.S.-Mexican Responses to Mexican Labor Migration, 1942-1955,* Ph.D. Dissertation submitted to the Department of History, University of California, Los Angeles, 1988.

Under the conditions created by the termination of the agreement, the specific content of bilateral cooperation preferred by Mexican authorities was—and remained for almost a decade—quite clear. The Bracero program had allowed for some degree of bilateral participation in controlling the flow. After 1964 Mexican official positions focused on the need to negotiate a new agreement similar to the one unilaterally ended by the United States. At that time this seemed not only the best way to participate in the management of the flow but also the most certain way to achieve the two policy objectives referred to above: maintaining the flows, and protecting the migrants.

The experience of the late 1960s made clear that the termination of the program had not stopped the migration but had simply changed the legal status of the migrants, driving them underground. Therefore, concern over the loss of job opportunities receded, and migrant protection became the basic reason for Mexico's preference for a formal bilateral agreement. U.S. authorities, however, took no more than passing notice of Mexican preferences, which were never actually taken up in formal discussions or negotiations.

Opting for the Status Quo

After 1974 Mexican authorities modified their basic stance: They no longer pushed for a new Bracero-type agreement. The context in which this change occurred is worth examining, since the change raised a debate that, while previously limited to academic circles, now permeated the highest echelons of the Mexican government. It started with Mexican authorities detecting movement in North American positions regarding this issue. In preparation for the new U.S. President's first visit to Mexico, the Ford administration sent signals that seemed to suggest a willingness, for the first time in almost a decade, to discuss the possibility of a new Bracero agreement. However, instead of rejoicing, Mexican authorities decided to respond coolly to such overtures. This reaction was related to the timing of the perceived U.S.-attitude change. The fact that it came not only on the heels of the first news of oil discoveries in southeastern Mexico, but also at a crucial moment for Washington's policies toward Arab oil producers, raised concerns that went beyond the Bracero issue. The new and more understanding U.S. attitude was seen by crucial Mexican actors as representing an attempt to link migration to other issues in the bilateral relation. This potential for the United States to use immigration as a foreign policy instrument was to become one of the more permanent Mexican concerns during the two decades that led to IRCA. In the specific context of 1974, this potential helped to bring about a basic change in Mexican preferences.

The perceived change in U.S. position prompted an internal discussion about the nature of the migration flow and the policy options open to governments to control or at least manage it. It has already been pointed out that experience itself proved that a formal agreement was not necessary to "keep the valve open." The belief that such an agreement would facilitate the protection of Mexican nationals was also shaken in the course of internal debate. The history of the Bracero program, underlined distinguished scholars that were able to attain presidential-level attention, did not warrant such belief.[6] As a result, the legal status of the flow started to be perceived in Mexican policymaking circles as only partly related to the adequate protection of Mexican nationals in the United States.[7]

---

[6]Ernesto Galarza was the most prominent scholar. See Jorge Bustamante, "Mexican Migration: The Political Dynamic of Perceptions," in Clark W. Reynolds and Carlos Tello (eds.), *U.S.-Mexico Relations; Economic and Social Aspects* (Stanford, Calif.: Stanford University Press), 1983.

[7]This belief never became fully consensual in those circles. Former ambassador to Washington Hugo Margain, for example, continued to defend his preference for a formal agreement on the grounds that it would facilitate protection activities undertaken by Mexican representatives in the United States.

The last rationale for preferring a formally bilateral and binding document had begun to crumble. The satisfaction of Mexican authorities with the status quo in this area—particularly, as will be discussed below in relation to existing alternatives—became increasingly clear. Undocumented labor was, after the mid-1970s, the dominant concern of Mexican scholars and officials in relation to migratory flows between their country and the United States. Almost no official statement or academic study was made in Mexico or, for that matter, in the United States (also concerned with "illegal workers") regarding other types of migratory flows—which also reached considerable size during those years. Demands for formal agreements were dropped. Protection gradually became the basic link between immigration and Mexican foreign policy.

Dominant Assumptions in Mexico Since the Mid-1970s

After the change that took place around 1974, Mexican arguments began to be based on a series of assumptions that made previous positions regarding a specific bilateral approach increasingly irrelevant. Three such assumptions, closely related ones, seem particularly germane for the topic of this paper.

First is *the definition of the problem as a labor market question*. Without denying the role of historical and even social factors, such as those associated with tightly knit family and community networks, Mexico saw the phenomenon as fundamentally economic in nature, a response to the simultaneous pressures of push and pull factors that created powerful economic forces and realities.

The second assumption, closely related to the first, was *the difficulty of exerting governmental control over this type of nongovernmental flow*. Markets may be regulated, channeled, and even partially managed, but attempting to rule them out of existence seems a rather futile exercise. Such was the underlying Mexican argument in this case.

The third and final assumption emphasized *the objective need of U.S. agriculture and economy for such workers*. The reasoning in this case went something like this: North American labor markets are clearly segmented, and the kind of labor provided by undocumented workers displaces only a very limited number of North American workers. If Mexican undocumented labor were not available, the consequences would include, in addition to a limited increase in job opportunities, further mechanization of production processes, transfer of some operations offshore, and, in some cases, inability of small- and medium-sized producers to compete. Even if specific labor markets were negatively affected, the migrant's overall impact on the U.S. economy was positive. This, Mexicans frequently argued, was recognized even in U.S. legislation, which, through the so-called Texas Proviso, made it legal to *hire* "illegal workers" just as *harboring* them was considered outside the law.

EXPLAINING MEXICO'S APPARENT INCONSISTENCY

If we now return to the subject that leads off this paper, the seeming inconsistency of the Mexican position, the key role of the above assumptions emerges quite clearly. The assumptions are, in fact, not only the fundamental source of the Mexican position after 1974, but also the key reason for the difficulties in translating a bilateralist stance into efforts to influence U.S. debate.

On Common Ground?

The first impact of dominant perceptions was related to the extremely limited common ground for discussion between representatives of both countries. Mexico's basic assumptions were so far from the perceptions which dominated North American debate during those years that there was not even a shared definition of the problem. The points of departure were in fact too different to allow for minimum common understanding.

Mexico's basic assumptions implied that the objective of a bilateral approach should be *the regulation of an unavoidable flow*. After an increasingly restrictionist mood started to emerge in North American debate during the early 1970s, it became extremely difficult to process through U.S. domestic politics almost any of the forms such a proposal might take. Whenever an initiative for a temporary-worker program was presented, for example, the kinds of numbers involved for it to be meaningful put it beyond the grasp of even the most "heterodox" participants in the North American debate.

North American debate, on the other hand, generally preferred a bilateral approach leading to termination of the flow, not management of it. Since the bilateral approach that Mexicans favored seemed to be out of the cards, it was practically impossible for any meaningful dialogue to take place. Given Mexico's basic satisfaction with the existing reality, the status quo seemed preferable to available alternatives.

The Worst Will Never Come

The Mexican attitude was that while a "positive" change in the status quo was not a possibility, a "negative" one was also not likely. This seemed to be the most important conclusion, regarding U.S. governmental behavior, derived from the key assumptions listed above: Given the fact that labor migration played positive roles, at least in the short term, for the Mexican as well as the North American economy, the "valve" not only should but could be expected to remain open. However, the tone of the immigration debate in the U.S. Congress introduced some disturbing nuances. In fact, as the Simpson-Mazzoli versions of the bill were barely defeated in the early 1980s, the United States (understood as the aggregate of those diverse interests and actors participating in the immigration debate) was increasingly viewed as fully capable of harming—if not totally disregarding—its own "objective" interests. But these changed perceptions regarding likely U.S. responses were not enough to convince Mexican authorities of the need to actively "intervene" in U.S. legislative debate. The thrust of their argument, in fact, remained unchanged: U.S. authorities would not *want* to stop such flows, and even if they wanted to they were *incapable* of doing it.

During the 1980s, this basic Mexican assumption translated into the conviction that it would be very hard to pass any law and that any law passed would not have real teeth. If any measure was approved, it would be expected to include so many loopholes as to make it one more example of a "symbolic" law.[8] The tortuous way followed by legislative reform on this topic since the early 1970s was seen as confirmation of that belief. As a consequence, there seemed to be no need for a concerted effort on the part of Mexicans to become actively involved in North American legislative discussions.

The passing of IRCA in late 1986—which took not only Mexican authorities but many observers on both sides of the border by surprise—introduced a new set of considerations. The

---

[8]This concept is used here in the sense presented in Kitty Calavita, *California's "Employer Sanctions": The Case of the Disappearing Law*, Center for U.S.-Mexican Studies, University of California at San Diego, Research Report Series No. 39, 1982.

de facto rules of the game embodied in the Texas Proviso, for example, were replaced by U.S. recognition of the role of pull factors and the attempt to turn their attraction off through employer sanctions. Before generally describing the new context created by this and other features of IRCA, the picture of the reasons behind Mexico's apparent inconsistency must be completed. The role of wider Mexican beliefs—also dominant during those years—is discussed below regarding bilateral relations in general and, more specifically, the dangers associated with "intervening" in U.S. domestic politics.

The Dilemma of Nonintervention

In the course of whatever type of bilateral consultations that took place during the 1970s and 1980s, Mexican authorities repeatedly expressed their decision to respect the "sovereign right" of the United States to pass legislation on this question without attempting to influence the U.S. policymaking process. Two principal reasons may explain that decision. First, Mexican officials were not particularly satisfied with the specifics of their nonintervention approach, but *once relevant U.S. political actors had decided to deal with the problem through domestic legislation,* not much could be done regarding Mexican input into such a process.[9] Consultations were, as a result, seen as minor components of a basically unilateral exercise, and there was little incentive for paying serious attention to them.

Second, a more general concern about the desirability for nonintervention in U.S. domestic politics led to the same conclusion. Nonintervention has been a central tenet of Mexican foreign policy. It has historically reflected a deep concern that outside governments may try to become active and open participants in Mexican domestic politics. Mexican authorities have in fact never formalized any kind of lobbying scheme in Washington. Reticence about participating in domestic North American debates during the period under examination was thus not limited to matters of immigration.

The notion that Mexico's behavior in this area was, in good measure, an example of a much more general behavior pattern complements the argument this paper has tried to make. In the author's opinion, however, it is the key assumptions, which guided Mexican perspective in the mid-1960s and in the mid-1980s and which were so different from U.S. assumptions, that should be considered as the explanatory factor for Mexican preference. As the basic outline of a complex story shows, however, assumptions and perceptions did change from one sub-period to the next. Will they change again in the immediate future as a result of the new realities introduced by IRCA? This is the question discussed in the next section.

IRCA AND MEXICAN PERCEPTIONS

To evaluate the impact that IRCA may have on Mexican preferences regarding a bilateral approach to migratory flows, one must have a concrete picture of Mexican policy objectives in this area. Maintaining the flows and protecting Mexican workers in the United States have been considered here to be the two crucial goals. This section assumes that *temporary* worker presence in the United States is the option that best resolves the tension between short- and long-term Mexican interests affected by migratory flows.[10]

---

[9]As noted previously, a similar, earlier attempt during the last stages of the Bracero program had not succeeded (García y Griego, *The Bracero Policy Experiment*).

[10]This assumption is not unrelated to the direction of more recent Mexican debate on this issue. In it, the notion of the "escape valve" has tended to be supplemented by the notion of "the other side of the coin": human capital

Two different time periods will be explored regarding the ways in which this more specific policy objective may be affected by IRCA. First, the most immediate Mexican reactions and concerns after its passing will be identified. Second, the possibility of future changes in Mexican attitudes will be explored.

Immediate Reactions After the Passing of IRCA

Immediately after the passing of IRCA in late 1986, two different sets of attitudes could be identified in Mexican discussions of the new context thus created. On the one hand, there were those who contended that the new law would not have a significant impact on the migratory flows. This line of reasoning recast a well-known argument: The strength of economic and social realities driving the flows is such that it would be impossible to stop them.[11] As long as wage differentials remain what they are, the basic factors that explain the flows will remain in force. Legislative efforts may introduce some changes in the characteristics and even dimensions of the flows, but they will be few among many variables that must be taken into account.[12]

On the other hand, some concern was expressed—along quite different lines—regarding the potential repatriation of significant numbers of Mexican workers. As U.S. authorities undertook the effort to stop undocumented migration—widely perceived south of the border as doomed to fail—some Mexican observers believed that a drastic implementation of the law, to the point of massive expulsions, could be possible during the short term. In spite of frequent reassurances on the part of various U.S. officials that no such actions would be undertaken, historical precedents pointed in the opposite direction and seemed to provide serious basis for that concern.[13]

Is Mexico Modifying Its Assumptions?

As this second immediate concern has failed to materialize, new discussions have begun south of the border regarding IRCA's potential impact on Mexican interests. In this author's opinion, the basis for reconsidering Mexico's dominant assumptions must be the realization that—in spite of any ardent restrictionist argument—IRCA's main objective is not to stop the flow but to control and regulate it. This simple point means that, for all the rhetoric surrounding it, IRCA is closer to Mexican objectives than most Mexicans expected. Mechanisms such as the expanded H-2A provisions, the Special Agricultural Worker (SAW) program, and the Replenishment Agricultural Worker (RAW) provisions clearly indicate that important U.S. interests want to keep open the possibility for sizable numbers of migrants to participate in the U.S. economy. There is, however, a downside to this situation, as seen from a Mexican perspective. The most important problem lies in the nature of the mechanisms introduced to achieve this objective.

---

flight. This has helped clarify the tension between short-term and longer-term Mexican interests. In the short term, migration serves to ease pressures on the Mexican labor market, but in the longer term it is clearly in Mexico's interest to keep such workers at home. This was one of the issues raised in the course of the public hearings organized by the Mexican Senate during the first semester of 1985.

[11]Such an argument has not subsided. See, for example, the statements of Ofelia Woo Morales, Coordinator of the "Zapata Canyon Project" at the Colegio de la Frontera Norte, Tijuana, Mexico, reproduced in Araceli Dominguez, "Ni la Zanja Evitará el Flujo de Ilegales a EU: Colegio de la Frontera Norte," *Excelsior,* Sección en los Estados, p. 1, January 27, 1989.

[12]Other important factors would include, for example, changes in the cost/benefit relation of the potential migrant's decision to go or stay, introduced, say, by the Mexican economic crisis.

[13]Mercedes Carreras de Velasco, *Los Mexicanos que Devolvió la Crisis* (México: Secretaria de Relaciones Exteriores), 1976.

The Question of Unilateral Temporary-Worker Programs

The three programs mentioned above share a common characteristic: They have not only been unilaterally designed but will be unilaterally managed by the United States. This unilateral implementation of some of IRCA's provisions could become a new, and quite different, source of Mexican concern.[14] The possibility of such a development, however, is related not only to the law's intended objectives but also to the ability of North American authorities to implement it. A significant success on their part would open a clear opportunity for change in Mexican perceptions—a change that could bring about different Mexican definitions of the specific content of a viable bilateral approach.[15]

Questions must be directed at IRCA's individual provisions before considering U.S. capacity to actually implement them. First, are the mechanisms and programs incorporated in IRCA amenable to some kind of binational management? Second, how relevant are they to Mexican policy objectives? The H-2A program provides a good example of some of the issues raised by the latter question. H-2A deals with temporary employment—the kind of migratory flow identified by Mexico as a likely preferred alternative. Its permanence—as opposed to the "one shot" nature of SAW and RAW—also suggests future potential. In this author's opinion, if H-2A becomes a significant mechanism for temporary migration in the not so distant future, one may expect attempts to incorporate a Mexican (or in more general terms any sending country's) input into that program. This, however, will depend on the degree of success achieved in implementing the law—the only way in which H-2A could become a "significant mechanism."

Possible Bilateralism Based on the Degree of IRCA's Success

A cursory review of two extreme possibilities provides a useful way to organize this discussion. First, if IRCA can be implemented in its entirety, workers admitted under SAW and RAW will eventually be able, once documented, to move to other lines of activity. This may in turn have a significant impact on the numbers that an H-2A program would have to cover. A clear potential for change in perceptions lies here. Once IRCA proved to be working and producing these kinds of results, Mexicans would quite likely prefer a bilateral approach, which would give them some say in the program's specifics.

It is quite plain that changes in Mexican attitudes and preferences would not guarantee that a bilateral approach could occur. It takes two to tango and the United States has not been interested in dancing either. A critical question, then, would be whether U.S. attitudes

---

[14]The unilateral nature of these provisions is problematic not only because of the basic fact that the flow involves *Mexican* nationals and is affected by events and policies adopted *in Mexico by the Mexican government.* A rather unexplored dimension of the phenomenon is also involved: Whoever is charged with distributing a rather scarce good by choosing candidates for any of those programs has important instruments of social and political control placed in his hands. The peculiar "recruitment" of Mexican workers in Mexican territory by U.S. authorities in the context of the SAW program, for example, presents an odd spectacle. Mexican authorities have decided not to press this point more from a decision to maintain cordial relations than from agreement on the merits of the policy.

[15]As with the successive versions of IRCA when proposals to increase Mexican quotas for legal immigration were dropped, the preoccupation with the unilateral application—but application after all—of some North American legislative provisions has been until now a concern only to some scholars and "attentive publics" rather than a new Mexican perception. This paper explores some of the conditions under which this preoccupation may reach such status. Of course, some factors militate against the possibility that it may be incorporated as a new and widely shared Mexican perception. There will probably be opposition to initiatives aimed in this direction. After all, they amount to participation in the management of frameworks defined and designed unilaterally.

have also changed as a result of IRCA.[16] Evaluations of North American ability to exercise unilateral control over the flows are crucial. They also hinge on the type of success that IRCA may achieve. A fully successful unilateral program, our first extreme, would not easily be changed into a bilateral one by North American legislators. However, in the second extreme, if IRCA did not seem to be working, one U.S. alternative would be to try the bilateral approach espoused by Mexican and some North American observers. Thus, the most favorable context for changing perceptions in both the United States and Mexico lies in a situation in which IRCA works but not too well. This might open the possibility for joint management of a "front door" for legal—in particular temporary labor—migration.

Even the context created by limited IRCA success would not necessarily lead in the direction of a more bilateral approach. North American reactions would surely include proposals for even more stringent legislation. Which alternative would prevail has to be considered an open question. However, two parallel developments provide elements that are predisposed toward the bilateral alternative. First, the work of the Commission for the Study of International Migration and Cooperative Economic Development has been positive.[17] Second, the political climate in overall intergovernmental relations has also been positive. Although this started during the last two years of the Reagan administration, it became dominant after the practically simultaneous inaugurations of Carlos Salinas de Gortari and George Bush.[18]

Relative success in implementing IRCA is, however, only one factor (even if in this author's opinion the most important) that may contribute to developing the attitudes necessary to achieve some form of bilateral approach. Other developments could lead in similar directions. The crucial point here is the degree to which national policy objectives identified in relation to those other developments could be served by bilateral efforts.

Other Sources of Bilateralism

What may be some of these national policy objectives? On the U.S. side, the need to join with Mexico in an effort directed at third-country migrants may become the most relevant. This is clearly not an easy policy to agree on. For Mexico, efforts to control migration from Central American countries will affect relations with those countries. It is possible that Mexico would deal with this policy question through agreements with the governments of the isthmus and not necessarily with the United States. This kind of collaboration was included as one of the results of the Seventh Meeting of the Mexico-U.S. Binational Commission, held in late August 1989 in Mexico City, which indicates not only the positive overall climate achieved in bilateral dealings but also the potential for some kind of bilateral approach implicit in the emergence of third-country migration through Mexico.[19]

---

[16]Particularly important would be modifications in U.S. perceptions regarding on the one hand the nature and size of the flow and on the other U.S. governmental ability to unilaterally control it. There are indications that some changes have already taken place in the former. The debate on numbers, for example, has been helped by statistics garnered as a result of the amnesty program.

[17]Consultations under the auspices of the Commission have led to interesting potential developments. There is considerable satisfaction in Mexican policymaking circles with the tone of the exchanges that have already taken place; their concrete results, however, are still to be felt.

[18]This factor creates both possibilities and doubts. Will this friendly attitude resist the complexities of bilateral dealings? Could it overflow to the management of specific issues such as migration?

[19]Other than presidential summits, the Binational Commission is the highest level of intergovernmental dialogue and negotiation between the two countries. Its seventh meeting, for example, was attended by nearly half of President Bush's cabinet. See Secretaria de Relaciones Exteriores/Departamento de Estado: Comunicado de Prensa: VII Reunión Binacional México-Estados Unidos de América, Tlatelolco, Mexico City, August 7, 1989. As should be clear from the body of this paper, however, this specific kind of bilateralism neither results from IRCA nor adequately deals with the issues that have dominated this issue for over two decades.

Regarding Mexican policy objectives, a different possibility may be noted that reflects the continued relevance of one policy objective presented at the beginning of this paper. Bilateralism may be seen as an instrument to improve the protection of the rights of Mexican migrants in the United States.[20]

This protection may become increasingly important if working and living conditions deteriorate for the remaining flows. The degree of IRCA's success is, again, relevant. However, even if employer sanctions do work, there are reasons not to expect a complete drying of migratory flows.[21] If Mexicans continue to migrate to the United States under those conditions, they may be driven further underground and, as a result, the need for Mexican governmental protection may in fact increase.

In this particular case, however, there do not seem to be compelling reasons to expect U.S. authorities to assist in protection activities as long as undocumented migrants are involved. They would quite probably consider this type of bilateralism as directly conflicting with their intention to discourage such migration. The possibility that bilateralism may become a useful instrument in this regard is thus closely related to the potential for some kind of future "front door bilateralism."

However, *joint binational actions* may originate outside the area of migratory flows but still affect them. Some nonimmigration flows considered undesirable may provide the necessary incentives to convince at least some Mexican authorities to collaborate. Drug interdiction is the most likely candidate, as demonstrated by the operations jointly undertaken by U.S. and Mexican authorities in early 1989.[22] Even if there is no relation between immigration and these other flows, efforts to curb any of them will involve border controls which cannot be expected to discriminate among them. This alone may bring about binational activities which, though originating in dynamics other than those emphasized here, would have an impact on migratory flows. One might call such a result "indirect bilateralism."

A final point of caution must be raised. As the previous discussion shows, even if both the Mexican and the North American governments have objectives regarding migratory flows that could be furthered by joint activities, it seems quite likely that the goals will receive different emphases on each side of the border. Policy objectives have not been and may not be identical for both countries in the foreseeable future. As a result, some of the previous problems related to the specifics of bilateralism may be recast.

Not only the passing of IRCA but also several other developments open *the possibility* of bilateralism in the not so distant future. IRCA, however, clearly dominates. Its relevance for Mexico-U.S. relations, in fact, will not be limited to its impact on Mexican perceptions of joint efforts to manage migratory flows. As a coda to the main argument here, the last section covers the example of legalization programs in order to briefly suggest some potential impacts on wider bilateral dealings.

---

[20]Mexico's Under Secretary of Foreign Relations, Sergio Gonzalez Galvez, has publicly discussed the possibility that the Salinas administration may propose to negotiate a bilateral treaty safeguarding the rights of Mexican workers in the United States. Arthur Golen, "Mexico Asks Safeguards for Workers," *The San Diego Union*, June 17, 1989, pp. A-1 and A-20.

[21]For example, networks will still be at work and one may expect that at least part of those flows could find a space in the "informal economy" of some U.S. urban centers.

[22]See Jorge Bustamante's comments in "'Operativo' Conjunto," *Excelsior*, February 27, 1989, p. 6-A.

UNINTENDED CONSEQUENCES: IRCA, LEGALIZATION, AND MEXICO-U.S. RELATIONS

IRCA may impact Mexico-U.S. relations in quite unpredictable ways. A brief review of the implications of only one of IRCA's main components—legalization provisions—clearly illustrates this. Available information indicates that these provisions will cover an important number of Mexicans both as part of the amnesty program and as a consequence of SAW— Mexican applications represent by far the largest numbers in both cases. A significant proportion of those migrants that are actually admitted will probably become more permanent, move from their present jobs, and eventually opt for U.S. citizenship.

The impact of this new wave of legal migrants on Mexico-U.S. relations will vary over time. The impact may be quite interesting even before the migrants become U.S. citizens. In the immediate future, for example, political participation in Mexico by Mexican nationals who legally reside in the United States may become a contentious issue for North American actors. Those U.S.-resident Mexicans may push for the recognition of their right to vote in Mexico's national elections—a widespread practice in several other nations. Such a demand has already been made and may be expected to intensify in the future. We have also had clear examples in the recent past of its possible support by U.S. citizens, who would be in a position to try to bring it into discussions between Mexico City and Washington, D.C.

Voting rights by themselves would be only part of the issue. If the migrants' previous decision to "vote with their feet" gives any indication, it would seem fair to assume that a significant proportion of that vote would go to opposition parties. Both the demand itself and its likely results, then, could affect bilateral dealings, even at the intergovernmental level.

If the new migrants succeed in altering some of the behavior patterns that have characterized previous migrants and if they opt for U.S. citizenship, a significant wave of legal migration may result from the citizens' family-reunification provisions presently included in U.S. legislation.[23] "Documented" migration may become a significant factor in relations between the United States and Mexico during the next decade. In the longer term, the consolidation of a Mexican-American community interested in affecting not only U.S. policy but Mexican policy and U.S.-Mexican relations will pose new challenges to both governments.

Legalization programs and their implications also illustrate a more general point: IRCA's impact on U.S.-Mexican relations may be quite contrary to the expressed intentions of some of its principal sponsors. One of the driving forces of legislative reform in this area was the need, as then Attorney General William French Smith put it, "to regain control of [U.S.] borders." Successful implementation of the legalization provisions would bring about a final paradox in this regard—which in a sense reflects the complexities of attempting to reign over deep economic and societal processes.

Given the concentration of Mexican migrants in areas close to the border, we will probably have an even more active and lively border in the future as a result of legislative changes. After all, crossing the border will no longer involve significant risks for this latest wave of immigrants into the United States. Increased interaction between the economies and societies of Mexico and the United States is something that many people in both countries do not particularly appreciate. If migration issues give us any clue, stopping the process will be very difficult.

---

[23]There are several factors at work here. Among them are the number of applications that will be finally approved, the extent to which these will include family units, and the practice of moving to the United States and waiting for legalization procedures there.

MEXICAN IMMIGRATION, U.S. INVESTMENT, AND U.S.-MEXICAN RELATIONS[1]

David F. Ronfeldt and Monica Ortíz de Oppermann
The RAND Corporation

Americans have long viewed illegal immigration from Mexico as a problem that needed a solution. Mexicans have long argued that worker migration is not a problem but a natural, beneficial phenomenon of history and economics. Thus, illegal immigration remained a contentious and seemingly insolvable issue for U.S.-Mexican relations when in 1986, to the surprise of virtually everybody everywhere, the U.S. Congress approved the Immigration Reform and Control Act (IRCA).

The Immigration and Naturalization Service (INS) has implemented the law's amnesty and legalization provisions quite well, and there are reasons to expect that IRCA-related issues will continue to be managed in a friendly, pragmatic manner. But at the same time, IRCA has created new uncertainties and difficulties for bilateral relations and has led to some disturbing possibilities. Immigration issues may yet become divisive enough to generate serious social and political reactions in the United States and to harm U.S.-Mexican relations as a whole.

ISSUES AS MIRROR IMAGES

It would be useful, therefore, to anticipate the likely effects of IRCA over the long term. But how can this be done? The law has just begun to take hold. It is still early for researchers to identify its current effects, let alone project them into the future.

An alternative method—the one used in this study—is to identify an instructive analogue. One such analogue might be formed using the recent laws of some West European countries to restrict worker migrations from the Middle East. But their relevance here seems limited, partly by the fact that the U.S.-Mexican relationship is unique. The nature of the "silent integration" developing between our two countries suggests looking for an analogue within the relationship itself.

This study turns to foreign investment in Mexico and constructs an analogue based on an observation made years ago but not explored until now: The research questions and policy issues that Americans raise about immigration are very similar to those that Mexicans raise about foreign investment in their country. For example, both issues have given rise to debates about job displacement and the distortion of cultural values.[2]

It is not only the policy debates that are virtual mirror images of each other. Similarities also appear between the principal laws that each country has enacted for the issue of most concern to it. But whereas the United States passed IRCA in 1986, Mexico enacted its Law to Promote Mexican Investment and Regulate Foreign Investment (LIME) in 1973. What the United States is now feeling and doing about illegal immigration, Mexico experienced over a decade ago regarding foreign investment. The evolution and effects of LIME since 1973 may

---

[1]This paper expands on the briefing that Dr. Ronfeldt presented at the conference and summarizes points that will be elaborated and analyzed by Ronfeldt and Ortíz in a forthcoming report.

[2]See Kevin McCarthy and David Ronfeldt, "Immigration as an Intrusive Global Flow: A New Perspective," in Mary M. Kritz (ed.), *U.S. Immigration and Refugee Policy: Global and Domestic Issues*, Lexington Books, D. C. Heath and Co., Lexington, Massachusetts, 1983, esp. pp. 385–387.

thus be analyzed as a historical analogue to the future of IRCA. To the extent the analogue is valid, it may indicate

- how IRCA may affect Mexican immigration flows,
- how IRCA and its implementation may evolve over time,
- how policy dialogue in and between our two countries may be changed.

The comparison may represent more than an analogue. It may imply that people in both countries should rethink their views of each other and start developing shared criteria for comprehending the process of integration that is occurring along the borderlands and potentially across the entire North American region. This study shows that assertive laws like LIME and IRCA may arise from nationalism but may finally become instruments for accommodation. After all, Mexican immigration and U.S. investment are key dimensions of interdependence—two flows that must continue and work for both countries in order for relations to function well over the long term.

AT FIRST GLANCE: OBVIOUS ISSUE DIFFERENCES

The two issues may initially look like apples and oranges. In the immigration area, the key actors are people—many of them poor workers who are isolated, powerless, and often subject to exploitation and abuse. The United States is said to be "a nation of immigrants"—most of whom have been welcome and have done very well. Yet policy debates are filled with fears about how the growing stock and flow of immigrants, particularly those who enter illegally from Mexico, may affect the U.S. economy and society.

In contrast, the key actors in the foreign investment area are corporations—many of them wealthy, well-organized, and powerful. Mexico has often welcomed foreign investment, but it has also resisted being overrun by foreign investors. At the time LIME was passed in 1973, there was widespread concern that the growing stock and flow of foreign investment, particularly from U.S.-based multinational corporations, would prove detrimental to Mexico's economy and sovereignty.

The two countries are also dissimilar in relation to both issues. The United States, obviously the more powerful country, has alternatives besides Mexico for importing foreign labor and exporting U.S. capital and technology. If Mexico were to cease supplying labor to the United States or welcoming U.S. investors, the United States might experience some adverse economic effects, but they would not be devastating.

Mexico is more vulnerable to external conditions. It has few alternatives to the United States as a major source of capital and technology, and it has no real alternative as a destination for migrant labor. If the United States were to seal its borders and U.S. investors were to go elsewhere, the adverse effects on Mexico could be dramatic.

Because of such differences, the two issues are normally analyzed separately. When they are discussed together, it is often because an economist is examining production factor exchanges (the labor component of immigration and the capital and technology components of investment are basic factors of production). Or a policy analyst or government official may be proposing to link issues and negotiate tradeoffs, as in the notion that the United States should promote investment in Mexico in order to create new jobs and reduce migration pressures there.

The laws each country has enacted—LIME in 1973, IRCA in 1986—also look very different. They arise from different countries and legal systems, in different decades, and they respond to different problems.[3] Whereas IRCA focuses on illegal immigration, LIME makes no issue of illegal foreign investment. The determination of what is legal and what illegal varies greatly between the two countries and their laws.

IRCA is a new law that aims to reduce the number of persons residing illegally in the United States, stem the flow of illegal immigration, and halt the employment of undocumented aliens. It is a long, complicated document containing detailed requirements for implementation in several phases by the INS. The most prominent provisions aim to

- extend amnesty to, and provide for the eventual permanent residence of, illegal aliens who had resided continuously in the United States since January 1982 or who had worked in agriculture's perishable crops industry for 90 days between May 1985 and May 1986;
- prohibit employers from hiring undocumented workers, require employers to verify the legality of all new hires, and set civil and criminal penalties that may be applied against employers of undocumented workers.

In addition, IRCA provides for the expansion of enforcement programs to halt future illegal immigration, especially along the border with Mexico; it seeks to prevent discrimination by employers who may avoid hiring "foreign-looking" workers who are citizens or otherwise legally in the United States; it authorizes federal compensation for some costs that state and local agencies incur in providing public services to the population granted amnesty; and it contains provisions to assure a continued supply of labor for agricultural employers who rely on undocumented workers.

In contrast, LIME is 17 years old and much shorter and less complex than IRCA.[4] In many respects, it represents not so much a new law as a codification and toughening of existing laws. In particular, it reasserts the classic restrictions on foreign investment that have long represented major achievements of the Mexican revolution and mainstays of the nation's mixed economy:

- The prohibition of foreign investment in "strategic sectors"—e.g., petroleum, basic petrochemicals, railroads, telecommunications, electricity—that were reserved exclusively for Mexican state enterprises.
- The prohibition of foreign investment in "sensitive sectors"—e.g., radio, television, transportation (land, air, and sea), and gas distribution—that were reserved for Mexican private as well as state enterprises.

Elsewhere, according to LIME, foreign participation should not exceed 49 percent of the capital and control of an enterprise—a rule that became a hallmark of the process known as "Mexicanization."

The law was imprecise about implementation, and it entrusted to a new consultative body, the National Commission on Foreign Investment (CNIE), decisions to authorize specific investments. Even foreign takeovers of Mexican businesses—a vital concern at the time—had to be authorized by the CNIE. LIME also required every foreign investment, old and new, to register with a new National Registry on Foreign Investment.

---

[3]The discussion here focuses on the original laws. Modifications—e.g., Mexico's recent statute about foreign investment, and current U.S. proposals to amend IRCA—are discussed later.

[4]LIME is based on the constitutional point that foreign investors are aliens—which could be taken to mean that it too is an immigration law.

104

LIME allowed for flexibility and authorized the CNIE to grant exemptions to the 49 per- cent (or other specified) limit if that was in Mexico's interest. Furthermore, the law did not tamper with the continuation of the maquiladora (in-bond assembly plant) program along the U.S.-Mexican border.

DIMENSIONS OF ISSUE SIMILARITY

Despite the differences, the comparison is not completely between apples and oranges. Table 1 highlights data on each issue area at the time the respective law was passed. In both cases, large stocks—in one case compared with total population, in the other with total capital stock—are of relatively similar size. Moreover, the neighboring country accounts for the larg- est share of the stocks and flows, which are concentrated regionally and by sector and which account for large capital returns to the sending country. Viewed in terms of these measures, the two issues—Mexican immigration to the United States, and U.S. investment in Mexico— seem to be of roughly similar size, visibility, and importance in each country.

Furthermore, similar kinds of perceptions and arguments permeate policy analysis and dialogue across both issues in both countries. Comparable statements exist on both sides of the border to illustrate the similarities identified below.

Negative Economic Arguments

First, on the negative side, it appears that the economic arguments against heavy immi- gration into the United States and against foreign investment in Mexico are nearly identical. The most basic fear in both countries is usually that foreigners will displace local citizens— from their jobs in the case of immigration, from their businesses in the case of foreign invest- ment.[5] This in turn leads to higher level concerns about how a nation's economy may be dis- torted and its autonomy limited. (See Table 2.)

Another similarity appears in concerns about the effects on class structure and government-funded programs. Some Americans worry that immigration is creating an under- class that will burden U.S. welfare and education programs. Likewise, some Mexicans have

Table 1

DIMENSIONS OF SIMILARITY

Category	Foreign-Born Population in the U.S. (Circa 1986)	Foreign Investment in Mexico (Circa 1973)
Stocks	Total = approx. 6% of U.S. pop.	Total = 3% Mexican capital
Neighbor's share	Mexicans = 30% of total	U.S. = 77% of total
Share of annual inflow	Mexicans = approx. 50% of undoc.	U.S. = 52% of total
Regional concentration	U.S. Southwest	Central Mexico
Sectorial concentration	Urban services	Manufacturing
Return capital flows	Large remittances to Mexico	Large profit repatriations to the U.S.

[5]For example, similar displacement concerns may be found in "Iniciativa de Ley para Promover la Inversión Mexi- cana y Regular la Inversión Extranjera," *Comercio Exterior*, enero 1973, pp. 16–25; and Ray Marshall, "Immigration in the Golden State: The Tarnished Dream," in David Simcox (ed.), *U.S. Immigration in the 1980's: Reappraisal and Reform*, Westview Press, 1988. Marshall was U.S. Secretary of Labor (1977–1980).

Table 2

ECONOMIC ARGUMENTS AGAINST IMMIGRATION
AND FOREIGN INVESTMENT

Distortions to the Economy	Immigration in the U.S.	Foreign Investment in Mexico
Displaces jobs/business	x	x
Lowers wages/profits	x	x
Limits technological advance	x	x
Harms local competition	x	x
Creates underclass/overclass	x	x
Hurts balance of payments	?	x
Undermines national autonomy	x	x

worried that foreign investors, particularly from the U.S.-based multinational corporations, will form a power elite—an overclass—that could constrain Mexico's autonomy. Meanwhile, it is believed that foreign firms take advantage of domestic policies to protect internal markets and subsidize industrialization.[6]

The debate in Mexico has made an issue of the balance-of-payments effects. Many Mexicans believe that foreign investors take out of the country—e.g., through repatriations of profits, through transfer payments for licensed technologies and services—much more than they put into it, especially if they raise most of their capital in Mexico rather than bringing it in.[7]

A similar issue has not arisen in the immigration area. Mexican immigrants remit a lot of money home. But this is not regarded as having a serious negative effect on the balance of payments of the large U.S. economy, even though in absolute terms the immigrants may remit more money than U.S. firms do.

Negative Cultural Arguments

Cultural concerns are also quite similar, as indicated by Table 3. For example, both countries have strong concerns that a growing influx of foreigners will undermine national identity and solidarity. It is said that the nation's culture and its traditions will be contaminated rather than enriched by the spread of foreign values, ideas, languages, and life-styles.[8]

Some analysts have claimed that IRCA was motivated partly by a strain of racism and discrimination in U.S. society, a desire to limit the presence of "little brown people." As far as we know, LIME has never been called racist. But our discussions with Mexican analysts indicate that support for LIME was motivated in part by a desire—perhaps not racist, but somewhat racial in basis nonetheless—to limit the presence of "gringo" businessmen in Mexico.

---

[6]See Miguel S. Wionczek, *Inversión y Tecnología Extranjera en América Latina,* Editorial Joaquín Mortiz, 1971, which points out how foreign firms may benefit from cheap energy and transportation services.

[7]For an example of the "decapitalization" critique, see José Luis Ceceña, *México en la Órbita Imperial,* Ediciones El Caballito, México, D.F., 1970.

[8]For example, compare remarks by former Under Secretary of Industry and Commerce (1970–1974) José Campillo Saínz, speech delivered in New York, September 12, 1973, *Mexican Newsletter,* No. 14; and Otis Graham, Jr., "Immigration and the National Interest," in Simcox, *U.S. Immigration in the 1980's,* p. 127.

106

Table 3

CULTURAL ARGUMENTS AGAINST IMMIGRATION
AND FOREIGN INVESTMENT

Disruption of National Culture and Identity	Immigration in the U.S.	Foreign Investment in Mexico
Introduces alien values, life-styles	x	x
Generates ethnic/racial tensions	x	?
Creates assimilation problems	x	x

Negative Political Arguments

Comparing the political perceptions yields another set of similarities, indicated by Table 4. As one Mexican scholar has noted, "The problem of foreign direct investment is considered by the Mexican government as being very delicate from the political point of view"—a statement that also pertains to immigration in the United States.[9] The concerns go beyond minor violations of the law, like the falsification of U.S. immigration documents or the use of Mexican prestanombres (name-lenders, front men) by foreign investors.

Thus some Mexicans have worried, based on the history of Mexico before the Revolution of 1910, that alliances will form between foreign investors and domestic political and business leaders that are detrimental to the nation's economic development and political independence. In turn, some Americans are concerned that the influx of immigrants from Mexico may eventually enable Spanish-speaking politicians to emerge across the Southwest and create a Quebec-type enclave. In both countries, one may find statements that the nation will lose control of its borders and that national sovereignty is at risk.[10]

Table 4

POLITICAL ARGUMENTS AGAINST IMMIGRATION
AND FOREIGN INVESTMENT

Burdens to the Political System	Immigration in the U.S.	Foreign Investment in Mexico
Stresses infrastructure, services	x	x
Generates crime and abuse	x	?
Causes political challenges	x	x
Weakens control of borderlands	x	x
Creates dependency on foreigners	x	x
Jeopardizes sovereignty, security	x	x

[9]Wionczek, *Inversión y Tecnología Extranjera*, p. 148.

[10]Similar concerns about the potential loss of sovereignty may be found in Bernardo Sepúlveda, "Política Industrial y Empresas Transnacionales en México," in Bernardo Sepúlveda Amor, Olga Pellicer de Brody, and Lorenzo Meyer (eds.), *Las Empresas Transnacionales en México,* El Colegio de México, 1974; and Council of Economic Advisers, *Economic Report of the President,* U.S. Government Printing Office, Washington, D.C., February 1986.

For people who hold some of the foregoing views, Mexican immigration into the United States or U.S. investment in Mexico may be a problem. Those who identify with almost every item on the lists may believe they add up to a threat. They may feel that their nation is being invaded, that its viability, even its soul, is at stake. They may start using the language of national security to convey their concerns.[11]

Positive Arguments

As outlined in Table 5, the array of positive perceptions and arguments regarding immigration and foreign investment is mostly economic. Here again, there is a good match across the two issues and countries.

For example, many Mexicans recognized, even in the highly nationalistic climate of the 1970s, that foreign investment could improve Mexico's productive capacity by bringing new capital and technology into the country, increasing employment opportunities, and opening up new markets. Likewise, it is often argued in the United States that the immigrant workers benefit the U.S. economy, partly because they take low-wage, low-skilled agricultural and urban service jobs that might otherwise go unfilled.[12] In both cases, the strongest arguments about positive effects often come not from the receiving but from the sending country.

It is not easy to find cultural and political arguments in favor of high levels of immigration or investment from a foreign source, even though that source is a neighbor. Because of the strength and scope of negative perceptions in the United States, "It's a tricky problem

Table 5

ARGUMENTS IN FAVOR OF IMMIGRATION
AND FOREIGN INVESTMENT

Category	Immigration in the U.S.	Foreign Investment in Mexico
Economic Benefits		
Creates jobs and businesses	x	x
Expands markets	x	x
Raises the standard of living	x	x
Introduces new technologies	?	x
Fosters regional development	x	x
Aids productivity, competitiveness	x	x
Improves balance of payments	No	x
Social and Political Benefits		
Generates taxes, other payments	x	x
Brings new ideas	?	x

---

[11]For example, Campillo Saínz, "Mexican Thesis on Foreign Investment," Ministry of Industry and Commerce, Mexico City, October 14, 1972, provides a rare, early example of a Mexican official cautiously using the word "security." An extreme U.S. example is The Federation for American Immigration Reform (FAIR), *Ten Steps to Securing America's Borders,* Washington, D.C., January 1989.

[12]For example, see Kevin F. McCarthy and R. Burciaga Valdez, *Current and Future Effects of Mexican Immigration in California,* The RAND Corporation, R-3365-CR, May 1986, p. 77.

being for immigration in this country."[13] It has been just as difficult to be for foreign investment in Mexico in the past.

Similar Patterns of Ambivalent Views

The preceding discussion has contrasted the negative and positive views, as though people identify primarily with one side or the other. Yet many if not most people hold ambivalent views. Here too there are similar patterns of perception and analysis in both countries.

One key analysis pattern is to balance the benefits against the costs and risks in what appears to be a moderate, pragmatic manner. But this may lead to many kinds of nuanced conclusions. Whatever the flow under discussion, assessments exist in both countries that (1) likely political and cultural costs outweigh any likely economic benefits and (2) to the contrary, economic and other benefits exceed all clear costs and risks.[14]

Analysts who conclude that costs and benefits are mixed—for whichever country or issue area—often proceed in terms of one or all of the following additional patterns:

- The flow is "structurally necessary" as an economic factor of production for the receiving country.
- The effects depend on the "conditions" under which the flow occurs.
- Government policy should strengthen the positive effects and counteract the negative ones.
- Policy should take into account the "absorptive capacity" of the country and should attend to the process of "adaptation" and "adjustment" that takes place between the immigrant or investor and the country.

These patterns typically culminate in a pragmatic concept of "limits," below which the country may accommodate and benefit from the flow and above which negative effects are likely to multiply. The language of limits is increasingly part of the policy debates in both countries.[15]

Out of Dialogue Emerge the Laws

In sum, immigration and foreign investment have generated conceptually similar policy dialogues in both countries—albeit running in contrary directions. Yet these dialogues are not just conceptual; they have had practical effects in the form of the laws each country has instituted to deal with its particular concerns.

As discussed in the next section, points of similarity extend to the laws and their effects on policy debate. The debates leading to LIME and IRCA are so similar that what has happened to LIME since 1973 may prefigure what will happen to IRCA in the future.

---

[13]From an undated interview with Rep. Patricia Schroeder, by The Alexis de Tocqueville Institution, Stanford, California.

[14]For an example of a view in which the benefits may exceed the costs, see Joel Kotkin, "Fear and Reality in the Los Angeles Melting Pot," *Los Angeles Times Magazine*, November 5, 1989. Another like-minded article from the popular press is Pete Hamill, "Along the Tortilla Curtain," *Esquire*, February 1990, pp. 39–41.

[15]For example, see comments by Jorge Bustamante in a roundtable discussion published as "México/Estados Unidos: La Nueva Vecindad," *NEXOS*, No. 143, noviembre 1989, pp. 25–32.

COMPARING THE LAWS

Origins

In both countries, the laws follow upon many years of rising flows, fairly light controls on those flows, and constant public controversy about the effects of the flows. Public opinion is aroused not only by the increases in flows from all sources, but specifically by the increase from the neighbor, which grows faster than flows from other sources and climbs to a very high share of the total.

As a result, feelings intensify that one's country is too open, too accommodating, too hospitable to foreigners—even though the principal flow is from the neighboring country. Fears spread that if trends continue, one's country risks being overrun, invaded, flooded by unwelcome foreigners.

A protectionist, defensive nationalism gains strength. None of the underlying concerns are new, and the ensuing policy debates do not settle whether people's concerns are real or a matter of perception. But a threshold is crossed. A consensus emerges that the existing laws are ineffective and being flouted. Policymakers conclude that a strong new law is needed to protect the nation's interests.

Both LIME and IRCA were thus enacted in periods of heightened nationalism. But they were formulated through different national processes that are difficult to compare—and in the case of LIME, difficult to document. LIME issued from the executive branch of Mexico's relatively closed political system, and it reflected strong input from left-leaning intellectual sectors. The debate around LIME is noteworthy for the absence of analyses emphasizing the positive contributions of foreign investment and opposing efforts to restrict it.

In contrast, IRCA issued from the open U.S. congressional process, after a lot of political activity among diverse interest groups and with odd alliances of conservatives and liberals joining the coalitions that finally supported IRCA. The debates around the law gave rise to numerous analyses both for and against making a major effort to restrict illegal immigration.

Content: Blends of Nationalism and Pragmatism

Both laws stand out as landmark pieces of nationalistic legislation because of their intent to stem a foreign influx. But neither law represents a comprehensive reform. As noted earlier, LIME mostly codified and toughened existing legislation. IRCA focuses only on law governing illegal immigration and leaves legal immigration for future reform.

Both laws define the problems mainly in economic-displacement terms. LIME explicitly refers to concerns that foreign investment will displace Mexican businesses and limit Mexico's autonomy. IRCA clearly reflects concerns about undocumented workers taking jobs away from American laborers. Cultural, political, and security concerns play crucial roles in the debates, but they are left unstated in the laws.

Both laws begin by requiring the immediate registration of aliens—investors in one case, immigrants in the other—to legalize and document their presence. And both laws set new penalties for violations by local citizens and resident aliens. LIME threatened sanctions against Mexican prestanombres (name-lenders) who acted as front men for foreign investors seeking to circumvent Mexican law. IRCA provides for sanctions against employers who hire undocumented workers.

Despite this envelope of nationalism, neither law was as tough as it might have been. Both were the result of domestic compromises—IRCA apparently more so than LIME—and reflect the fact that important interests in both countries were served by continuing the flows.

As a result, the internal details for implementing both laws were quite pragmatic and accommodating. For example, LIME was not made retroactive against established firms where foreigners held more than a 49 percent interest. IRCA allowed "grandfathering," whereby employers were not to be penalized for undocumented foreign-born employees who had been hired, recruited, or referred to them before November 6, 1986.

Moreover, both laws contain loopholes or allow for exceptions so that needed capital or labor can flow continually. Mexico's CNIE was given great flexibility for negotiating the terms of specific investments and could also grant exemptions to the 49 percent limit on foreign participation—especially if the investor agreed to introduce new technology, create new jobs, open up new export markets, and/or locate in one of the less developed regions of Mexico. Whereas LIME left the maquiladora system alone, IRCA created a functional equivalent in the form of its provisions for Special Agricultural Workers (SAWs), Replenishment Agricultural Workers (RAWs), and the category of workers known as H-2As. Together, they allow for the legal migration into the United States of thousands of Mexicans who could claim to qualify as agricultural workers.

Initial Effects

Similarities of the laws extend to their effects during their first few years (see Table 6). The laws quickly became the centerpieces in exercises of heightened nationalism; the pragmatism behind the laws received little notice. The laws look tough, restrictive, protectionist—and in many ways they are. LIME, even though it mostly codified existing laws, represented an assertiveness as new as IRCA's.

Just before and after the law was approved, an alarmed outcry arose in the neighboring country that it was being targeted in an unfair, unfriendly, unilateral manner. Officials and commentators there declared that the law-making country had a right to decide whether it wanted to receive the flow—be it foreign investment or immigration. They showed respect for the principle of nonintervention in internal affairs. They claimed that the flow responds to a natural demand—whether for capital in Mexico or labor in the United States—and claimed that the new law probably would not have much effect. But they also lamented that they were not consulted about the new law. For example, a famous speech by the U.S. Ambassador to Mexico in 1972 charged that LIME would change "the rules of the game"—a point that might well summarize subsequent, more cautious Mexican reactions to the enactment of IRCA.[16]

Table 6

INITIAL EFFECTS OF LIME AND IRCA

Category	LIME	IRCA
Law initially looks very tough	x	x
Outcry arises in neighboring country	x	x
Officials reassure neighbor	x	x
Law not aimed specifically at neighbor	x	x
Law not meant to stop flow	x	x
Law not as tough as other countries'	x	x
Law allows for exceptions	x	x
Worst-case scenarios do not come true	x	x
Short-term effects on the flow unclear	x	x

---

[16]Ambassador Robert McBride asked whether the rules were changing in a speech to the U.S.-Mexico Businessmen's Committee, Acapulco, October 12, 1972. The text was reprinted in Spanish as part of special sections in *Comercio Exterior,* October 1972, pp. 937–944 and 945–951, that also contain a rejoinder by Campillo Saínz and critical comments by Jesús Puente Leyva, Leopoldo Solis, Samuel I. del Villar, and Miguel Wionczek.

While acknowledging that the rules of the game had changed, officials from the legislating country hastened to reassure their neighbor about the law. They said it was not really aimed at the neighbor (though of course it was). They said it was not meant to halt the flow but only to regulate and channel it. As Mexican officials repeatedly said about LIME, in a wonderful phrase that could also be applied to U.S. justifications of IRCA, the law was "not restrictive, but selective."[17]

Moreover, the officials added, the new law was not as tough as it could have been; other countries had tougher laws. Mexico defended LIME in terms of a broader third-world trend to exert nationalist controls over foreign investment. Likewise, IRCA was said to reflect a trend that started in Western Europe to restrict immigration and refugee flows.

In addition, the officials noted that the implementation of the law would take time and would be done in a friendly, pragmatic manner that allowed for appeals and exceptions. Meanwhile, the worst case scenarios that critics painted did not come true. LIME did not lead to the exclusion of U.S. investors. And IRCA did not result in massive deportation of aliens, an oversupply of unemployed workers along the border, and a drop in living standards in Mexico.

Finally—today with IRCA and previously with LIME—no clear, dramatic effect on the flow in the near term can be attributed to the law. It turns out that researchers find it quite difficult to tell what kinds of effects such a law is having. The first year or two, a dip may occur because people who might have invested in Mexico or migrated illegally to the United States hesitate due to fears and uncertainties created by the law and its enforcement. But no drastic reductions occur. After all, the framers of both laws neither wanted nor expected to halt the flow in question.

WHAT LIME MAY IMPLY ABOUT IRCA'S FUTURE

The foregoing parallels provide a basis for treating the experience with LIME as an analogue for projecting IRCA into the future. To the extent that the analogue is valid, the following may be expected.

Evolution and Administration of the Law

The evolution of LIME since 1973 indicates—for IRCA—that nationalism will give way to pragmatism.

- At first, administrative and other problems may hound the implementation of the law. Over time, its terms will be simplified and eased.
- New technical and professional cadres may arise whose command of the issues will moderate the policy debate.
- Compromises will be made to accommodate new flows that serve important interests. Exceptions may become the rule.
- National interests and objectives will be redefined to emphasize the benefits over the costs and risks of the flows.

---

[17]"The Government of Mexico hasn't proceeded arbitrarily with the investor from abroad. . . . The law is not restrictive, but selective. We want the flow of foreign investment to continue, but not indiscriminately." Fausto Zapata, *Notas sobre el Sistema Político y la Inversión Extranjera*, The Johns Hopkins University Press, Washington, D.C., January 29, 1974.

LIME's evolution has been completed by the enactment in 1989 of new regulations (herein named RELIME) that dramatically liberalize the law and open Mexico to greater foreign investment. Will IRCA be superseded someday by a counterpart to RELIME? Will the United States welcome and ease immigration from Mexico to a degree that may seem radical today? Unlikely as it may seem, these are the conclusions that we ultimately infer from this analogue. How and why this might be the case is further explained below.

Effects on the Size of the Flows

LIME has surely had a limiting effect. Without it, foreign investment would probably have been higher. But it is unclear how much higher. And it is difficult to attribute changes in the flows to the law, which is only one of the factors that investors consider. Economic and political conditions in Mexico are actually more significant.[18] Will IRCA's impact on the immigration flow be viewed similarly?

If IRCA has effects parallel to LIME's, immigration flow size from Mexico will exhibit the following pattern:

- An initial temporary, marginal decline in the illegal flow as a result of the new law. (This has occurred.)
- A return to increased flows (legal and illegal combined) because of structural factors apart from the law.[19]
- Continued growth in the total stock from Mexico, which will remain a primary source of foreign-born persons but will account for a smaller share than before IRCA.

If, as some demographers predict, labor shortages occur soon in the United States, then it may decide to permit additional labor migration from Mexico—just as Mexico liberalized LIME because of capital shortages. This might occur through the adoption of temporary worker programs or of an "open border" policy (freer flow of labor) in connection with expanding the U.S.-Canada free trade pact to include Mexico.

Effects on the Characteristics of the Flows

LIME aimed to alter the characteristics of investment flows so that they would serve the interests of the nation and not just of the investors. IRCA does not specify what kinds of immigrants are desirable. But IRCA is heading toward a parallel effort that would alter the characteristics of immigration flows, as evidenced by two Congressional bills—one by Senators Edward Kennedy and Alan Simpson, the other by Representative Howard Berman—that propose to overhaul U.S. law on legal immigration.

Parallels appear in the terms—written into LIME, softened in RELIME, and now used in the U.S. debate on immigration law—that give preference to those

---

[18]See Richard S. Weinert, "Foreign Capital in Mexico," in Susan Kaufman Purcell (ed.), *Mexico–United States Relations,* Proceedings of the Academy of Political Science, Vol. 34, No. 1, New York, 1981; and José I. Casar, "Mexico's Policy on Foreign Investment," in Riordan Roett (ed.), *Mexico and the United States, Managing the Relationship,* Westview Press, Boulder, Colorado, 1988.

[19]For a structural explanation of why Mexican labor is needed in the United States and why immigration may increase regardless of the legal situation, see, among other sources, Wayne Cornelius, "Mexican Migration to the United States," in Purcell, *Mexico–United States Relations,* pp. 71–72. As far as we can determine, no Mexican counterpart to an analyst like Cornelius existed in Mexico's debate about foreign investment in the early 1970s. Such a counterpart would have argued that there were structural reasons for investment to continue and that a restrictive law was inadvisable and likely to fail.

- who represent new stock, independent of firms or families already well represented in the receiving country;
- who will introduce new capital, skills, and technologies that the country needs;
- who will establish job-creating businesses in areas that have received few investors or immigrants in the past.

LIME aimed to attract new firms to Mexico and limit the expansion of established firms (i.e., U.S.-based corporations) that were propagating through subsidiaries and branches. The parallel issue for U.S. legislation is family reunification.

LIME has had marginal effects, and our study suggests that it may take years of effort to affect the characteristics of a major flow like foreign investment or immigration. By analogy, IRCA will result in similarly marginal changes, along with a long debate as to whether IRCA or other factors explain the changes.

Moderation and Maturation of the Policy Dialogue

LIME, like IRCA, reflected nationalist desires to resist the trend toward integration between our two countries. But because of the experience with LIME, the policy dialogue about foreign investment now seems much more advanced, moderate, pragmatic, and mature than the immigration dialogue does. LIME has become a vehicle not of rejection but accommodation. As indicated by the recent enactment of RELIME, a new nationalist mentality is emerging in Mexico that views foreign investment more in terms of the benefits than of the costs and risks.

Will IRCA have similar, paradoxical effects on U.S. thinking and behavior toward immigration from Mexico? For that to happen, the law must work to some degree. Then the edge may wear off the divisive issues, the anti-immigration mood may peak, and a new era of qualified openness toward Mexico may develop.

After a policy dialogue matures in the context of growing interdependence, officials from our two countries may agree to a bilateral framework agreement for the flow(s) in question. This occurred with trade and investment in 1989, but our two countries seem far from a comparable understanding on immigration issues.

Meanwhile, understanding the phenomenon of mirror issues suggests that accepted nationalist mindsets should be questioned in both countries. Many Americans think that Mexican immigration is bad, but U.S. investment is good for Mexico. Many Mexicans think that U.S. investment is bad, but Mexican immigration is good for the United States. This study suggests a different logic: The two flows may be equally good or bad for both countries.

Figure 1 summarizes the challenge. As interdependence deepens toward social and economic integration, one goal should be harmonizing the views of both flows in both countries.

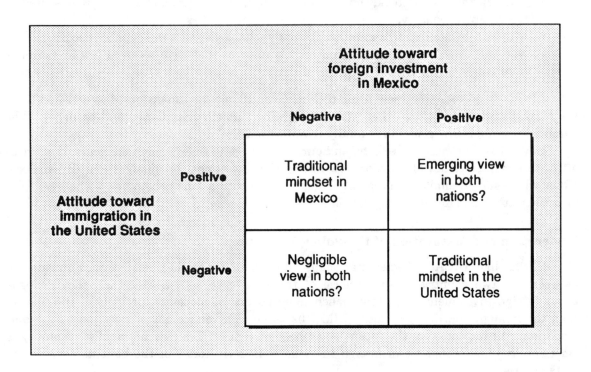

Fig. 1—A matrix of mindsets for foreign investment in Mexico and
immigration to the United States

EMIGRATION AS A SAFETY VALVE FOR MEXICO'S LABOR MARKET: A POST-IRCA APPROXIMATION

Manuel García y Griego
El Colegio de México

INTRODUCTION

It has been argued that labor immigration to the United States, especially that of undocumented workers, has functioned as a "safety valve" for Mexico's growing labor force. Though rarely defined, the safety valve metaphor has been used to refer to (1) the reduced pressure on Mexico's labor market as a result of net migration to the United States and (2) the alleviation of poverty that presumably results from the remittances sent home by temporary workers. Furthermore, it is generally assumed that these economic benefits of emigration diminish the pressure on the Mexican political system and, indeed, that the safety valve's very existence could be a determinant of Mexico's political stability. In accordance with these views, in 1988 several members of the U.S. Congress with a special interest in Mexico wrote: "The United States acts as a safety valve for Mexican unemployment, preventing the buildup of social and political instability . . ." (Center for Strategic and International Studies, 1989, p. 17).

This statement is an echo of similar arguments that have been made numerous times, both in Mexico and in the United States, since about the 1930s. However, three developments of the 1980s have given the safety valve metaphor a new resonance.

First, since 1982, the Mexican economy has entered a downward spiral. Petroleum prices have dropped sharply, Mexico has found it difficult to service its debt—even with massive rescheduling and creative attempts at debt financing, and the national economy has deteriorated markedly. The urban work force, especially, has been hard hit; unemployment has risen and real wages have plummeted. Economic crisis has been accompanied by political strains, though not of the magnitude many expected.

A second development of the 1980s is the sharp growth in the number of deportable Mexicans located by the U.S. Immigration and Naturalization Service (INS) between 1982 and 1986. Many observers, especially Washington officials, interpreted this as an indication that the Mexican economic crisis was pushing a growing number of Mexican workers into the United States.

A third development occurred in 1986. The culmination of a decade of debate and controversy was the passage, by the U.S. Congress, of the Immigration Reform and Control Act (IRCA), which sought to curb illegal entries and legalize part of the undocumented population. To some observers it has appeared as though the "safety valve" may be closing when Mexico most needs it.

If these arguments are correct, the adoption of IRCA should have represented a substantial threat to Mexico's interests. And indeed, during the period of U.S. immigration policy debate leading up to IRCA and to its early implementation, Mexican public opinion reacted as if in fact IRCA represented such a threat. In May 1987, for example, many in the Mexican public misconstrued the start of the legalization phase as a first step toward mass deportations. Earlier, during the passage of the Simpson-Mazzoli bill in the House of Representatives in

June 1984, the Mexican public had expressed a similar reaction.[1] The Mexican government developed contingency plans for a large return migration. Neither the alarm expressed by the Mexican public nor analysts on either side of the border, however, have explained adequately why the Mexican government did not act vigorously to keep the valve "open" if undocumented emigration really played such a role in Mexico's politico-economic system.

This may be an appropriate time to reexamine the safety valve and to estimate its dimensions. This paper shall attempt to construct two indicators of what could be considered the "labor force safety valve." First, on the basis of a regional population projection whose methodology is discussed below, the paper defines one such indicator as the difference between the labor force growth that would have occurred in the absence of net emigration, by age and region in Mexico, and the actual labor force growth that occurred with net migration to the United States. This is termed the labor force increase avoided in Mexico by net immigration to the United States. Annualized estimates are presented for each five-year period between the years 1980 and 2000 for total immigration and for the undocumented labor force. The second indicator is the ratio of the Mexican-born immigrant labor force resident in the United States, by age, to the total Mexican-born work force, which includes those workers that reside in Mexico and those that reside in the United States. This indicator constitutes an approximate measure of the conditional probability that a Mexican-born worker of a certain age will reside in the United States (given that he or she is already in the labor force of either country).

The construction of these indicators is made possible by extant data on undocumented Mexican migration to the United States and certain data available to the public on the number of Mexican-born persons that applied for legalization as pre-1982 entrants and obtained an I-687 temporary residence visa under IRCA. Because these are the only indicators developed here, the paper identifies several components that might be considered for a more complete analysis. These are (a) the migration of temporary workers to the United States who ostensibly reside in Mexico; (b) the remittance flows of other residents in the United States or of temporary workers; (c) an analysis of how far the United States is likely to go toward "closure" of the valve; (d) an analysis of the nature of the effort that would be required to generate jobs in Mexico if the labor force safety valve were to be closed; and (e) an analysis of the potential political consequences of a closure of the valve. Also, in part for these reasons, the Mexican population legalized as Special Agricultural Workers (SAWs) is omitted from this analysis. Having limited the discussion to two indicators, this paper must leave unresolved several broader questions of the concept and significance of the safety valve.

Nonetheless, a quantitative discussion, whose subjects are (1) the dynamics of Mexico's labor force during the last two decades of the twentieth century and (2) the significance of migration to the United States in terms of growth, is useful as a first approximation. Three questions are addressed in this paper. First, what has been the degree to which emigration has diminished the growth of Mexico's national and regional labor force? The second and third questions arise in the context of the current implementation of IRCA; this context is that 1.2 million pre-1982 entrants have obtained temporary residence as legalized undocumented Mexicans and that employer sanctions have not yet noticeably reduced post-1986 undocumented migrant flows. Therefore, what has been the impact of legalization of the labor force safety valve? And third, if current emigration rates were to hold constant until the year 2000, what

---

[1]A commentary on the alarm expressed in the Mexican media in May 1987 can be found in Bustamante (1987). A reaction to the June 1984 debate is found in García y Griego and Giner de los Ríos (1985), which attempted to answer the implicit question of whether Mexico's economy was vulnerable to changes in U.S. immigration policy. References to Mexican public reaction in June and July of 1984 are mentioned on p. 222.

would be the magnitude of the safety valve that could be closed as a result of the effective enforcement of employer sanctions? By addressing these questions, it is hoped that light can be shed on the broader question of the politico-economic role of labor emigration for countries of origin and their vulnerability to changes in the immigration policies of receiving countries.

METHOD

This exercise builds on several existing datasets and on past attempts to estimate the total flow of both legal and undocumented Mexican migration to the United States. One source is the estimate of the total Mexican-born population counted in the 1980 U.S. census, developed by Robert Warren and Jeffrey Passel, which utilizes the census results, INS data on legal immigrants and naturalizations, and a residual method for estimating the number of undocumented residents in the United States (Warren and Passel, 1987; Passel and Woodrow, 1984). Warren and Passel's estimates of the 1980 Mexican-born and undocumented Mexican population resident in the United States are used as a point of departure for deriving the 1980 base population and also to estimate emigration rates from Mexico to the United States during 1975–1980.

A second source is an unpublished estimate using a similar methodology, prepared in 1989 by Karen Woodrow and Jeffrey Passel and based on the 1988 Current Population Survey (CPS). This source is important because it largely corroborates the results of the third source and is used to calibrate this paper's estimates of the net migration of Mexicans to the United States during the 1980s. The third source is a regional projection of the population of Mexico, which this author prepared recently as an estimate of the supply of immigrants to the United States (García y Griego, 1989). This projection, which incorporates currently accepted assumptions for Mexican regional fertility and mortality and which estimates five-year migration patterns between two regions in Mexico and the United States, constitutes an attempt to model regional and national-level internal migration within Mexico and international migration between Mexico and the United States. It adopts the alternative fertility and the mortality assumptions of the INEGI-CONAPO[2] projections of Mexico's population by state, 1980–2010 (INEGI-CONAPO, 1985). A fourth source is the currently available data on legalizations under IRCA (U.S. Immigration and Naturalization Service, 1989). Final sources are the U.S. and Mexican 1980 censuses, from which are derived the age-sex and region-specific labor-force participation rates employed in this demographic exercise (INEGI, 1986; and U.S. Bureau of the Census, n.d.).

The exercise reported here extends the regional population projection (the third source) with three modifications. As a result, the estimates of the Mexican regional population, national population, and emigrant population in the United States differ somewhat from those presented in the two alternative hypotheses presented in that source (García y Griego, 1989). The model presented here is closest to Hypothesis I in the earlier projection, which assumed that the 1975–1980 interregional migration rates held constant throughout the projection period.

The first modification was to increase immigration rates to the United States from both regions in Mexico by 15 percent uniformly across all sex-age groups from the rates observed in 1975–1980. This was done because we now know from Woodrow and Passel's analysis of the June 1988 CPS that a larger Mexican-born population was found in the United States than

---

[2]INEGI is the Instituto Nacional de Estadística, Geografía, e Informática, and CONAPO is the Consejo Nacional de Población.

would have been the case had migration rates held constant. An increase in the immigration rates to the United States of 15 percent, in conjunction with the other two modifications discussed below, produced 1985 and 1990 Mexican-born populations in the United States that, when interpolated at June 1988, approximate the 4,085,000 Mexican-born that Woodrow and Passel found in the CPS.[3] This 15 percent increase results in an estimated 4,474,000 Mexican-born persons residing in the United States in June 1990.

A uniform 15 percent increase in immigration rates is, of course, not the only possible explanation for why the 1988 Mexican-born population is larger than we would expect on the basis of the 1980 population and previously observed 1975–1980 migration trends. Return migration to Mexico could have decreased substantially, and our estimates of the mortality of the Mexican-born population for the 1980–1990 period could be too high. (Here and in the model discussed in García y Griego, 1989, the mortality of the Mexican-born in the United States is assumed to be identical, by age and sex, to that of the specific region in Mexico that sent 70 percent of the emigrants of the 1970s. See Fig. 1.) Even extraordinary decreases in assumed mortality and return migration rates, however, would not have been sufficient to produce the net increase in Mexican-born population observed during 1980–1988. The absolute numbers of return migrants and deaths were already relatively small. Moreover, the obligatory increase in emigration rates between 1975–1980 and 1980–1988 is more than plausible, given economic trends in Mexico and the United States. Indeed, a 15 percent increase between those two periods suggests that emigration probabilities from Mexico to the United States have increased modestly, considering the magnitude of the economic changes in Mexico during that time. (Figure 1 summarizes the principal assumptions adopted in this exercise.)

Although this increase is inescapable if we accept the 1988 CPS-based estimate, it is quite possible, of course, that the increase was not uniform across age-sex groups and proportional in each of Mexico's two regions. The regional division of Mexico, adopted in García y Griego (1989) and continued here, separates eight core sending states (region 1) from the rest of the country (region 2). Region 1 is the combined area of the states of Baja California, Chihuahua, Durango, Guanajuato, Jalisco, Michoacán, San Luis Potosí, and Zacatecas. These states contributed about 70 percent of the migrant flow to the United States during the 1970s, and several of them have sent large proportions of migration since the 1920s. It is hypothetically possible, of course, that emigration rates from region 1 remained unchanged and that all of the increased emigration resulted from region 2. More likely is that both regions experienced some increase. Because there is no quantitative basis for assuming that region 2's emigration rates increased to a greater degree than region 1's, here the increase is allocated uniformly. In the event that region 2's emigration rates rose somewhat higher than 15 percent, then the national estimates presented here should not be affected significantly, although the magnitude of the labor force emigration safety valve for region 1 would be overestimated.

The second and third modifications are related. The regional population projection prepared previously by this author did not separate undocumented from legal residents and it ignored as inconsequential the difference between the size of the Mexican-born population resident in the United States on April 1 and on June 30, 1980. The revised population projection model attempts to estimate the Mexican-born persons resident in the United States according to immigration status. "Legal residents" include naturalized U.S. citizens, legally resident aliens, and Mexican-born pre-1982 entrants legalized under IRCA (I-687 temporary

---

[3]Actually, according to Woodrow and Passel's unpublished estimates, the CPS reported 3,867,000 Mexican-born. They determine, however, that about 218,000 persons of Mexican origin misreported their nativity; these subsequently were allocated to the Mexican-born.

- **Mortality.** Region 1's[a] male life expectancies at birth for 1980–85, 1985–90, 1990–95, 1995–2000 are, respectively, 65.14, 66.36, 67.89, 68.95. Females: 70.86, 72.48, 73.85, 75.01. Region 2's male life expectancies at birth are, respectively, 63.72, 65.57, 66.89, 68.14. Females: 70.34, 72.22, 73.8, 75.1. These are identical to those estimated by INEGI-CONAPO. The (1) mortality of the Mexican-born population in the U.S. and (2) age-specific mortality of the legally resident and undocumented populations are assumed by the author to be identical to those of region 1.

    SOURCE: INEGI-CONAPO (1985). Identical to assumptions in García y Griego (1989).

- **Fertility.** Total fertility rates for women in region 1 for 1980–85, 1985–90, 1990–95, 1995–2000 are, respectively, 4.40, 3.52, 3.05, 2.88. Region 2: 3.84, 3.18, 2.85, 2.73. The fertility of the Mexican-born population in the U.S. is not of interest because its offspring is not Mexican-born.

    SOURCE: INEGI-CONAPO (1985). Identical to assumptions in García y Griego (1989).

- **Migration rates, I.** Certain age-sex-specific migration rates estimated for 1975–80 are assumed to remain constant between 1980–2000. These include the probability of changing residence from region 1 to region 2 and from region 2 to region 1 (both flows are within Mexico) and the probability of returning to Mexico from the United States. Internal migration rates are estimated using the 1980 Mexican census, published and unpublished tabulations. Return migration is estimated using the 1980 Mexican census and unpublished tabulations from the 1970 census (methodology described in García y Griego, 1989). Return rates for undocumented and legal immigrants are assumed identical, by age and sex.

    SOURCE: García y Griego (1989).

- **Migration rates, II.** Emigration rates from regions 1 and 2 are estimated for 1975–80 on the basis of Warren and Passel (1987). The observed rates in 1975–80 are increased uniformly by 15% to arrive at an estimated 4,085,000 Mexican-born residents in June 1988.

    SOURCE: Warren and Passel (1987). Hypothesis I rates in García y Griego (1989) increased by 15%.

- **Legal immigration to the U.S.** Mexican-born male immigrant survivors in 1985 (admitted 1980–85): 189,000. Females: 144,000. Mexican-born male immigrant survivors in 1990 (admitted 1985–90): 217,000. Females: 169,000. Pre-1982 legalized male survivors in 1990: 698,000. Females: 528,000. Assumed levels of legal immigration in 1990–95 and also 1995–2000: 220,000 male survivors at the end of the 5-year period; 170,000 females. These assumptions hold Mexican legal immigration in 1985–90 constant during the 1990s.

    SOURCES: U.S. Immigration and Naturalization Service, *Statistical Yearbooks*; and U.S. Immigration and Naturalization Service (1989).

- **1980 base populations.** Mexico's population is taken directly from INEGI-CONAPO's correction and adjustment (INEGI-CONAPO, 1985). U.S. resident Mexican-born

Fig. 1—Key assumptions used in the projection of Mexico's population
and migration to and from the United States, 1980–2000

population is estimated by Warren and Passel (1987) and adjusted by the author (see text). Additions are made of 40,000 males age 30–64 in 1980 (assumed, on the basis of IRCA legalization applications, to have been missed by the 1980 U.S. census) and 47,000 Mexican-born (11,000 legal residents resulting from net effects of immigration, return migration, and deaths between April 1 and June 30, 1980).

     SOURCE: García y Griego (1989); also see text.

- **Labor force participation.** Regions 1 and 2: 1980 rates are calculated from the Mexican census, by age and sex. These rates are assumed constant during 1980–2000 and are employed to calculate the number of workers that Mexico did not incorporate into its labor force due to net migration. U.S. Mexican-born: 1980 rates are calculated, by age and sex, from unpublished tabulations of the U.S. census. Rates are held constant over time (1980–2000) and assumed identical for legal and undocumented residents.

     SOURCES: INEGI (1986); U.S. Bureau of the Census (n.d.); also see text.

^aRegion 1 consists of eight core sending states in Mexico (Baja California, Chihuahua, Durango, Guanajuato, Jalisco, Michoacán, San Luis Potosí, and Zacatecas), and region 2 consists of the remaining 24 states.

[a]Region 1 consists of eight core sending states in Mexico (Baja California, Chihuahua, Durango, Guanajuato, Jalisco, Michoacán, San Luis Potosí, and Zacatecas), and region 2 consists of the remaining 24 states.

Fig. 1—continued

resident visas). Undocumented Mexican-born residents of the United States are the residual. Moreover, initial runs of these projections demonstrated that the relatively small number of migrants expected to have entered during the three months after the 1980 U.S. census could affect the results significantly and also that a correction of the 1980 census-based estimate was necessary.

The second modification, then, was that the 1980 base population for the Mexican-born in the United States was adjusted forward to June 30, 1980. The third modification was that 40,000 males between the ages of 30 and 64 in 1980 were added to Warren and Passel's estimate of 2,531,000 Mexican-born counted in the 1980 census. This correction was necessary because the very high participation in the pre-1982 IRCA legalization program of the Mexican male population age 30 and over would result in more legal residents in 1990 in those age groups than the total Mexican-born estimated at that point using the 15 percent emigration rate increase. It was assumed that legalization rates, though high, would have to fall somewhat short of 100 percent in these age groups.[4] The amount of the adjustment due to return flows, deaths, and net immigration between April 1 and June 30, 1980, was 47,000 for both sexes. Hence the Mexican-born population resident in the United States during mid-1980 is estimated at 2,618,000. The legally resident population was adjusted similarly: Warren and Passel's estimate of 1,400,000 on April 1, 1980, was adjusted by 11,000 to account for the net effects of deaths and legal immigration; this yields 1,411,000 legal residents during mid-1980.

The two components of the Mexican-born population, legal and undocumented residents in the United States, are conceptualized as follows. The total Mexican-born population resident in the United States grows as a result of net flows, which are estimated directly from migration rates among regions 1 and 2 and the United States. These rates are the five-year

---

[4]More precisely, it was assumed that the fraud rates in those age groups was lower than the proportion of Mexican-born eligible persons who did not apply for legalization. The female participation in the legalization of pre-1982 entrants was also very high in these age groups. It was not so high, however, as to suggest significant census underenumeration in 1980. A more detailed analysis of the legalized population and the expected stock of pre-1982 entrants in early 1988 could suggest a census correction for the Mexican female population and a somewhat larger correction than introduced by this author for the Mexican male population.

probabilities, by age and sex, that a Mexican-born person will change residence among these areas. As previously mentioned, the rates for 1980–2000 are those which will result in a Mexican-born population in 1988 that approximates the CPS-derived result. Legal immigrant survivors are calculated on the basis of (1) data on legal immigrants admitted and (2) assumptions regarding mortality and rates of emigration from the United States. Age-sex-specific mortality for Mexican legal immigrants is assumed to be identical to that of the total Mexican-born. Legal immigration can be the result of physical immigration to the United States (an applicant waiting in Mexico obtains his or her immigrant visa and moves to the United States), but most of it actually reflects a change in status of undocumented Mexicans already resident in the United States. This exercise produced negative growth of the undocumented population in some age-sex groups during 1985–1990; this was not the result of net return migration of undocumented residents to Mexico, but the result of the legalization of undocumented residents after IRCA.

The purpose of this exercise is to estimate the effects of emigration on the growth of the Mexican-born labor force in Mexico and the United States. Obtaining this estimate requires the adoption of several uncorroborated assumptions. The first problem, after the age-sex totals of the population have been derived, is to determine activity rates by age and sex. These rates were estimated in what is perhaps the most direct manner. Age-sex-specific activity rates were calculated from the 1980 Mexican census for the total populations in region 1 and region 2. The work force under 15 years of age was ignored. These activity rates were assumed to be constant, by age and sex, for the two decades of the projection (1980–2000). From unpublished tabulations of the 1980 U.S. census, age-sex-specific labor-force participation rates were derived for the Mexican-born population age 15 and over. These rates were also assumed to be constant over the two decades, and furthermore the same rates were assumed to hold for legal residents and undocumented Mexican-born.

These assumptions undoubtedly introduce some errors into the labor force estimates, though for several reasons these errors are not likely to be large enough to affect the general interpretation offered here of the labor force safety valve. First, one might expect that the female labor-force participation rates would rise during this period and therefore that the growth of the labor force in both Mexico and among the Mexican-born in the United States is somewhat understated. The male labor-force participation rates are not likely to change noticeably, however, and this component of the labor force can be expected to represent a substantial majority throughout the period. Second, the 1980 activity rates in Mexico, especially for women, have been shown to be inconsistently high when compared with other sources. The overestimate of economic activity in the 1980 Mexican census appears to be the result of a comparatively overbroad definition of labor participation. Thus, the activity rates employed here may result in an overestimate of the 1980 Mexican labor force and in a small underestimate of that of the 1990s.

Finally, it is probable that the undocumented population has, on the average, higher labor force participation rates than those of the Mexican-born. This exercise may both overestimate the size of the legally resident labor force and underestimate somewhat the size of the undocumented Mexican resident labor force. Even so, it is worthy of note that the male participation rates cannot be very different since they are all in the .90 to .95 range between the ages of 20 and 49; it is the differential female rates that are most likely to affect the result. Even so, according to the 1980 U.S. census the labor-force participation rates of Mexican-born women are quite high: between .45 and .53 between the ages of 20 and 49.

ESTIMATES OF MEXICO'S POPULATION AND THE MEXICAN-BORN POPULATION IN THE UNITED STATES, 1980–2000

Table 1 presents the general results of the exercise. Mexico's 1980 population[5] grows from almost 70 million in 1980 to nearly 85 million in 1990 and slightly over 101 million in the year 2000.[6] The Mexican-born population resident in the United States starts at 2,618,000 in 1980 and grows to 4,474,000 in 1990. The numbers presented for the period after 1990 should be interpreted with caution. They represent what could be expected to happen if 1980–1990 trends were to continue until the end of the century, assuming that the emigration rates observed during the 1975–1980 period and increased by 15 percent during the 1980s were to hold constant.

As may be noted in Table 1, Mexican legal immigration has grown at the expense of undocumented immigration during the 1980s, although all of this occurred in 1985–1990 and resulted from IRCA's legalization process. The 1980 undocumented Mexican population resident in the United States, 1,208,000, is estimated to have grown to 1,437,000 by the end of the decade; the legal resident population, however, is estimated to have risen from 1,411,000 to 3,038,000. The slow growth of the undocumented population and the fast growth of the legally resident population are two sides of the same coin. The legalization of about 1,226,000 pre-1982 migrants estimated as survivors in 1990[7] increases the legally resident population and decreases the undocumented population by this amount. (This number does not include 1,064,100 Mexican SAW applicants, who are assumed to be mostly residents of Mexico.) In addition, 386,000 Mexican immigrants are estimated to have been admitted in 1985–1990 and survived to June 1990; these are also included in the 1990 legally resident population presented in Table 1. What this table shows, in effect, is that the IRCA pre-1982 legalization, though large, was still somewhat smaller than the net undocumented immigration of residents into the United States during the decade.

The lower part of Table 1 presents estimates of the components of change for each of the Mexican populations in the United States. Deaths increase sharply for the Mexican-born population, from 94,300 in 1980–1985 to 142,400 in 1995–2000, notwithstanding the assumption of a slowly declining mortality rate during this period (see Fig. 1, mortality assumptions). This growth in the number of deaths, of course, is attributable to the increased size of the Mexican-born population. The ratio of deaths to population, or the implied crude death rate, is much higher for legal residents than for undocumented residents. This is entirely due to the different age distributions; the legally resident population has large groups over the age of 40, whereas the undocumented population declines sharply after that age.[8]

---

[5]The 1980 total population for Mexico reported in Table 1 is somewhat larger than that presented in the 1980 Mexican census. The difference is due to an INEGI-CONAPO estimate of the 1980 census undercount and adjustment to midyear (INEGO-CONAPO, 1985).

[6]INEGI and CONAPO, utilizing the same fertility and mortality assumptions adopted here, arrive at 103,996,000 persons resident in Mexico in the year 2000. The difference between this estimate and that in Table 1 is entirely due to different assumptions of net international migration between 1980 and 2000. My assumptions result in somewhat higher levels of net immigration to the United States and exclude foreign-born residents in Mexico that entered after 1980.

[7]These are the estimated June 1990 survivors of 1,235,800 Mexican citizen applicants for I-687 temporary residence visas (pre-1982 legalization program). The number of applicants is reported in U.S. Immigration and Naturalization Service (1989). The SAW applicant numbers come from the same source.

[8]It should be noted that the mortality of migrants during the projection interval is assumed to be that of their region of origin, and, furthermore, all migrant deaths are charged to the region of origin. This means that, in this exercise, the Mexican-born population in the United States does not record the deaths of the 0–4 age group within the United States, and therefore the crude death rates implied in Table 1 pertain only to the population age 5 years and over.

Table 1

PROJECTION OF MEXICO'S POPULATION AND MIGRATION TO AND FROM THE UNITED STATES[a]
(In thousands)

Category	1980	1985	1990	1995	2000
Population at midyear					
Mexico (total)	69,655	77,429	84,973	92,775	101,050
Region 1[b]	18,154	19,658	20,973	22,262	23,615
Region 2	51,501	57,771	64,000	70,514	77,434
Mexican-born in U.S.	2,618[c]	3,517	4,474	5,470	6,461
Legal residents	1,411	1,590	3,038	3,147	3,253
Undocumented residents	1,208	1,927	1,437	2,322	3,208

Category	1980–1985	1985–1990	1990–1995	1995–2000
Components of change of Mexican-born residents in the U.S.				
Total Mexican-born				
Deaths	94.3	107.1	121.1	142.4
Return migration (survivors)	171.2	231.6	289.7	343.8
Immigration (survivors)	1,164.5	1,295.4	1,405.9	1,477.8
Legal residents				
Deaths	75.8	80.2	109.4	123.4
Return migration (survivors)	77.3	85.0	170.8	160.8
Immigration (survivors)[d]	332.4	1,612.8	390.0	390.0
Undocumented residents				
Deaths	19.0	26.9	11.7	19.0
Return migration (survivors)	93.9	146.6	118.9	183.0
Immigration (survivors)	832.1	−317.4	1,015.9	1,087.8

SOURCE: Population projection by the author, 1980–2000. See text.

[a]Numbers are rounded independently.

[b]Region 1 consists of eight core sending states in Mexico (see text), and region 2 consists of the remaining 24 states.

[c]Revised upward from Warren and Passel (1987) by adding 40,000 males age 30–64 missed in the U.S. census and the 47,000 net increase estimated during April, May, and June 1980. See text and Fig. 1, assumptions regarding 1980 base populations.

[d]See Fig. 1, assumptions regarding legal immigration to the United States.

Immigration of Mexican-born survivors is estimated to rise from 1,164,500 in 1980–1985 to 1,477,800 in 1995–2000 (if immigration rates hold constant). Return migration grows sharply, from 171,200 in 1980–1985 to 343,800 in 1995–2000. Since return migration rates are also held constant (these correspond to the rates observed in 1975–1980), this increase is entirely due to the growth of the Mexican-born population resident in the United States. Though not represented in Table 1, these northbound and southbound flows translate to an average annual net migration of 199,000 Mexican-born survivors in 1980–1985, 213,000 in 1985–1990, 224,000 in 1990–1995, and 227,000 in 1995–2000.[9] The initial increase in migration during the 1980s is attributable to a growth of the base population in Mexico (especially in

---

[9]The net immigration of survivors is defined here as the difference between immigrant survivors and return migration survivors (Mexican-born in both cases). This net immigration into the United States, less the deaths of the Mexican-born, is the increase during the interval.

region 1) that provides migrants to the United States; the leveling off of net migration means that the slow growth of the young adult population in Mexico's sending regions is almost balanced by the growing return migration as the Mexican-born population in the United States grows to 5 and 6 million. The slow growth of the legally resident population after 1990 is explained by (1) the constant levels of legal immigration assumed after 1985 (apart from the pre-1982 legalization that occurred between 1985 and 1990) and (2) the growing number of deaths and return migration from this much larger population in 1990.

The undocumented resident population presents a number of characteristics worthy of note. During 1980–1985, according to Table 1, new entrants totaled 832,100; this translates to an average annual net flow of 143,000 immigrant survivors. During 1985–1990 there were an estimated −317,400 new entrant survivors; this negative number results from the legalization of 1.2 million pre-1982 undocumented Mexicans. During the first half of the 1990s this model projects 1,015,900 new entrants; during 1995–2000, 1,087,800. Because of the estimated growth of return flows, however, annual net immigration of undocumented Mexican residents in this model is expected to level off between 169,000 and 171,000.

These flows, of course, are not inevitable. What they do suggest is that current trends, if extended into the future, would produce new flows of undocumented Mexican residents (temporary migrants excluded) slightly larger than those observed during the 1980s prior to IRCA. Put another way, these numbers suggest a benchmark against which to evaluate the effectiveness of IRCA in the 1990s—such effectiveness might be measured by the degree to which a decline in net undocumented Mexican migration was recorded from these expected levels, attributable to IRCA itself. Returning to our discussion of the safety valve, we may note that if IRCA were to reduce illegal entries substantially, these numbers would be an approximate measure of the maximum additional population growth that would occur in Mexico resulting from U.S. efforts to stop illegal entries. This measure, however, is less significant than that of the net flow of undocumented workers, discussed below.

Several events other than IRCA enforcement could alter this estimate of undocumented migration during the 1990s in either direction. An increase in legal migration without a change in emigration rates from Mexico will result in smaller undocumented flows (under this assumption, the total number of Mexican-born migrants would be the same). This exercise assumes that the number of legal immigrants remains approximately constant between the years 1985 and 2000 (390,000 survivors at the end of each five-year period; see Fig. 1). This could be an underestimate, for two reasons. As additional Mexican legal immigrants naturalize, visa applications for immediate relatives of U.S. citizens can be expected to grow. This growth is not limited by current legislation, although some previous versions of legislative proposals before the 101st Congress could have limited the number of such visas for any one country. A second reason is that SAW temporary residents will soon obtain legal immigrant status, and RAW (replenishment agricultural worker) visa holders could obtain such status in the early 1990s, thus taking pressure off of undocumented immigration.

A final set of considerations would focus on economic conditions in the United States and Mexico. A sharp recession in the United States would reduce undocumented flows and could even produce a temporary return flow to Mexico; a sharp increase in labor demand for Mexican workers would result in the opposite effect. In the latter event, immigration rates to the United States would rise, as they did between 1975–1980 and 1980–1988. A further deterioration of the Mexican economy would increase migration pressures, especially outside of the eight core sending states. It is not clear, however, that emigration rates are sensitive to regional or national economic conditions in Mexico. The estimated 15 percent increase between 1975–1980 and 1980–1988 is modest, considering that most of the oil boom years occurred during the former period and that an unprecedented economic crisis occurred during most of the latter period.

LABOR FORCE SIZE AND GROWTH AND THE SAFETY VALVE

Table 2 presents estimates of the labor force derived from this projection. Mexico's national labor force (both sexes, age 15 and over) is estimated to rise from 22 million in 1980 to 40 million by the year 2000; this extraordinary growth of the labor force is entirely attributable to a concomitant increase in the working-age population. The Mexican-born labor force in the United States has grown even more quickly and, if immigration rates and age-sex distribution assumptions hold, could grow from 2.6 million workers in 1990 to 4 million in the year 2000. The undocumented resident work force grows unevenly because of legalization under IRCA during 1985–1990. The labor force grows slightly during the 1980s, from 666,000 to 737,000, and if assumptions held during the 1990s, it would grow to 1.3 million in 1995 and 2 million by the year 2000. The implied increases in the Mexican-born labor force are not the same as the number of workers lost from the Mexican labor force due to net emigration, because the activity rates of the working-age population in the United States, especially of

Table 2

PROJECTION OF MEXICO'S LABOR FORCE AND MEXICAN-BORN WORK FORCE IN THE UNITED STATES[a]
(In thousands)

Category	1980	1985	1990	1995	2000
Labor force at midyear					
Mexico (total)	22,092	26,246	31,027	35,719	40,072
Region 1[b]	5,476	6,346	7,314	8,193	8,994
Region 2	16,616	19,900	23,712	27,526	31,078
Mexican-born in U.S.[c]	1,426	1,994	2,640	3,329	3,990
Legal residents	760	910	1,903	1,986	2,019
Undocumented residents	666	1,084	737	1,343	1,971

Category	1980–1985	1985–1990	1990–1995	1995–2000
Average annual growth of Mexican-born labor force resident in Mexico and in the U.S. (age 15 and over)				
Mexico (total)	830.8	956.2	938.4	870.7
Region 1	174.1	193.6	175.7	160.2
Region 2	656.6	762.6	762.8	710.5
Total Mexican-born	113.5	129.2	137.9	132.2
Legal residents	29.9	198.8	16.5	6.6
Undocumented residents	83.6	−69.6	121.4	125.5

SOURCE: Population projection by the author, 1980–2000. See text.

[a]Numbers are rounded independently.

[b]Region 1 consists of eight core sending states in Mexico (see text), and region 2 consists of the remaining 24 states.

[c]Labor-force participation rates were estimated from unpublished tabulations of the 1980 census of the Mexican-born immigrant population. See Fig. 1, assumptions regarding labor force participation.

Mexican-born women, are considerably higher (as observed in the 1980 U.S. census) than those of the Mexican population resident in Mexico.

The average annual growth of the labor force for each of the regions and categories is also summarized in Table 2. The Mexican national-labor-force growth is supposed to have peaked in 1985–1990, although, as mentioned previously, it is possible that the growth is understated somewhat for the later periods. In either event, national-labor-force growth should average between 830,000 and 960,000 during this 20-year period. The growth of the U.S. Mexican-born labor force, by contrast, could peak in 1990–1995 and then decline slightly at the end of the 1990s. In any event, the average should be between 114,000 and 138,000 annually.

It may be noted that the average annual growth of the Mexican-born legally resident work force in the United States declines sharply in the 1990s. (The growth during 1985–1990, of course, is much higher than that of 1980–1985 because of IRCA legalization.) This decline is entirely explained by the assumed constant level of legal immigration (390,000 survivors at the end of each five-year period, as noted above) and by rising levels of return migration and deaths. Return migration increases because of the growth of the legally resident population due to legalization; deaths grow mainly because of the aging of the legalized population admitted in 1985–1990. By 1995–2000 the admission of 390,000 immigrant survivors barely increases the legally resident work force by 6,600 as a consequence of rising deaths and return migration. This growth estimated for the 1990s is likely to be somewhat higher for legal residents and lower for undocumented workers to the extent that SAW and RAW workers establish residence in the United States. Other factors, such as changes in U.S. immigration legislation and in economic conditions, can also alter these flows.

In the absence of such perturbing factors, the challenge faced by the implementation of IRCA's employer sanctions could be partly represented by the average annual increase estimated in the undocumented resident work force—121,400 in 1990–1995 and 125,500 in 1995–2000. This does not include the size or growth of the population of undocumented workers that reside in Mexico and work temporarily in the United States (many of whom applied for SAW visas) and that also could be expected to increase in size or growth during the 1990s.

If we assume that the estimates presented in Table 2 are approximately correct, it should then be possible to discuss the magnitude of the safety valve afforded by the net migration of Mexican workers. The first indicator of the safety valve is the magnitude of the Mexican labor force growth avoided due to net emigration. This indicator is constructed by taking the difference between the size of the Mexican labor force that would result in the absence of net emigration during any five-year projection period and the actual size of the labor force estimated with emigration. The activity rates assumed for the migrants that did not leave are identical, for each age-sex group in each region, to those estimated for the rest of the population. The safety valve estimated below is thus slightly lower than the increase in the Mexican-born resident work force in the United States, mainly because Mexican-born females resident in Mexico have lower labor force participation rates than those resident in the United States.

Table 3 summarizes the results. The so-called safety valve, measured in terms of labor force growth that did not occur in Mexico due to net migration, begins at an average 90,000 per year in 1980–1985 and rises to 108,000 per year in 1995–2000. If net migration had not occurred during 1980–1985, the labor force would have grown by 10.8 percent over the amount that actually occurred; the proportions are similar for other periods and rise to about 12.4 percent in 1995–2000.

The bulk of the growth avoided in Mexico is attributable to net undocumented emigration. Table 3 shows, however, that the *decline* in labor force increase avoided by

Table 3

AVERAGE ANNUAL LABOR FORCE INCREASE AVOIDED IN MEXICO BY NET EMIGRATION TO THE UNITED STATES[a]
(In thousands)

Category	1980–1985	1985–1990	1990–1995	1995–2000
Annual labor force growth avoided in Mexico (age 15 and over)				
Due to total net migration	90.3	100.4	107.0	108.5
Due to net legal migration	25.2	174.5	22.0	23.0
Due to net undocumented migration	65.1	–74.2	85.0	85.5
Annual labor force growth avoided in region 1 (age 15 and over)[b]				
Due to total net migration	57.5	63.5	67.4	67.7
Due to net legal migration	17.1	118.2	15.0	15.7
Due to net undocumented migration	40.3	–54.6	52.4	52.0

SOURCE: Population projection by the author, 1980–2000. See text.

NOTES: The numbers refer to annual averages over each 5-year period and are the number of workers that would have entered the Mexican labor force (both regions or region 1) if net migration were zero for all age-sex groups and the labor-force participation rates were those observed in regions 1 and 2 in the 1980 census. Numbers for 1990–1995 and 1995–2000 assume that emigration rates for 1980–1990 hold constant (see text).

[a]Numbers are rounded independently.

[b]Region 1 consists of eight core sending states in Mexico (see text), and region 2 consists of the remaining 24 states.

undocumented migration due to IRCA legalization in 1985–1990 (74,200) more than offsets the increase avoided in 1980–1985 (65,100).

One of the consequences of the legalization of pre-1982 undocumented Mexican immigrants appears to be that most of the safety valve flow was legalized, leading to this point: Post-1981 undocumented migrant worker survivors in 1990 will be fewer in number than the undocumented workers resident in the United States 10 years earlier. The first consequences of IRCA's legalization of pre-1982 entrants have been contrary to those expressed by Mexican public opinion of the U.S. immigration debate formed from afar. Rather than "closing" the valve, IRCA has ensured that part of it will remain open as long as economic conditions permit. Table 2 suggests that the undocumented labor force resident in the United States in 1990 is slightly smaller that the legally resident work force in 1980. Similarly, whereas in 1980 the undocumented and legally resident work forces were roughly of the same size (666,000 undocumented workers compared with 760,000 legally resident workers), in 1990 legal workers were nearly three times as many as undocumented workers.

However, if past migration trends were to continue during the 1990s in the absence of new legalization efforts, this situation could change. The Mexican national-work-force growth that was avoided because of net emigration in the 1990s (which would occur if 1980s emigration rates held constant) would be 85,000 per year—slightly under 10 percent of the labor force growth occurring with emigration. Put another way, the relative size of the safety valve during the 1990s, if emigration rates hold constant, would be similar to that recorded between 1980 and 1985. This is not surprising, given that emigration rates and activity rates are held constant throughout this period of estimation. But it does underscore (1) the approximate magnitude of the undocumented work force increase to be suppressed by employer sanctions if IRCA is to accomplish its objectives and (2) the magnitude of the impact on labor force growth in Mexico if that increase actually were to be averted. Table 3 shows that the principal impact of such a closure of the safety valve would be on region 1, where the labor force would grow by an additional 52,000 workers per year in the event that net migration to the United States were to reduce to zero. This is about 30 percent of the actual labor force growth in region 1 (175,700 per year in 1990–1995, according to Table 2). An increase of 32 percent instead of 2.3 percent of the labor force in eight Mexican states in one year cannot be conceived of in terms other than a severe regional crisis.

Before we arrive at the simple conclusion that closure of the labor force safety valve would, indeed, be a calamity for the core sending states in region 1, several qualifications are in order. First, the likelihood of an abrupt and complete closure of the valve is quite small; i.e., the absorption of this number of additional workers by Mexico's labor market in these eight states *in one year* is an unrealistic assumption. Second, it is reasonable to expect that not all of these workers would remain in this region—indeed, most of them would perhaps migrate within Mexico to large urban areas in region 2 (outside of the eight core sending states). Part of the utility of Table 3, then, might be that it provides a first approximation of the magnitude of the internal labor flows, from region 1 to region 2, that Mexican labor markets hypothetically would have to absorb. This second qualification means, in principle, that although region 1 might be *sensitive* to a partial or complete closure of the safety valve, the central question of whether it is *vulnerable* to such a possibility is best answered at the national level.

A final qualification has to do with the possible expansion of the number of RAW or H-2A workers admitted under IRCA and the settling out of SAW workers as residents in the United States. There is too little information on this subject at this time to present quantitative measures of how these programs might interact. However, returning to the estimate of 85,000 undocumented workers annually for the 1990s, it is clear that if a sizable fraction of this number of SAW workers were to settle in the United States annually and were replaced by a like number of RAW or H-2A workers, then the safety valve could continue to operate in mostly legal terms throughout the 1990s. (The total number of Mexican SAW applicants—1,064,100—hypothetically could accommodate such a settling out process, although the reportedly widespread fraud in this program makes it possible that the total number of applicants granted temporary residence may not rise much higher than 400,000.) This line of reasoning, however, is still uncertain.

Another way to measure the safety valve is to compare the Mexican-born labor force in the United States with the total labor force born in Mexico, including those that reside in Mexico and in the United States. The previous indicator presented in Table 3 was mainly useful as a measure of marginal change, e.g., what might happen if part or all of the net flow of workers to the United States were to be suppressed by IRCA's employer sanctions or some other set of circumstances. The indicator to which we now turn (presented in Figs. 2 and 3) allows us to consider (1) the total impact of past migration to the United States on the Mexican work force and (2) the still unlikely possibility that IRCA enforcement will produce large return flows of undocumented residents to Mexico.

To this end, the total Mexican-born labor force (TMBLF) is defined as the combined total of the Mexican-born labor force resident in Mexico and resident in the United States. The proportion of Mexican-born workers resident in the United States is then estimated. Figure 2 shows these proportions, by age, as they rise for most age groups between the years 1980

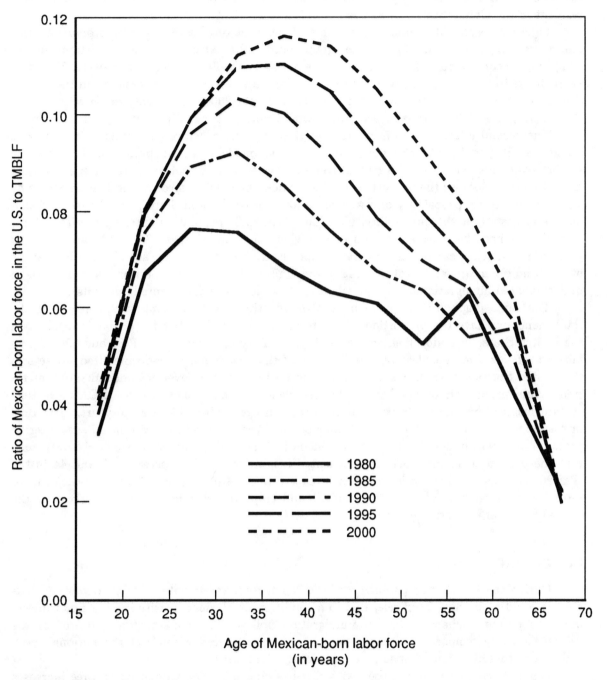

SOURCE: Population projection by author.

NOTES: The x-coordinate values are set to the average age of each group. For example, the 15–19 age group has an x value of 17.5 years. The final value, 65+, is assumed to have an average age of 70 years. TMBLF = total Mexican-born labor force.

Fig. 2—Proportion of the total Mexican-born labor force that constitutes the
Mexican-born labor force in the United States, by age of worker, 1980–2000

130

and 2000. The proportion of the TMBLF that is the *undocumented* Mexican-born workers resident in the United States, by age, is presented in Fig. 3.

Figure 2 suggests two effects over time. The most obvious is that the proportion rises almost uniformly over time for all age groups except the extremes. The proportions rise to what may be considered rather high levels as early as 1990. For every group between 20 and 54 years of age in that year, the proportion of the Mexican-born labor force resident in the United States is between 8 percent and 10 percent. By the year 2000—if current trends were to continue during the 1990s—the same age groups would range between 8 percent and 11.6 percent.

The second effect is the distribution of this proportion across age groups. It should be noted that, in part because this output comes from a model, the distribution tends to become smooth over time. However, the general trend is toward a more peaked distribution around the ages of 30–44. Because the proportion of the Mexican-born labor force in the United States by age is a conditional probability of a worker residing in the United States, the change in distribution suggests that this probability, like that of the male population entering the labor force in either country, becomes a function of age where the central ages—30 to 44—are the peak years of activity. In essence these curves demonstrate how regular the age distribution can be of the conditional probability of working in the United States under conditions of high levels of undocumented immigration or its equivalent (legalization of undocumented migrants).

The same graph was prepared by subtracting the legally resident work force from the total; hence we have the proportion of the total Mexican-born labor force that is resident in the United States in undocumented status (Fig. 3). A comparison of the 1980 and 1985 distributions reflects a more-or-less regular increase of the proportion of undocumented workers in the United States across all ages—precisely the result of a high level of undocumented migration. This proportion dropped markedly between 1985 and 1990 due to IRCA's pre-1982 entrant legalization—major drops occurred across all ages, especially after 25 years. The 1990 undocumented work force shows proportions below those recorded for 1980 for all ages after 25 years. The 1990s, under the assumptions made in this model, suggest a strong recovery such that the peak proportions reach unprecedented heights for all ages between 15 and 44 in the year 2000. Under this scenario, between 6 percent and 7.4 percent of the total Mexican labor force in these age groups would be resident and employed as *undocumented* workers in the United States at the end of the century.

CONCLUSION

During the 1970s, the significance of the "labor force safety valve" for Mexico was debatable; it could easily have been relegated to a condition of Mexican sensitivity, but not vulnerability, to potential changes in U.S. immigration policy. The impact of a "closure" of the valve—excluding temporary workers—would have been relatively small at the national level. Only the potential regional impacts were obviously significant.

It is now clear that during the 1980s this has changed. The annual labor force increases avoided by net immigration to the United States are larger, both in absolute and relative terms, and these are also critically more significant in the context of a festering economic crisis. A subtle but important change has occurred during the decade. The Mexican-born labor force in the United States, through steady growth, has nearly doubled, from 1.4 to 2.6 million workers. The cumulative effect of this is significant. For each age group between 25 and 44, the proportion of the Mexican-born work force resident in the United States has increased between 2 and 3.2 percentage points over the decade. The average, for all work-force

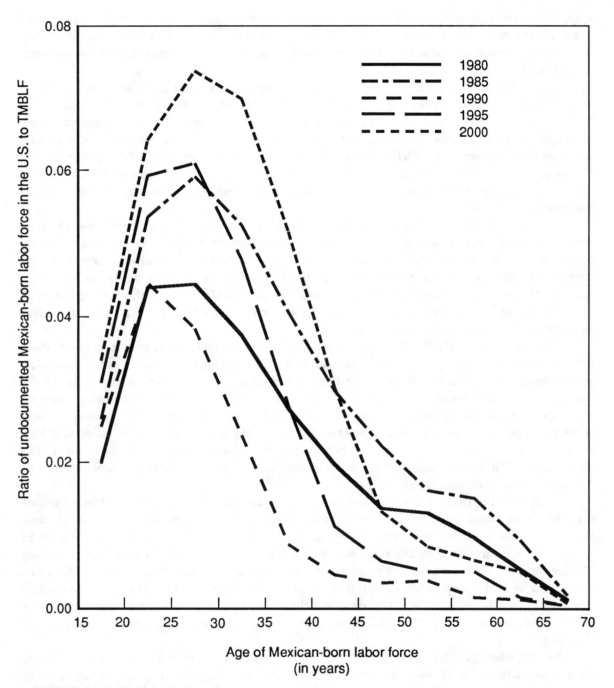

SOURCE: Population projection by author.

NOTES: The x-coordinate values are set to the average age of each group. For example, the 15–19 age group has an x value of 17.5 years. The final value, 65+, is assumed to have an average age of 70 years. TMBLF = total Mexican-born labor force.

Fig. 3—Proportion of the total Mexican-born labor force that constitutes the undocumented Mexican-born labor force in the United States, by age of worker, 1980–2000

ages, grew from a proportion of 6.1 percent in 1980 to 7.8 percent in 1990. Emigration has had a significant effect on the diminished growth of the Mexican labor force during the past decade, and the proportion of the work force resident in the United States approaches unprecedented levels.

The legalization of 1,235,800 pre-1982 Mexican entrants, an initial consequence of IRCA, thus presents an irony. Instead of facing an immediate threat of mass deportation, Mexico has had to cope with the promise of mass legalization. Almost as if by accident—certainly the high participation rates of undocumented residents in the legalization program were not generally expected—a good part of the "labor force safety valve" has been legalized. Rather than closing the valve, IRCA has ensured that part of it can be closed only by changes in U.S. economic conditions. Mexico would appear to be less vulnerable to immigration control in 1990 than it was ten years earlier.

This situation could change, however, during the 1990s, if recent past trends were to continue. In an important sense this exercise demonstrates how net flows of undocumented migration, which may strike most observers in the public debate as quite modest or as underestimated though perhaps accurate, have a significance belied by conventional interpretations. An annual labor force increase avoided in Mexico by net immigration to the United States of up to 85,000 undocumented workers during the 1990s may seem small, but its cumulative effect over the decade would be far from insignificant.

However, just as IRCA's legalization has made Mexico less vulnerable to an immediate closure of the valve, likely increases in the number of SAW and RAW visa holders that settle as residents in the United States may continue to legalize the valve in the early 1990s. Increases in H-2A admissions—which so far have not occurred—could have a similar effect on the temporary migration flow, about which we know less at this time. IRCA, therefore, suggests a second irony. At the same time that Mexico would appear to be more vulnerable to a reduction in emigrant flows, because of labor force growth and economic crisis at home, the legalization of substantial numbers of Mexican workers in the United States reduces that vulnerability to an uncommon degree.

Until recently, IRCA has been interpreted widely as a threat to Mexican interests because it could close a "labor force safety valve." This perception could be reexamined on the grounds that emigration is viewed too narrowly, as an instrument that reduces economic pressure in Mexico, rather than as a complex multifaceted phenomenon that has benefits *and* costs for Mexico (and the United States). Moreover, the mass legalization provided for under IRCA was considered by many proponents of immigration control to be in the U.S. interest. Even when this problem is viewed narrowly, however, in light of the impact of IRCA's legalization on the safety valve, the perception that IRCA was unavoidably a threat to Mexican interests seems simplistic.

Nevertheless, proponents of the safety valve metaphor could argue that all IRCA has done is to postpone the threat, given that (1) undocumented migration appears to have continued unabated and (2) employer sanctions could in the future diminish such flows. Indeed, the projection given here suggests that continued flows of undocumented workers taking up residence in the United States will be slightly higher in the 1990s than in the 1980s, on the assumption that migration rates hold constant. Legalization has diminished the probability that in the short run U.S. efforts to curb illegal entries will have a severe impact on Mexico's employment situation, but it has laid bare Mexico's exposed position in the 1990s.

To diminish that exposure, the Mexican government would appear to have two alternatives. First, and most often discussed, is the possibility of U.S.-Mexican bilateral management of the legal flow of Mexican workers. This would appeal to Mexico because it would reduce the uncertainties of undocumented migration, it could give Mexico an opportunity to emphasize the migration of temporary workers rather than permanent settlers, and it could afford important legal protections. It also has some disadvantages, perhaps the most important being that the logic of the situation would seem to require Mexican efforts to restrain the departure of citizens who enter the United States illegally. This alternative is basically hypothetical since, notwithstanding Mexican dilemmas, the United States appears to have little interest in this course of action.[10]

The second major alternative, currently being explored by a U.S. commission created by IRCA, would appear to focus on economic development schemes to reduce migration pressures. Prior to the passage of IRCA, it did not make sense for Mexico to divert scarce public investment and development resources—which have been diminished dramatically anyway by its economic crisis—to the regions that send migrants to the United States. These regions are not those in most urgent need of development assistance. A cursory examination of what migration trends could be in the 1990s, and the more real possibility that this flow could be disrupted, may alter Mexican perceptions of such interests.

REFERENCES

Bustamante, Jorge A., "La Ley ya Es Vigente; Mañana sólo Reciben las Solicitudes," *Excélsior* (Mexico City), May 4, 1987, pp. 1A, 9A.

Bustamante, Jorge A., "U.S. Immigration Reform: A Mexican Perspective," in Susan Kaufman Purcell (ed.), *Mexico in Transition; Implications for U.S. Policy; Essays from Both Sides of the Border,* New York: Council on Foreign Relations, 1988, pp. 69–80.

Center for Strategic and International Studies, *The Congress and Mexico: Bordering on Change; a Report of the CSIS Congressional Study Group on Mexico,* Washington, D.C.: Center for Strategic and International Studies (Vol. XI, No. 8 of the Significant Issues Series), 1989.

García y Griego, Manuel, "A Bilateral Approach to Migration Control?" in Susan Kaufman Purcell (ed.), *Mexico in Transition; Implications for U.S. Policy; Essays from Both Sides of the Border,* New York: Council on Foreign Relations, 1988, pp. 81–91.

García y Griego, Manuel, "The Supply of Mexican Migrants to the United States, 1990–2010: A Demographic Analysis," in Wayne A. Cornelius and Jorge A. Bustamante (eds.), *Mexican Migration to the United States: Process, Consequences, and Policy Options,* San Diego, California: Center for United States–Mexican Studies, University of California, San Diego, for the Bi-Lateral Commission on the Future of United States–Mexico Relations, 1989.

García y Griego, Manuel, and Francisco Giner de los Ríos, "Es Vulnerable la Economía Mexicana a la Aplicación de Políticas Migratorias Estadunidenses?" in Manuel García y Griego and Gustavo Vega (eds.), *México-Estados Unidos, 1984,* Mexico City: El Colegio de México, 1985, pp. 221–272.

---

[10]A discussion of the politics of bilateral management of Mexican labor migration emphasizing the obstacles appears in García y Griego (1988). A discussion focusing on the attractiveness of bilateralism appears in Bustamante (1988).

Instituto Nacional de Estadística, Geografía, e Informática, *X Censo General de Población y Vivienda, 1980; Resumen General* (two volumes), Mexico City: INEGI, 1986.

Instituto Nacional de Estadística, Geografía, e Informática and Consejo Nacional de Población, *Proyecciones de las Población de México y de las Entidades Federativas: 1980-2010*, Mexico City: INEGI and CONAPO, 1985.

Passel, Jeffrey S., and Karen A. Woodrow, "Geographic Distribution of Undocumented Immigrants: Estimates of Undocumented Aliens Counted in the 1980 Census by State," *International Migration Review*, Vol. 18, No. 3, Fall 1984, pp. xxx–yyy.

U.S. Bureau of the Census, "Foreign-born Immigrants; Tabulations from the 1980 U.S. Census of Population and Housing," Mimeographed, Washington, D.C., n.d.

U.S. Immigration and Naturalization Service, *Statistical Yearbook of the Immigration and Naturalization Service*, volumes for fiscal years 1980-1988, Washington, D.C.: Government Printing Office, 1981-1989.

U.S. Immigration and Naturalization Service, Statistics Division, Office of Plans and Analysis, "Provisional Legalization Application Statistics," Mimeographed, Washington, D.C., July 20, 1989.

Warren, Robert, and Jeffrey S. Passel, "A Count of the Uncountable: Estimates of Undocumented Aliens Counted in the 1980 United States Census," *Demography*, Vol. 24, August 1987, pp. 375–393.

THE DOMESTIC AND FOREIGN POLICY CONSEQUENCES OF MEXICAN AND CENTRAL AMERICAN IMMIGRATION: MEXICAN-AMERICAN PERSPECTIVES

Rodolfo O. de la Garza
University of Texas at Austin

Nestor Rodríguez
University of Houston

Harry Pachon
Pitzer College

The presence of Mexican and Central American immigrants, including but not limited to those legalized by the 1986 Immigration Reform and Control Act (IRCA), will have long-term multiple effects on Mexican-American communities across the Southwest. This paper describes the patterns of relations that are already developing between these two immigrant groups and Mexican Americans. It then assesses the impact these immigrants may have on Mexican-American political life, with particular attention to how Mexican-American concerns may be affected regarding U.S. policy toward Mexico and Central America.

In the early 1980s, researchers in Texas analyzed these questions with regard to Mexican immigrants and Mexican Americans (Browning and de la Garza, 1986). Several developments suggest the wisdom of revisiting these issues. First, Central Americans constitute a new and distinct presence that is only now beginning to be felt. This population differs from Mexican immigrants in terms of being much more varied linguistically, ethnically, and racially. Their motivations for immigrating are also more varied. Central Americans, thus, may relate to and influence Mexican Americans differently from the way Mexican immigrants do.

A second factor is the changed immigration milieu created to a significant degree by IRCA. IRCA enabled approximately 2 million Mexican and Central American immigrants to legalize their status and, after five years, enjoy all the benefits of American society, including citizenship. IRCA also forced those immigrants who are not eligible for amnesty further underground.

A third factor is the recognition by Mexican-American organizations, especially the National Association of Latino Elected and Appointed Officials (NALEO), that these immigrants, most of whom are of Mexican origin, represent an untapped political resource whose mobilization is essential to the ultimate political empowerment of Mexican Americans (and all Latinos) in the United States. Historically, Mexican-American organizations have been at least ambivalent, if not hostile, toward Mexican immigrants (Allsup, 1982). NALEO, however, recognized that the battle for Mexican-American and Latino political power in general had to be fought on two fronts. The first, which was well under way (García and de la Garza, 1977), involved attacks on the historical barriers to Latino political participation. The second involved naturalizing resident aliens who constitute one-third of all adult Latinos in the nation. NALEO saw incorporating this population into the Latino political community as the last major obstacle to Mexican-American and Latino political empowerment.

The final factor that has changed is that since 1980 a new, albeit inchoate, political dimension has been developing among Mexican and Central American immigrants, and its intensity, content, and extent are unclear. The conditions under which these populations will influence Mexican-American political concerns, will mobilize autonomously, or will be mobilized by Mexican Americans or others because of these attitudes are also unknown. What is clear, however, is that there now exists among this generation of immigrants an interest in homeland politics and U.S. policies toward the homeland that previous immigrants did not share. This creates the potential for influencing Mexican-American politics in new ways that are already becoming manifest.

This paper, then, begins with a description of relations between Mexican and Central American immigrants and Mexican Americans in Houston and South Texas. While these relations may or may not be typical, they do offer insights that may guide our thinking about these processes in other areas. The second section addresses the naturalization process, i.e., the process by which immigrants become citizens. The final section reviews recent developments illustrating the consequences of recent immigration for Mexican-American domestic and international political life.

SOCIAL, ECONOMIC, AND CULTURAL RELATIONS

Research in Houston and the Rio Grande Valley offers insights into how Mexican and Central American immigrants are affecting various aspects of Mexican-American society (Rodríguez, 1989). It must be noted at the outset that there are important differences in the frequency and quality of contact between Mexican Americans and each of the immigrant groups. Contact may be very limited either because of cultural and racial differences, as in the case of blacks from the Honduran Caribbean coast and Mayans, or because of class differences, as in the case of elite Mexican immigrants. Second, relations are strongest between low-income Mexican Americans and these immigrants.

These differences aside, both Mexican and Central American immigrants are helping to reproduce the most traditional segment of the Mexican-American subculture. Intermarriage and the transfer of Spanish-language-based cultural elements are important parts of this process of social reproduction. In Houston and in other places where Mexican and Central American immigrants have come in close contact with large numbers of Mexican Americans, intermarriage between the immigrants and Mexican Americans has been an almost inevitable result. In many cases, these intergroup unions involve low-income immigrant males and Mexican-American females, and the intermarriage setting is an established Mexican-American barrio (Rodríguez, 1989).

The Mexican and Central American impact on the reproduction of the traditional cultural segment of the Mexican-American subculture occurs at formal and informal levels. At the formal level, Mexican and Central American immigrants are playing a significant labor role in the operation of ethnic enterprises in Mexican-American communities (Hansen and Cárdenas, 1988). Both immigrant groups supply low-wage labor for Mexican-American businesses such as restaurants, bars (including immigrant women working as taxi-dancers), dance halls, yerberias (herbal stores), and spiritualist shops (catering to curanderismo—nonmedical healing—and other spiritual practices). Owners of such ethnic businesses hire Mexican and Central American immigrants partly because they speak Spanish, the language of many customers. But the attraction of Spanish-language proficiency is more than its communicative function. Spanish is also the *container* of the cultural elements on which the ethnic businesses base their operations. In Mexican-American restaurants, the recipes of popular dishes conceptually exist in Spanish. It takes a person experienced in Spanish-language-based cuisine to understand

and carry out the authentic preparation of these dishes. This experiential factor is what separates a barrio restaurant from a fast-food American-type Mexican restaurant. The differences in products are readily evident. For example, so-called Mexican restaurants outside Mexican-American neighborhoods usually do not offer popular folk dishes such as menudo and tripas. The importance of Spanish-language conceptualization is maximized in yerberias and spiritualist shops of curanderismo, where cultural practice would be rendered inoperative in any attempt to transfer meaning into an English-language form.

To the extent that Mexican and Central American immigrants work in the ethnic businesses cited above, their social-cultural impact on Mexican Americans is significant, because these businesses lie at the bedrock of the most traditional (least acculturated) segment of the Mexican-American subculture. Thus, in areas with a high concentration of more traditional Mexican Americans, this intergroup impact can be very significant.

At the informal level, Mexican and Central American immigrants similarly affect Mexican Americans through their contribution to Spanish-language maintenance. While many Mexican Americans learn Spanish from each other, some practice Spanish in daily contacts with Mexican and Central American immigrant neighbors, co-workers, fellow students, etc. (Rodríguez, 1989). The linguistic impact of the immigrants may also be indirect, i.e., the immigrants constitute a clientele that spurs growth in Spanish-language media, affecting Mexican Americans in the process. Cases in which Mexican and Central American immigrants refer to their U.S.-born children as "chicanitos" also suggest an awareness among these newcomers of a social-cultural transformation related to the Mexican-American population.

Bringing quantitative concerns into consideration and taking the perspective of the proportion of an immigrant group that interacts with Mexican-American institutions such as families and ethnic enterprises, differences emerge between the impact of Mexican immigrants and of Central American immigrants on the Mexican-American subculture. The differences are related to immigrant settlement patterns (see Rodríguez, 1987).

In the Houston area, which has about half a million Mexican Americans and large numbers of Mexican and Central American immigrants, it is clear that Mexican immigrants have more involvement than Central Americans with Mexican-American institutions (Rodríguez, 1989). This reflects the different settlement patterns of the respective immigrant populations. Since the 1910s Mexican immigrants have generally settled in areas commonly described as the old Mexican-American barrios, which were founded in the 1910s and 1920s. Coming in the 1980s, Central Americans have tended to settle outside these barrios, often in areas with little or no Latino presence prior to their arrival (Rodríguez, 1987). Consequently, Mexican Americans participate more with Mexican immigrants than with Central American immigrants in community activities such as church and recreation.

National and cultural diversity among Central Americans further complicates the immigrant differential impact on the Mexican-American population. For example, Salvadorans, Latino Guatemalans, and Latino Hondurans may have greater settlement among Mexican Americans than Guatemalan Mayans and blacks from the Honduran Caribbean coast. While a few young Mayan men have married Mexican-American women, the large majority of the two Mayan groups that have settled in the Houston area (one group comes from the department of Quiché and one from Totonicapán) reside outside Mexican-American neighborhoods.

Black Hondurans have settled mainly in the city's poor black neighborhoods. These Hondurans speak Spanish but have monolingual English-speaking blacks for neighbors. What little interaction they have with Mexican Americans usually occurs at work. While some Mayans attend Catholic or Protestant churches with Latino members, the black Hondurans maintain a religious distance from Mexican Americans and other Latinos. In musical culture, they remain firmly attached to Afro-Caribbean music such as reggae (Rodríguez, 1987).

In the main, therefore, Mexican immigration has a greater social-cultural impact than Central American immigration on Mexican Americans. Yet additional quarters of the game remain to be played out. For example, an expansion of Central American business entrepreneurship into Mexican-American areas could easily increase relations between Central American immigrants and these Mexican Americans. This is a practical expectation, as Mexican Americans continue to be the largest group of potential Latino customers.

Economic Comparisons

The discussion above points out that both Mexican and Central American immigrants provide labor for Mexican-American businesses such as restaurants and bars. To be sure, the labor impact also seems to vary by immigrant group. That is, more Mexican than Central American immigrants seem to be working in Mexican-American-owned businesses, but exceptions exist based on the specificity of social networks that lead to employment in Mexican-American businesses. The two immigrant groups also form clienteles for these ethnic businesses, although these clienteles are of different sizes.

Fieldwork in the Houston area indicates that members of both immigrant groups can be found as co-workers of Mexican Americans. In many cases Mexican Americans become the supervisors and trainers of these immigrant workers (Rodríguez, 1989).

Mexican-American employers and co-workers sometimes share the view that Central American immigrants are better workers than Mexican immigrants. They attribute all the super-worker characteristics to Central American immigrant workers that have been used to describe undocumented Mexican workers. Basically, Central American immigrant workers are thought to work harder and complain less. Central Americans also make this comparison themselves. To the extent that the work commitment of migrants is inversely related to the number of visits to their places of origin, at least prior to IRCA, Central Americans may have been better workers, since it was more difficult to make undocumented trips to Central America than to Mexico.

Mexican and Central American immigrants differ in their economic impact on Mexican Americans by degree and area. In Houston, differences in settlement patterns lead to a difference in the extent to which each group becomes economically involved with Mexican Americans. As mentioned above, Mexican immigrants have a greater settlement rate among Mexican Americans than do Central Americans. For over half a century Mexican immigrants have been part of the economy in the Mexican-American barrios. Central Americans have come into these communities only since the early 1980s, and in smaller numbers (Sheldon et al., forthcoming).

Diversity among Central American immigrants also leads to differential impact on Mexican Americans. Salvadorans and Hispanic Guatemalans and Hondurans have more economic interaction with Mexican Americans than do Mayans and black Hondurans. Among the latter two groups, Mayans have more economic contact with Mexican Americans, but only indirectly. Only a segment of the Mayan immigrant population in the city has Mexican-American co-workers (Rodríguez, 1989).

In the lower Rio Grande Valley, which has a high Mexican-American population in both proportion and density, economic relations between Central American immigrants and Mexican Americans may reach a greater proportional level than exists in Houston. For example, sociologist Rogelio Nuñez reports that in some Valley areas, owners of Mexican-American drinking places have extensively hired Central American immigrant women to do the service jobs that were previously the domain of Mexican immigrant women (Nuñez, 1989). Yet, the transient nature of Central Americans in this border area may keep economic relations between Mexican Americans and Central Americans tentative.

Commonly, the question of Latino-immigrant economic impact on Mexican Americans revolves around the issue of job competition or displacement. Although most studies have focused on Mexican immigrant workers in exploring this impact (see Browning and de la Garza, 1986), the question can be asked if Central American immigrants present a new economic threat for Mexican Americans, given these newcomers' different migration circumstances. It is reasonable to suggest that the refugee nature of Central American immigration may have introduced a greater number of skilled workers than Mexican immigration does. That is, political turmoil in Central America may have motivated a greater number of professionals, technicians, and other skilled workers to migrate to the United States than economic pressure may have done in Mexico. The result of this difference would be that Central American immigrants would compete more with Mexican-American skilled workers than with other immigrants.

A glance at statistics on Mexican and Central American immigration (legal and undocumented) suggests that this difference can only have significance in terms of proportions rather than absolute numbers, because Mexican immigration is much greater than Central American immigration. In the recent immigrant-legalization program, 97,000 Mexicans applied for legal status in Houston, compared with 30,000 Central Americans (U.S. Immigration and Naturalization Service, 1989a). This large imbalance makes it improbable that Central American skilled workers outnumber Mexican-immigrant skilled workers.

Yet, Central Americans have gained professional and other skilled positions in Houston in the mid-1980s. For instance, Central Americans work in professional levels in the city's radio, television, and educational industries. Mexican Americans would have filled these "Hispanic" positions prior to the mid-1980s. The perennial question, of course, is whether Central Americans take these jobs from Mexican Americans or whether they fill new jobs created by the increasing presence of Latino immigrants. At this point, the question remains unanswered.

To summarize, Mexican Americans may face greater competition from Central American immigrants than from Mexican immigrants for skilled jobs but only in a proportional sense. Presently, Central Americans do not appear to have brought skills missing among Mexican immigrants, skills that might negatively affect the employment status of Mexican Americans.

It may be worthwhile to reflect on the economic impact of the two immigrant groups from the perspective of their business segments. The question is then, "Is there a difference in the capital investments of the two immigrant business segments that produces a differential economic impact on Mexican Americans?" The complete answer to this question requires a level of financial-investment data that is not presently available, but the following observations may lead to interesting insights.

In Houston the business segment of the Mexican immigrant population has two parts. One consists of wealthy families that maintain financial and social-elite ties to Mexico. When this segment invests in Houston, it does so in businesses located in the most affluent commercial areas of the city, which cater to a middle- and upper-class clientele. This segment has no significant relations with the Mexican-American community (Rodríguez, 1989; see also Briseno, 1989). The second segment consists of less affluent but upwardly mobile families that come

140

from a working- and middle-class background in Mexico. This segment invests in small businesses in the city's Latino areas and maintains ties to the Mexican-American population. A social and economic gulf separates these two segments.

The Central American business segment in the city is different. While containing some very wealthy individuals, it seems to lack the small-business entrepreneurial sector found among Mexican immigrants that penetrates Mexican-American communities. So far, only a few Central American–owned businesses exist in Mexican-American neighborhoods. These tend to be small and service-oriented, e.g., an insurance firm, a notary office to help immigrants fill out immigration papers, and a long-distance telephone service for calls to Mexico and Central America. Outside Mexican-American areas, there has been a rise in Central American businesses that send packages and money orders to Central America.

Future developments could lead to the growth of a Central American entrepreneurial sector that could significantly expand into the city's Mexican-American areas. A further increase in instability in Central America could produce a greater transfer of entrepreneurial capital to Houston, as well as to other Latino areas in the country. Continued growth of the Central American immigrant population in the city could attract Central American entrepreneurial capital and lead to the establishment of a Central American ethnic business community. For example, a large, Anglo-owned supermarket chain currently provides the ethnic business functions that an internal business community could provide.

Clearly, these immigrant populations are interacting with and affecting Mexican Americans in multiple ways. Their presence is now so clearly felt that efforts are under way to increase the rates at which they become naturalized citizens so as to maximize their integration with Mexican Americans. The following section describes this effort.

THE NATURALIZATION PROCESS

Immigrants are a large and growing proportion of the Latino population of the Southwest. Despite changes in 1965 restricting Latin American immigration, between 1972 and 1985 more legal immigrants came to the United States from Mexico than from any other country, and more than half a million entered between 1980–1987 (U.S. Immigration and Naturalization Service, 1989b). By 1980, there were also an estimated 2 million Mexican undocumented aliens residing in the country. Thus, according to the 1980 census, 25 percent of the nation's Mexican-origin population was foreign born, and approximately 58 percent of it had arrived since 1970. Combined with the influx of immigrants from other Latin American countries, these totals illustrate the potential significance of this population for Mexican-American political life.

The total political effect these immigrants have depends on whether they are undocumented aliens, resident aliens, or naturalized citizens. Because their mere presence increases the population base used to determine electoral districts from councilmanic to congressional levels, all immigrants are a factor in Mexican-American politics (de la Garza and DeSipio, 1989). The more secure their status, the greater their potential for influence, however. Thus, the undocumented aliens have the most tenuous situation and the least political significance (de la Garza and Flores, 1986). Resident aliens have a much greater potential for involvement, but they are limited to non-electoral participation should they choose to be politically active. It is only the naturalized citizen who may fully participate in the political process.

Mexican Americans, recognizing that Latin American immigrants are potential allies, have initiated efforts to accelerate their naturalization rates so as to incorporate them into the

Mexican-American political community. This initiative is intended to alter the historic pattern among Mexican immigrants, who have the lowest naturalization rate of any immigrant group. While 66 percent of all immigrants were naturalized in 1980, only 35 percent of Mexican immigrants became citizens. Table 1 illustrates the average length of time between immigration and naturalization for Mexican, European, and Asian immigrants.

Some evidence exists that the rate for Mexican naturalizations has increased in the past three years. However, the percent of non-naturalized Latinos in states that have been the traditional ports of entry for Mexican immigrants is indicative of the magnitude of noncitizenship that still exists among Mexican immigrants. (See Table 2.)

Reasons for Low Naturalization Rates Among Mexican Immigrants

As DeSipio (1987) noted, there is a dearth of contemporary social-science research literature on naturalization. Within the extant literature, specific research on Mexican-immigrant naturalization patterns is even further limited. Only two large-scale datasets exist; both treat naturalization as a dichotomous variable ("Is respondent a U.S. citizen?") and neither probes the attitudes and experiences of Mexican immigrants regarding U.S. citizenship (California Tomorrow, 1988). Other studies deal with either small samples or are impressionistic in nature (DeSipio, 1987). Yet, together this research identifies the following factors as contributing to low Mexican naturalization rates:

1. Because of the proximity of the U.S./Mexico border, the Mexican immigrant has a sojourner attitude and therefore little interest in naturalization;
2. The sense Mexican immigrants have of being "outsiders" and subject to discrimination in the United States discourages them from applying for U.S. citizenship;

Table 1

LENGTH OF RESIDENCY PRECEDING NATURALIZATION
FOR SELECTED IMMIGRANT GROUPS

Year of Naturalization	Origin of Immigrant Group	Years of U.S. Residency Preceding Naturalization
1969	Mexico	14
	Europe	8
	Asia	6
1974	Mexico	16
	Europe	9
	Asia	6
1983	Mexico	13
	Europe	11
	Asia	7
1986	Mexico	14
	Europe	9
	Asia	7

SOURCE: NALEO Education Fund, *Background Statistics on Immigration*, 1987.

142

Table 2

U.S. CITIZENSHIP STATUS OF ADULT LATINOS IN THE
FIVE SOUTHWESTERN STATES, 1980

State	Latinos over Age 19		
	Total No.	No. of Noncitizens	Percent Noncitizens
Arizona	238,225	38,347	16.1
California	2,570,144	973,603	37.9
Colorado	189,456	10,630	5.6
New Mexico	270,740	12,333	4.6
Texas	1,621,838	277,544	17.1

SOURCE: NALEO Education Fund, *1988 National Roster of Hispanic Elected Officials.*

3. Low educational levels of Mexican immigrants hinder all aspects of the Immigration and Naturalization Service (INS) naturalization process;
4. Bureaucratic obstacles in the naturalization process disproportionately affect Mexican immigrants.

NALEO is in the process of releasing the results of a national Hispanic immigrant survey that may make it possible to determine the relative weight of these factors in accounting for the low naturalization rates among Mexican immigrants. Until then, any conclusions about the incidence and prevalence of Mexican attitudes toward U.S. citizenship are only speculative. We believe, however, that the sojourner nature of the Mexican immigrant has perhaps been overstated. Perceptions about Mexican resident aliens may be colored by studies focusing on the experiences of Mexican undocumented immigrants, who appear to be more transient in nature. Moreover, the recent apparent successes of the NALEO U.S.-citizenship telephone hotline (which has received more than 150,000 calls in three years, predominantly from Mexican immigrants) challenge the assertion that little interest in U.S. citizenship exists among Mexican immigrants. An apparent increase in Mexican-immigrant naturalizations is also indicated by the fact that Mexicans now rank among the top three immigrant groups being naturalized in the United States (U.S. Immigration and Naturalization Service, 1989a).

Two factors previously unaccounted for that appear to contribute significantly to these low rates are not attitudinal in nature and are amenable to being changed. They are the low educational level of Mexican immigrants and the bureaucratic obstacles that the INS presents to immigrants seeking citizenship.

The naturalization examination is threefold in nature: an oral review of the citizenship application; questions on U.S. history/civics; and an elementary English literacy test. Most Mexican immigrants come with only an elementary school education and even after six years have a limited knowledge of English (Portes and Bach, 1985). These patterns also characterize most Central American immigrants. Given these conditions, the citizenship application process and examination presents a challenge. For example, the standard naturalization application, the N-400, takes on average 40 minutes for a college graduate to complete; the standardized U.S. citizenship booklet is written at a 10th grade English reading level. Thus, for Mexican (and most other Latino) immigrants, the naturalization process is not simple. Rather, the citizenship exam often looms as an obstacle to be overcome that requires formal preparation, e.g., adult school classes, self-help material, and form-processing assistance that may cost the immigrant up to several hundred dollars. The INS, as a matter of policy, does not assist the immigrant with this process.

Although its middle initial stands for naturalization, the INS has long given low priority to citizenship-related activities. Only 10 percent of its budget is allocated to these, and the INS continues to view the initiation of naturalization as the responsibility of the immigrant. Moreover, as recounted in *The Long Grey Welcome*, David North (1985) discovered that the INS "official" denial rate of 3 percent annually for citizenship applications does not include the approximately 27 percent of naturalization applications rejected under the separate categories of "Returns" and "Non-files."

"Returns," the first step of potential bureaucratic denial, include those applications that are returned if they are incorrectly filled out, if the fingerprint cards are not satisfactory, or if photographs do not meet official standards. Approximately 13 percent of applications filed in 1987 were formally returned.

The second step involves the naturalization examination. The examination is required of all citizenship applicants and assesses the applicant's basic knowledge of U.S. history, U.S. civics, and speaking and writing in English. The examination is not standardized, but usually includes five to ten basic history and civics questions, a review of the information provided on the application form, and the writing of a simple sentence (North, 1985). For the vast majority of applicants, examples of the history and civics questions would include such questions as:

- Who was the first president of the United States?
- How many branches of government does the federal government have?
- When was the Declaration of Independence signed?
- Who is the Vice President of the United States?
- Who is the Governor of this state?

There are also reports of more difficult and arbitrary civics and history questions being asked by a small number of INS examiners nationwide such as:

- Who was the fifth president of the United States?
- What is the name of the wife of the Governor?

Applicants who do not satisfy the examiner are told that their applications will be rejected by the courts; however, they are also told that they may instead have their applications administratively denied or "non-filed" and begin the process anew. Approximately 14 percent of applicants in 1987 were classified as "Non-files."

In cities with large numbers of Latino immigrants, the overall Latino rejection ("Returns" plus "Non-files") rate is consistently several points higher than in cities with fewer Latino immigrants. The high number of rejections that all naturalization applicants experience, plus the fact that Latino/Mexican immigrants experience even higher rejection rates—perhaps due to discrimination or to insufficient preparation—underscore the need to view low Mexican naturalization rates as being influenced by the current administration of U.S. naturalization programs.

A successful naturalization drive would surely also result in an increase in Mexican-origin voters. How that would affect Mexican-American domestic and foreign policy concerns may be discerned from recent events that already reflect the influence of these immigrant populations.

POLITICAL CONSEQUENCES OF MEXICAN AND CENTRAL AMERICAN IMMIGRATION

The presence of large numbers of Mexican and Central American immigrants is affecting Mexican-American politics in several ways. As has been noted, it increases the population base on which electoral districts are based and thus influences increased Mexican-American office holding. This has generated major political battles with non-Latinos in the Southwest and nationally. The presence of these immigrants generates internecine quarrels regarding how the state should respond to this presence. Finally, because of the political concerns some of these immigrants now bring with them as well as their mere presence, these immigrants are influencing Mexican-American foreign policy concerns.

Immigration fueled the dramatic growth in the Latino population of the Southwest between 1970–1980 and was a major factor in increasing the number of Mexican-American Congressmen from four to nine. A similar pattern is likely to result following the 1990 census when from three to five new Mexican-American congressmen may be elected (de la Garza and DeSipio, 1989). Comparable effects are evident at state and local levels. Between 1973 and September 1988, the percentage increase in Mexican-American elected officials in Arizona, California, and Texas was 149, 102, and 185, respectively (NALEO, 1987).

These representational gains have generated a two-pronged backlash. Most noteworthy is the effort led by the Federation for American Immigration Reform (FAIR) to exclude undocumented aliens from the population base used to determine congressional districts (Bean and de la Garza, 1988). Although twice rejected by federal courts, the suit has made this issue part of the nation's political discourse and has exacerbated political tensions and created hostilities that will have a lingering effect.

The second prong of this reaction has been the U.S. English movement (de la Garza and Trujillo, forthcoming). Fueled by nativists, this negative reaction to Latino immigrants has since 1981 led 14 states to declare English their official language, and 11 more are considering similar action (Combs and Lynch, 1988). These victories are especially noteworthy because they have come despite bipartisan opposition and intense Latino counter-mobilization supported by Anglo political leaders.

Mexican Americans disagree among themselves regarding the incorporation of these immigrants. While there is no sign that they are supportive of increased immigration from both Mexico and Central America, they no longer rally against Mexican immigrants as they have historically. Furthermore, some organizations have taken strong pro-immigrant positions. For example, the Mexican American Legal Defense and Education Fund is a recognized advocate of immigrant rights, and NALEO is leading the effort to monitor IRCA and to naturalize Latino immigrants.

Mexican-American reactions to Central American immigrants are more diverse than their reactions to Mexican immigrants. In Houston, Mexican Americans participate in various community organizations providing social services and political support to Central American immigrants. These organizations include grass-roots and church-based groups, and the support they provide ranges from lobbying for political asylum for Central American refugees to providing a forum for Central Americans to inform the U.S. public of Central American affairs.

But the political mobilization of Mexican Americans over Central American issues does not always support Central American immigration. In the small town of San Benito in the lower Rio Grande Valley, for example, segments of the Mexican-American community mobilized in opposite directions concerning the presence of a hospitality center, Casa Oscar Romero, for newly arrived undocumented Central Americans (Nuñez, 1986). The Catholic social service office in nearby Brownsville organized and operated Casa Oscar Romero in a low-income barrio. After a couple of scrimmages between Central American and local Mexican-American youth, Mexican-American residents led by the mayor started a drive to oust Casa Oscar Romero from San Benito. Mexican-American opponents of Casa Oscar Romero also complained that undocumented Central Americans were receiving treatment not given to Mexican immigrants. To pressure the Catholic Church to remove it, some Mexican-American Catholics withheld their Sunday donations at Mass. Although some Mexican Americans supported the hospitality center, the city council, with heavy Mexican-American support, passed a resolution fining Casa Oscar Romero $100 for each day it remained in town. In 1988 Casa Oscar Romero moved to Brownsville, where it again caused the emergence of Mexican-American political mobilization on both sides of the issue (Nuñez, 1989).

Central American immigrants have affected Mexican-American foreign policy concerns in distinct ways. The Central American presence has led to some Mexican-American involvement with Anglos and other Latinos in the sanctuary movement (Rodríguez, 1989). This suggests that Central American immigration has not become a Mexican-American issue in the sense that this group is considered the appropriate base for public discussion of Central American immigration. Instead, the issue is discussed in a multiethnic setting organized around religious and humanitarian values and foreign policy interests.

Central American immigration has also stimulated some Mexican Americans to develop an interest in U.S. policies toward Central America. A few Mexican Americans have traveled with U.S. groups to observe conditions in Central America, and some Mexican-American university students and faculty have provided support to visiting Nicaraguan officials and to organizations such as CISPES (Committee in Solidarity with the People of El Salvador) that are concerned with U.S. involvement in Central America. Mexican-American congressmen have traveled to Nicaragua and returned with criticisms of the Sandinista government, while others such as officials of LULAC (League of United Latin American Citizens) have visited and returned with more favorable evaluations. Mayor Henry Cisneros was a notable dissenter to the Kissinger Report on Central America, and Tony Anaya, the former governor of New Mexico, has been outspoken in his stance against U.S. involvement in Central America.

Mexican immigration is having a similar impact on Mexican-American concerns regarding U.S. policy toward Mexico. Since at least 1980, there has been a segment of Mexican immigrants who have left Mexico for political as well as economic reasons. Unlike Guatemalans and Salvadorans, they are not refugees. They are, however, dissidents with strong resentments toward the incumbent regime. They are convinced the government and PRI (Institutional Revolutionary Party) are increasingly authoritarian, and they point to the 1988 presidential elections and to previous state-level elections in Nuevo León and Chihuahua as examples of how unresponsive and corrupt the system has become. These dissidents claim to have developed organizations in seven cities, but as of 1988 there was no evidence that they were coordinating their activities (de la Garza, 1988).

Before 1988, these groups had not made a concerted effort to recruit Mexican Americans to their cause. They were, instead, satisfied with harassing Mexican diplomats and trying to inform Americans in general about their views of events in Mexico (de la Garza, 1988). That changed with the 1988 Mexican presidential campaign. In that election, those organizations plus others that developed in response to the candidacy of Cuahtemoc Cárdenas, the principal opposition candidate, reached out to Mexican Americans, who responded with moral and financial support. In response to the Cárdenas appeal, some Mexican-American leaders publicly supported the petition of Mexican immigrants that immigrants be allowed to vote absentee.

The request was refused. More significantly, at its 1988 annual meeting California's Democratic Party passed a resolution introduced by Mexican Americans calling on the U.S. government to pressure the Mexican government to respect human rights and conduct honest elections. This infuriated a wide segment of Mexico's political elite, who called it "arrogant," "naive," and "interventionist" (del Olmo, 1988). Jorge Bustamante, perhaps Mexico's leading proponent of bettering relations between Mexicans and Mexican Americans, compared the resolution to attacks on Mexico by Senator Jesse Helms and displayed shock and dismay particularly because Mexican Americans had introduced it (Bustamante, 1988).

The extent to which Mexican Americans will continue to be attentive to Mexican political developments is uncertain. The experience of 1988 suggests that the potential for further involvement exists, and that it is more dependent on the behavior of Mexican immigrants and Mexican-American political priorities than it is on the official positions of the U.S. government, which in 1988 strongly supported Mexico's official candidate. Stated differently, Mexican Americans may join Mexican immigrants and mobilize in opposition to the Mexican government rather than follow U.S. policy and support the PRI.

CONCLUSION

The presence of Mexican and Central American immigrants is affecting Mexican Americans in a variety of ways. Culturally, the presence is reenforcing the most traditional sectors of the Mexican-American population. Economically, it is providing essential resources in the form of consumers and workers. To a lesser degree, it also provides capital and competition for jobs. Politically, it is the basis for increased representation and represents a major potential group of voters. It has also stimulated an increased concern for U.S. policy toward Mexico and Central America. Thus, Mexican Americans are different in important ways because of these immigrants, and those differences are beginning to be reflected in the roles Mexican Americans are playing in American society.

REFERENCES

Allsup, Carl, *The American GI Forum: Origin and Evolution,* Austin: Center for Mexican American Studies, University of Texas, 1982.

Bean, Frank D., and Rodolfo O. de la Garza, "Illegal Aliens and Census Counts," *Society,* Vol. 25, No. 3, March/April 1988, pp. 48–53.

Briseno, Olga, "Foreign Assets," *The San Diego Union,* April 4, 1989, p. D-1.

Browning, Harley L., and Rodolfo O. de la Garza, *Mexican Immigrants and Mexican Americans: An Evolving Relation,* Austin: Center for Mexican American Studies, University of Texas, 1986.

Bustamante, Jorge, *La Opinión,* June 1, 1988.

California Tomorrow, *A Smoother Path to Citizenship: Increasing Naturalization in California,* San Francisco, 1988.

Combs, M. C., and L. M. Lynch, "English Plus," *English Today,* Vol. 6, No. 4, October 1988, pp. 36–42.

De la Garza, Rodolfo, *The Impact of Relations Between Mexicans and the Mexican-Origin People of the United States on U.S.-Mexico Relations,* Paper prepared for the Bi-Lateral Commission on the Future of United States–Mexico Relations, University of California, San Diego, 1988.

De la Garza, Rodolfo, and Louis DeSipio, "Making Latino Numbers Add Up to Increased Representation: The Road to the 1990 Census, Reapportionment and Redistricting," Texas Population Research Center, University of Texas at Austin, No. 11.05, 1989.

De la Garza, Rodolfo, and Adela Flores, "The Impact of Mexican Immigrants on the Political Behavior of Chicanos: A Clarification of Issues and Some Hypotheses for Future Research," in Browning and de la Garza (eds.), *Mexican Immigrants and Mexican Americans: An Evolving Relation,* Austin: Center for Mexican American Studies, University of Texas, 1986, pp. 211–229.

De la Garza, Rodolfo, and Armando Trujillo, "Latinos and the Official English Debate in the United States," *Language and the State,* Centre for Constitutional Studies, University of Alberta at Edmonton, Canada, forthcoming.

Del Olmo, Frank, "Only Gringos with Spanish Surnames," *Houston Chronicle,* Sec. 4, June 12, 1988, p. 5.

DeSipio, Louis, "Social Science Literature and the Naturalization Process," *International Migration Review,* XXI, Summer 1987, pp. 390–405.

García, F. C., and Rodolfo O. de la Garza, *The Chicano Political Experience: Three Perspectives,* North Scituate, Mass.: Duxbury Press, 1977.

Hansen, Niles, and Gilberto Cárdenas, *Immigrant and Native Ethnic Enterprises in Mexican American Neighborhoods: Differing Perceptions of Mexican Immigrant Workers,* Austin: IUP/SSRC Committee for Contemporary Latino Issues, Center for Mexican American Studies, University of Texas, 1988.

National Association of Latino Elected and Appointed Officials (NALEO), *National Roster of Hispanic Elected Officials,* Washington, D.C., 1987.

North, David, *The Long Grey Welcome: A Study of the American Naturalization Program,* Washington, D.C.: NALEO Education Fund, 1985.

Nuñez, Rogelio T., personal communication, January 12, 1989.

Nuñez, Rogelio T., "Central Americans in a Texas Border Town: A Preliminary Analysis," Paper presented at the Southwestern Social Science Association Meetings, San Antonio, Texas, March 19–22, 1986.

Portes, Alejandro, and Robert Bach, *Latino Journey,* University of California, Berkeley, 1985.

Rodríguez, Nestor, "Fieldwork Findings of the Changing Relations Project (1988–1989)," Sociology Department, University of Houston, Texas, 1989.

Rodríguez, Nestor, "Undocumented Central Americans in Houston: Diverse Populations," *International Migrant Review,* Vol. 21, No. 1, Spring 1987, pp. 4–26.

Sheldon, Beth Ann, Nestor Rodríguez, Joe R. Feagin, Robert Bullard, and Robert Thomas, *Houston: A Study of Growth and Decline in a Sunbelt Boomtown,* Philadelphia: Temple University Press, forthcoming.

U.S. Immigration and Naturalization Service, immigration legalization statistics for Houston provided by the Houston District INS Office, January 17, 1989a.

U.S. Immigration and Naturalization Service, *1987 Statistical Yearbook,* Washington, D.C.: Government Printing Office, 1989b.

ALGUNOS IMPACTOS DE LA LEY DE REFORMA Y CONTROL DE INMIGRACIÓN (IRCA) EN UNA REGIÓN DE JALISCO DE FUERTE EMIGRACIÓN HACIA ESTADOS UNIDOS DE NORTEAMÉRICA

Jesús Arroyo Alejandre[1]
Universidad de Guadalajara

INTRODUCCIÓN

Existen algunas investigaciones sobre Jalisco como lugar de origen de la migración hacia Estados Unidos, desde el "clásico" de Taylor sobre el municipio de Arandas en 1932, hasta los más recientes entre los que destaca "Return to Aztlan" (Massey y colaboradores, 1987) y diversos estudios que se desarrollan actualmente sobre el tópico, algunos en comunidades rurales.[2] Parece haber consenso en que esta migración, basada en tradicionales redes de amistad y parentesco (Mines, 1984) que la "orientan," es laboral, temporal, predominantemente de hombres jóvenes y una parte importante es de carácter indocumentada.

Una estimación conservadora de la migración de jaliscienses hacia Estados Unidos es entre 200 y 300 mil personas que trabajan por temporadas de 4 a 6 meses, aproximadamente;[3] magnitud que representa cerca del 20 por ciento de la PEA del Estado. De acuerdo con este cálculo las remesas aproximadas se estimarían en alrededor de 200 millones de dólares anuales, es decir casi el 30 por ciento de las exportaciones totales de Jalisco.[4]

En 1986, con la implantación de la IRCA, se especuló sobre un regreso masivo de indocumentados; al paso del tiempo, como frecuentemente ocurre, se han planteado otras hipótesis más plausibles. La mayoría de ellas se refieren al impacto de la IRCA en Estados Unidos y México en general, pocas han analizado sus efectos en las comunidades rurales "de origen." En 1988 Cornelius, señalaba que en los debates sobre la efectividad de la ley no se estaba considerando información de primera mano sobre este ultimo tipo de impacto.

En los primeros trabajos de evaluación de la ley[5] se establece que uno de los propósitos centrales de la misma es controlar el flujo de indocumentados, pero que al menos para 1986 y 1987 no se había observado. Empero, a finales de 1988 y principios de 1989 se perciben opiniones y se llevan a cabo algunas acciones tendientes al cumplimiento de dicha ley (como una mayor vigilancia por parte de la patrulla fronteriza y la iniciativa de construcción de una zanja en la zona de San Diego-Tijuana) lo que probablemente puede repercutir en una mayor dificultad para la entrada y consecución de empleo de indocumentados.

---

[1]Este trabajo reporta resultados preliminares y parciales de un proyecto de investigación sobre "La Migración de Jaliscienses hacia Estados Unidos y el Desarrollo Regional en Jalisco," el cual es financiado por The Commission for the Study of International Migration and Cooperative Economic Development.

El autor agradece la colaboración en este trabajo de Adrián de León Arias y M. Basilia Valenzuela Varela.

[2]Véase Cornelius (1988) y Rodríguez (1989).

[3]Estimación basada en cálculos de la Organización Internacional del Trabajo (International Labour Office, 1987:1–2) y la encuesta del CONAPO en 1984 (CONAPO, 1986).

[4]Diversos estudios sobre Migración (Mines, 1981; Taylor, 1987) señalan que los inmigrantes envían un promedio de 1000 dólares anuales; basados en esta estimación, y suponiendo que un 20 por ciento de la migración total hacia Estados Unidos es de jaliscienses, es como se llega a este monto aproximado.

[5]Bustamante (1987), García y Griego (1987), varios autores en *Foro Internacional*, Vol. XXVII, No. 3, 1987.

Alba (1987:458) hace referencia a posibles impactos en la selectividad de los inmigrantes señalando que: "Los indocumentados que han legalizado su situación poseen características socioeconómicas más elevadas que el inmigrante medio, incluso por encima de los niveles socioeconómicos promedio." Además, que "el patrón migratorio, por generaciones de carácter temporal y rotatorio, podría ser empujado hacia un patrón más universal, es decir, desplazarse hacia una migración de carácter más permanente." La nueva ley tal vez obligue a decidir sobre se residencia entre México y Estados Unidos a quienes no deseaban hacerlo.

Con respecto a los efectos en las comunidades rurales, García y Griego y Giner de los Ríos (1985) plantearon algunos supuestos basados en comunidades definidas, hipotéticamente, según su capacidad de absorción de empleo y su dependencia económica de la migración. Por su parte, Taylor (1988) elabora un informe en 1985 básicamente a partir de su experiencia en dos comunidades en Michoacán y concluye que dada la estrecha dependencia de las comunidades rurales de la migración, la IRCA se enfrenta a presiones económicas en el origen que no puede controlar, en consecuencia, es muy difícil que esta migración sea permanentemente reglamentada en forma unilateral.

El Contexto de la Migración de Jaliscienses Hacia Estados Unidos

La evolución y las proyecciones de la población del estado de Jalisco y la Zona Metropolitana de Guadalajara (ZMG) se presentan en la gráfica 1, que muestra una gran concentración poblacional en la ZMG. En poca cuantía algunas otras ciudades menores como Ciudad Guzmán, Puerto Vallarta, Ocotlán, Lagos de Moreno, Tepatitlán y Autlán, también concentran la población estatal. Empero, todavía se encuentran dispersos alrededor de un millón de habitantes en 9,727 localidades rurales (de 2,500 habitantes y menos), muchas de ellas insuficientemente integradas desde el punto de vista territorial. El estado lo constituyen 124 municipios de los cuales, cuatro forman la ZMG: Gualalajara, Tlaquepaque, Tonalá y Zapopan.

El medio rural de Jalisco ha sido tradicionalmente una región de emigración; mientras que Guadalajara atrae grandes cantidades de migrantes, principalmente del interior de Jalisco y, en general, del Occidente de México. En los diez años anteriores a 1984 llegaron a la ZMG 279 mil personas; casi el 39 por ciento provenían del propio estado y alrededor de la mitad tuvieron su origen en el medio rural (Winnie y Velázquez, 1987). De 1950 a 1980 se experimenta una creciente emigración rural que se extiende a regiones más urbanas de Jalisco (Arroyo, 1989).

Para dar una idea de las magnitudes relativas de la migración de Jalisco hacia Estados Unidos reproducimos el cuadro 1 que se obtiene de diferentes estudios, como se señala en sus notas, no estrictamente comparables; pero tres de los cuatro tienen en común que usan muestras de inmigrantes indocumentados. De acuerdo con estos datos, después de Michoacán, Jalisco es el principal origen de este tipo de migración, aunque su participación relativa con respecto a otros estados del país, tiende a disminuir ligeramente a favor de Baja California Norte, Chihuahua, Guerrero, Estado de México y Oaxaca.[6]

---

[6]Existen algunos trabajos que revelan la creciente migración desde el Occidente de México hacia los estados del norte del país. Esto ha sido particularmente evidente en los ultimos 15 años, por lo que algunos estudiosos de la migración internacional han concluido que el Occidente de México contribuye directa o indirectamente con por lo menos el 70 por ciento de la migración a Estados Unidos (Cross y Sandos, 1981:73). Actualmente, en la encuesta que realiza el Colegio de la Frontera Norte en los principales puertos de entrada a Estados Unidos, todavía en julio de 1988 siguen Jalisco, Michoacán y Zacatecas como principales origenes de inmigrantes indocumentados (COLEF, 1988).

150

Cuadro 1

INDICADORES DE ORIGENES DE LA MIGRACIÓN MEXICANA HACIA ESTADOS UNIDOS POR REGIÓN Y ESTADO: 1926, 1973, 1978, 1984

Región y Estado de Origen	Por Ciento de Casos				Indice[a]			
	1926	1973	1978	1984	1926	1973	1978	1984[g]
Total[b]	100.0	100.0	100.0	100.0	100	100	100	100
Occidente de Mexico	61.4	68.6	54.1	36.9	247	339	275	196
Zacatecas	4.8	7.4	6.9	4.4	176	392	399	278
Michoacán	20.0	21.2	17.6	11.1	316	448	386	266
Jalisco[c]	14.7	26.2	14.5	10.0	194	392	225	155
Guanajuato	19.5	8.1	10.8	7.7	327	174	237	177
Nayarit	0.2	3.3	2.3	1.9	21	295	207	180
Colima	0.2	1.8	1.0	0.9	62	353	192	181
Aguascalientes	1.9	0.8	1.0	0.9	241	106	133	118
Pacífico Norte	3.7	16.0	10.0	18.2	76	227	140	257
Baja California Norte	0.5	8.4	3.8	10.2	84	466	207	597
Baja California Sur	[f]	0.1	0.1	0.1	[f]	33	30	36
Sonora	1.2	2.8	2.7	5.2	65	123	120	236
Sinaloa	0.2	4.7	3.5	2.7	83	174	126	96
Norte Interior	17.7	5.8	22.7	24.7	153	59	238	260
	17.7	5.9	22.6					
Chihuahua	4.4	1.0	11.2	15.7	148	32	380	552
Durango	5.9	3.9	4.9	3.5	240	209	281	202
Coahuila[d]	3.8	0.3	2.6	2.8	144	11	114	122
San Luis Potosí	3.6	0.7	3.9	2.7	104	26	155	93
Noroeste[e]	10.1	0.5	2.4	2.9	219	8	36	45
	10.0	0.5	2.3					
Nuevo León	8.0	0.2	1.2	1.7	318	5	33	46
Tamaulipas	2.0	0.3	1.1	1.2	98	11	39	43
Otras Regiones[e]	7.1	9.1	10.9	13.4	13	13	19	30
Guerrero	0.2	0.8	3.3	4.4	6	24	101	142
D.F. + Edo. México	5.3	3.0	3.1	5.1	19	13	13	39
Oaxaca	0.2	1.1	1.8	3.9	3	28	47	115
Otros Estados[e]	1.4	4.1	2.7	3.9	5	10	11	242

FUENTES: Winnie y De León (1987). Datos de 1984 incluídos por el autor con base en información de CONAPO (1986). Para 1978 (Bustamante-Martínez, 1979), cuadros 1-2. Encuesta a 5,271 entrevistados mexicanos repatriados, quienes habían sido detenidos como ilegales por el INS (U.S. Immigration and Naturalization Service). Para 1973, (Dagodag, 1975) y entrevista con el Dr. William W. Winnie. Datos de 3,166 formatos del INS de mexicanos indocumentados que habían sido detenidos dentro de la jurisdicción del Chula Vista Border Patrol Sector, el cual cubre los destinos de los tres estados de la Costa del Pacífico de los Estados Unidos. Para 1926, (Gamio, 1930). Datos obtenidos del estudio clásico de Manuel Gamio publicados en 1930. Se refiere a giros postales enviados a México. Para 1984, (CONAPO, 1986).

[a](Ni P/N Pi)x100, donde Ni es el número de casos en la muestra del Estado o región i; P es la población del país; Pi la población del Estado o la región i; y N es el total de casos en las respectivas muestras.

[b]El número de casos por Estado no se da aquí, pero está disponible en las fuentes. La muestra de 1978 incluía 5,271 casos, la de 1973, 3,166; y la de 1926, 23,845. Dada las diferencias en conceptos y enfoques entre las tres muestras, el número absoluto de casos es útil para propósitos del presente estudio sólo para la derivación de los valores relativos presentados en el cuadro.

[c]Dentro de Jalisco, para 1978, 219 de los 764 casos fueron el Area Metropolitana de Guadalajara, la cual, considerada aparte, tendría un índice de 103 comparado con 277 del resto del estado.

[d]Coahuila ocupa un lugar intermedio entre el Noreste y el Norte Interior, dada su posición geográfica, se ha dejado en el Norte Interior, a pesar de que sería preferible en algunos casos tratarlo como parte del Noreste.

[e]La encuesta de 1973 incluía 51 casos, los cuales no fueron obtenidos directamente por Dagodag. Si estos casos estuvieran concentrados en esta región, ello podría significar un incremento de su contribución a la migración en cuestión.

[f]Para 1926, los datos de Baja California Sur se incluyen juntos con los de Baja California Norte.

[g]Muestra de 9,631 entrevistas a personas de 15 años y mas de edad, de nacionalidad mexicana, quienes fueron devueltos a nuestro país entre el 5 y el 6 de diciembre de 1984 por los principales puertos fronterizos.

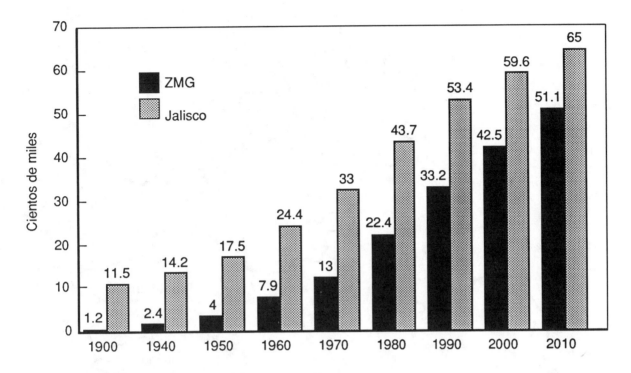

FUENTE: Censos de Población y Vivienda y Proyecciones de CONAPO, 1985. INEGI, 1985, e INESER, 1987.

Gráfica 1—Población de Jalisco y Zona Metropolitana de Guadalajara, 1900–2010

Del estudio realizado por CONAPO (1986) en una muestra de detenidos y deportados en los principales puertos fronterizos, construímos el cuadro 2 que da una idea general del perfil de este tipo de emigrantes residentes del estado de Jalisco. En este estudio se preguntó también a los detenidos y deportados su municipio de residencia. Con esta información construímos para Jalisco un índice de la migración de indocumentados de cada uno de sus municipios; aunque los datos se refieren a 1984 es, según nuestro conocimiento, el único indicador que nos permite estimar a nivel de municipio, la intensidad de este flujo poblacional.[7]

Este índice, junto con información de otros trabajos y nuestro conocimiento general al respecto obtenido de la observación de campo, nos permitió definir el área de estudio: localidades rurales y semiurbanas (de 300 a 5,000 habitantes) en municipios de alto rechazo poblacional hacia Estados Unidos, definidos como aquellos con indices migratorios mayores al promedio estatal. El número de municipios considerados de fuerte rechazo, según nuestro procedimiento, son 42, donde residen aproximadamente 710,000 habitantes, representando el 16 por ciento de la población jalisciense y alojan al 27 por ciento de su población rural. Esos 42 municipios estan distribuidos geográficamente en todas del estado de las nueves regiones (véase mapa 1 para las regiones). Su población de estudio se definió con propósitos de una investigación más amplia sobre migración y desarrollo regional (que se describe a grandes

---

[7]El índice se computó Idx = [(MDi/MDj)]/(PEAi/PEAj)] x 100 siendo MDi las personas detenidas o deportadas del municipio i; MDj el total de estas personas en el estado; PEAi la población económicamente activa del municipio; y, PEAj esta población del estado en conjunto.

Mapa 1—Nueve regiones del Estado de Jalisco

razgos al final de este trabajo). Empero, el ejercicio para definir el área de estudio y el análisis municipal de los datos de la encuesta de CONAPO de 1984 arrojan algunos hallazgos interesantes.

Construímos un índice de desarrollo socioeconómico comparativo municipal (NISEDEC) en base a variables[8] censales que miden aspectos económicos y sociales particulares de la

---

[8]Estas variables son: Porcentaje de población económicamente activa (PEA) que gana hasta una vez el salario mínimo; porcentaje de PEA en el sector agropecuario; porcentaje de población analfabeta mayor de 15 años; porcentaje de viviendas sin agua entubada; porcentaje de población mayor de 15 años sin primaria completa; porcentaje de vivien-

población del municipio, utilizando el método de análisis factorial para combinarlas y obtenerlo. Este índice se relaciona con el referente al rechazo poblacional en la gráfica 2, que muestra claramente que la migración hacia Estados Unidos tiene su orígen sobre todo en áreas con niveles socioeconómicos comparativos bajos y medios.[9]

Es interesante señalar que a nivel individual, la hipótesis común de varios estudios es que los migrantes internacionales tienen ingresos reales medios y altos. Lo anterior es aceptable cuando provienen de comunidades rurales y semiurbanas; pero los procedentes de ciudades son de ingresos reales medios y bajos. Sin embargo, si consideramos el nivel socioeconómico comparativo de *las regiones* de origen poco urbanizadas, como lo muestra la gráfica 2, en el caso de

Cuadro 2

CUADRO COMPARATIVO DE TRABAJADORES INDOCUMENTADOS
DEVUELTOS POR LAS AUTORIDADES DE LOS ESTADOS
UNIDOS DE AMERICA DICIEMBRE DE 1984
JALISCO Y NACIONAL

Categoría	Jalisco Porcentaje	Nacional Porcentaje
Sexo		
Hombres	85	89
Mujeres	15	11
Edo. de Permanencia en EUA por Edo. de Residencia en Mexico		
Arizona	2	7
California	91	55
Texas	5	34
Otros	2	4
Total	100	100
Nivel de Instrucción		
Primaria	63	60
Secundaria	19	18
Preparatoria	5	6
Profesional	1	1
Sin instrucción	12	15
Total	100	100
Estado Civil		
Solteros	60	57
Casados	36	36
Otros	4	7
Total	100	100
Posesión de Tierra		
Sí	31	42
No	69	58
Total	100	100

FUENTE: Encuesta en la frontera norte a trabajadores indocumentados deportados por las autoridades de los EUA en diciembre de 1984. CONAPO (1986).

das sin energía eléctrica; porcentaje de viviendas sin drenaje; paridez de la mujer de 25 a 29 años de edad; porcentaje de población que vive en localidades de menos de 5,000 habitantes; porcentaje de viviendas con uno y dos cuartos; y, tasa neta de migración.

[9]La mayoría de municipios con altas índices de rechazo también tienen comparativamente un alto porcentaje de población rural.

154

Jalisco los flujos migratorios hacia Estados Unidos provienen principalmente de regiones con nivel socioeconómico bajo y medio.[10] Lo anterior no necesariamente implica que logrando un mayor desarrollo de estas regiones se reduzca su emigración. Entonces, no se puede inferir una relación unívoca general entre migración y desarrollo regional. A pesar de ésto, esta relación depende de situaciones particulares: énfasis en el tipo de desarrollo;[11] intensidad en el uso del factor trabajo según las tecnologías predominantes en la producción regional a medida que toma lugar ese desarrollo; influencia de las redes de amistad y parentesco existente en cada región; de la vocación productiva regional; el grado y tipo de utilización de recursos de las regiones; de la integración y funcionalidad socioeconómica de los asentamientos poblacionales intra- e inter-regiónal; y, en general, de las oportunidades de desarrollo personal y familar que ofrecen las comunidades de origen.

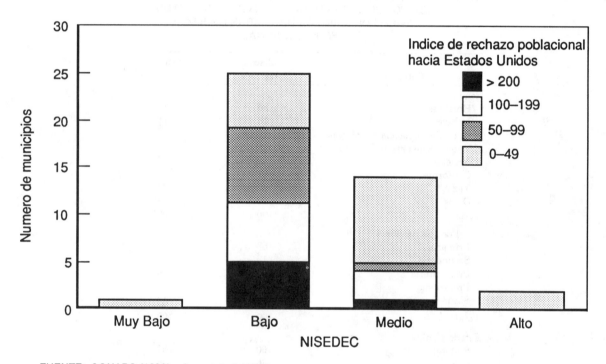

FUENTE: CONAPO (1986) y Arroyo et al. (1988).

Gráfica 2—Jalisco: municipios con alto índice de emigración indocumentada hacia Estados Unidos en relación con su nivel de desarrollo socioeconómico (NISEDEC)

---

[10]Según Cornelius las personas que emigraban ilegalmente en 1976 a Estados Unidos, estaban entre los ingresos medios y bajos y no entre los más bajos (Cornelius, 1978:20). Una década más tarde (Bustamante, 1987:21) asegura que no hay una relación causal directa entre pobreza y emigración y que inclusive se puede que actualmente está emigrando gente con mayuores ingresos.

[11]Agropecuario, agroindustrial, industrial manufacturero, servicios, agropecuario comercial moderno, agropecuario minifundista, etc.

Perfil General de Emigrantes Indocumentados Jaliscienses según la Encuesta del CONAPO, 1984

Los resultados de la encuesta del CONAPO de 1984 reitera hallazgos de otros estudios.[12] Los emigrantes indocumentados de Jalisco, y seguramente los documentados también, son jóvenes;[13] no existe una diferencia significativa entre las regiones del estado. Resalta la región Vallarta, recientemente entrante en la migración hacia Estados Unidos, con un porcentaje comparativamente alto de jóvenes entre 16 y 20 años; también que la región Guadalajara agrupa más del 50 por ciento de esta migración. Desde luego ésto se debe a que similarmente concentra la población total jalisciense; empero, se puede suponer que algunos inmigrantes de la ciudad de Guadalajara y de su "hinterland inmediato de influencia," al no encontrar oportunidades de empleo allí, deciden probar suerte en Estados Unidos (cuadro 3).

En cuanto al sexo, el predominio es de hombres y no hay diferenciación significativa entre regiones. Es entendible que por lo jóven de los emigrantes, sean casados y solteros en proporciones similares (cuadro 4). En este caso tampoco existen variaciones regionales significativas. El nivel educativo predominante es la primaria terminada, siendo los emigrantes de la región Guadalajara los que tienen un mayor nivel de instrucción escolarizada, incluyendo un porcentaje importante con nivel universitario.

El cuadro 4 apoya el supuesto de que este tipo de emigrantes, no sólo planean mejorar su ingreso (incluso su movilidad social al regresar a México) sino que probablemente muchos de ellos tratan de solventar una presión económica, pues los mayores porcentajes se encuentran en los grupos de personas quienes tienen 4 o más dependientes económicos familiares. Esto se puede interpretar como mayor presión económica sobre ellos para mantener a sus familias.

Aproximadamente un tercio de los emigrantes declararon que ellos o sus familias tenían tierras en México (cuadro 2). Aquellos que reportaron su residencia en regiones más urbanizadas o donde la agricultura es más comercial y moderna, en mayor porcentaje declararon no poseer (ellos o sus familias) tierras.

Cuadro 3

EDADES DE EMIGRANTES INDOCUMENTADOS JALISCIENSES POR REGIONES, 1984
(Porcentajes)

Región	15 o Meno Años	16 a 20 Años	21 a 30 Años	31 a 40 Años	Mas de 40 Años	Total
Colotlán	2	35	42	16	5	100
Lagos		21	51	19	9	100
Tepatitlán		32	47	11	9	100
Ameca	2	24	47	19	8	100
Guadalajara	1	34	46	11	7	100
Vallarta		41	34	7	17	100
Ocotlán		35	41	10	14	100
Autlán		24	64	5	7	100
Guzmán		20	54	18	8	100
Total	1	32	47	12	8	100

FUENTE: Encuesta del CONAPO 1984 (1986).

---

[12]Por ejemplo, CENIET (1982), Cornelius (1978), Cross y Sandos (1981), Massey et al. (1987).

[13]Cornelius (1978) con datos de 1976 asevera que el flujo migratorio estaba compuesto en su mayoría de personas jóvenes con edades promedio entre los 22 y 30 años de edad; por su parte en 1985 Cross y Sandos concluyen que la edad promedio de los migrantes era de 25 años y en 1987 Massey y colaboradores confirmaron esta tendencia.

Cuadro 4

PORCENTAJES DE HOMBRES A CASADOS Y CON MÁS DE 4
DEPENDIENTES EN EMIGRANTES INDOCUMENTADOS
JALISCIENSES POR REGIONES, 1984

Región	Hombres	Casados[a]	4 y Más Dependientes
Colotlán	79	51	44
Lagos	84	51	58
Tepatitlán	92	43	57
Ameca	81	37	59
Guadalajara	83	34	34
Vallarta	90	17	62
Ocotlán	92	41	59
Autlán	88	36	36
Guzmán	91	35	65
Total	85	36	48

FUENTE: Encuesta del CONAPO 1984 (1986).
[a]Otros son solteros.

Casi el sesenta por ciento de la población de referencia sólo había ingresado a Estados Unidos una vez y un tercio más entre 2 y 3 veces. En este aspecto no existen diferencias significativas entre regiones.

ALGUNOS IMPACTOS DE LA IRCA DESDE LA PERSPECTIVA DE LOS LUGARES DE ORIGEN EN JALISCO

En este apartado proponemos algunas hipótesis sobre los impactos de la IRCA en las áreas rurales y semiurbanas de amplia migración hacia Estados Unidos (como las hemos definido), basadas en la información obtenida de una encuesta de 67 migrantes visitantes en la navidad de 1988, quienes en alguna forma fueron afectados por la nueva ley de inmigración, y de entrevistas con "informantes clave." Ambos tipos de encuestas se aplicaron en 19 localidades de los municipios que presentan los más altos indices migratorios, los cuales se encuentran distribuidos en todo el estado. Desde luego que no se pretendió una representatividad estadística, pero sí se buscó diversidad geográfica y socioeconómica para un mejor sustento de las hipótesis.

Una opinión generalizada en los pueblos estudiados es que hubo un aumento considerable de emigrantes de visita con respecto a otras navidades, esto pudo observarse en todas partes de Jalisco, no sólo en esos pueblos. Asimismo, un número importante de personas con experiencia migratoria o sin ella habían obtenido documentos, incluso muchos de ellos aprovecharon la IRCA y se fueron con el propósito principal de obtenerlos. En la encuesta a emigrantes visitantes se encontró que casi el 85 por ciento de los entrevistados realizaron su último viaje durante el período de 1986 a 1988, más aún, en 1988 lo hicieron el 57 por ciento; y el 12 por ciento hizo su primer viaje a Estados Unidos durante el período de 1986–1988. También la opinión de informantes clave coincidió en este respecto.

De lo anterior, se puede inferir que el flujo migratorio de retorno y frecuencia de visitas continuará aumentando a raíz de la IRCA. Como corolario de ésto, un supuesto plausible es que la actividad económica de las comunidades en cuestión puede verse estimulada por este aumento siempre y cuando haya una mayor entrada de remesas e ingresos por concepto de migración, de lo cual no se tiene evidencia; aunque es probable que con la legalización las personas tengan acceso a trabajos más estables en Estados Unidos, no necesariamente mejor remunerados. Pues la opinión predominante de nuestros encuestados es que esperan una reducción en las oportunidades de empleos con salarios mayores al mínimo y una reducción general de los salarios en los mercados de trabajo tradicionales de inmigrantes temporales y no temporales de orígen mexicano.

Otra hipótesis interesante es que los efectos de la nueva ley están reforzando las "cadenas y redes migratorias" en el sentido de que las personas amnistiadas y quienes han conseguido documentos de legalización, pueden sentirse con mayores posibilidades de ayudar a sus amigos o parientes por haber conseguido documentos de legalización.

Entonces, en general, la nueva legislación aceleró el flujo migratorio de estas áreas; contrariamente a la creencia de que produciría un retorno masivo de emigrantes hacia sus comunidades de orígen en el periodo de implantación de la Ley. Así, el 79 por ciento de nuestros entrevistados arreglaron documentos con la IRCA, de estos, el 93 por ciento consiguió legalización a través del programa de trabajadores especiales agrícolas, y el resto obtuvo amnistía. Del total de los que lograrón documentación con la IRCA, el 83 por ciento inició sus trámites en Estados Unidos y 17 por ciento en México.

El uso y destino de las remesas ha sido un tema de discusión por parte de los estudiosos de este tópico. La pertinencia del mismo estriba en determinar hasta qué punto los ingresos provenientes de los trabajadores migratorios tienen impacto en el desarrollo (o crecimiento) económico de sus lugares de orígen. Lo que hemos encontrado al respecto en nuestros estudios, en primer lugar, es la dificultad de cuantificar dichas remesas, pues al parecer esta información en las encuestas no es muy confiable. Intentamos la cuantificación a través de los bancos locales pero una mayoría de las remesas se cambian de dólares a pesos a través de individuos, quienes por razones obvias no proporcionan información.[14] A pesar de esto, la opinión común es que entre el 50 y 70 por ciento de las familias de las localidades estudiadas viven de los ingresos de sus trabajadores migratorios. También, que la mayor parte del gasto es para manuntención y en segundo lugar para vivienda y enseres domésticos. Por lo poco diversificado de las economías locales y la concentración de la actividad económica en la ZMG y otras pocas ciudades medias en el estado,[15] las remesas tienen impactos no significativos en la actividad productiva de las localidades via efectos multiplicadores del gasto de consumo este concepto. Asi, gran parte de las remesas tienen su impacto económico multiplicador en la ZMG y otras ciudades "centrales" regionales. Sin embargo, en términos absolutos la mayor cantidad de emigrantes provienen de ciudades medias como Lagos de Moreno, San Juan de los Lagos, San Diego de Alejandría, la Barca, Colotlán, Ameca, Puerto Vallarta y hasta la ZMG, en éstas los mencionados efectos económicos son evidentemente más amplios.

De nuestra encuesta de casos, se observa el mismo destino de las remesas señalado arriba y por otros autores;[16] así, el gasto de manutención es predominante. Pero el gasto de pequeño comercio se encuentra en segundo lugar.

---

[14]Algunos tienen cuentas bancarias en Estados Unidos.

[15]Véase, Arroyo y colaboradores, 1988, quienes dan una descripción de la funcionalidad regional del sistema de ciudades de Jalisco y Colima, y de su desarrollo regional con énfasis en la importancia socioeconómica de los lugares centrales urbanos de estos dos estados.

[16]Desde Gamio (1930) ya se conocía este hallazgo y que ha sido corroborado por autores como Cornelius (1978), Diez-Canedo, (1984), CONAPO (1986), Massey et al. (1987).

Movilidad Ocupacional

Los emigrantes visitantes encuestados reportaron trabajar en Estados Unidos según el cuadro 5. En general, la agricultura sigue siendo la rama de actividad que absorbe la mayor parte de la mano de obra de mexicanos en Estados Unidos. Asimismo, nuestra información soporta otros hallazgos sobre el desplazamiento hacia mercados de trabajo más urbanos dentro de las ramas del comercio y los servicios. Además, parece que un efecto de la ley fue el cambio en la estructura de empleo de los que arreglan documentos; según nuestros datos, de los que consiguieron amnistía, el 25 por ciento cambió de empleo y de los que consiguieron permiso temporal de trabajador especial agrícola 29 por ciento también lo hizo. De la misma forma se muestra que probablemente cerca del 50 por ciento de quienes obtuvieron permisos especiales de trabajadores agrícolas no trabajaban en el campo.

Las regiones urbanas, semiurbanas y la ZMG paracen aumentar su importancia como lugares expulsores de mano de obra. De hecho, la encuesta de CONAPO de 1984 captó el 62 por ciento de los entrevistados con lugares de residencia en municipios que tienen ciudades de más de 40 mil habitantes. Empero, la ZMG era orígen del 52 por ciento de encuestados por el CONAPO. Por otro lado, según nuestras entrevistas en las zonas de fuerte rechazo, los informantes captan una tendencia a que personas calificadas y profesionistas estén integrándose al flujo de migración de trabajadores. Por ejemplo, en Guadalajara 200 maestros normalistas (de primaria) solicitaron licencia por un año para migrar al vecino país del norte, así como en al menos otros tres municipios en nuestra área de estudio. En el municipio de Ciudad Guzmán egresados del tecnológico, quienes obtienen un grado intermedio entre técnico especializado e ingeniero, también se van en busca de trabajo y mayores ingresos. Más aún, existe la opinión general, basada en el conocimiento de casos particulares, de que profesionistas egresados de las universidades, al no encontrar trabajo en México, están emigrando crecientemente.[17]

Con base en lo anterior, suponiendo la continuación de la crisis económica en México y el funcionamiento de lo que Diez-Canedo llama "mercados de trabajo simbióticos" de México y Estados Unidos, se puede plantear la hipótesis de que si la IRCA se aplica realmente a los

Cuadro 5

OCUPACIÓN EN ESTADOS UNIDOS DE LOS EMIGRANTES VISITANTES
(Diciembre de 1988)

		Antes de Arreglar Documentos	
Rama	Total	Amnistiados	Trabajador, Especial Agrícola
Agricultura	37	—	59
Comercio y servicios	25	50	16
Construcción	19	—	19
Manufactura	12	50	6
No trabajó	3	—	—
Otros	3	—	—
Total	100	100	100

FUENTE: Encuesta de 67 casos, diciembre 1988.

---

[17]Estas tendencias también son señaladas por El Colegio de la Frontera Norte (1988:6) que reporta como un hallazgos interesante el hecho de que los indocumentados tengan un nivel de escolaridad 5 años mayor que la media nacional.

empleadores estadunidenses, puede estimular la inmigración de mano de obra calificada de Jalisco, (técnicos y profesionistas) quienes utilizando sus redes de parentesco y amistad podrán conseguir empleo y probablemente permiso en el corto plazo; si suponemos que los empleadores están interesados en estos trabajadores y pueden hacer los trámites para su regularización. Sin embargo, por otro lado, los salarios generales pueden tender a bajar en actividades que usan mano de obra inmigrante. Y las personas indocumentadas tradicionales con bajo nivel educativo, provenientes del campo y con baja calificación, optarán por actividades de subempleo[18] y maquila domiciliaria en un tipo de "economía popular" dentro de Estados Unidos.

Se puede inferir que con la nueva legislación, se generalizará lo que llama Bustamante "sobreoferta" de mano de obra[19] hacia mercados de trabajo no tradicionales como algunos de técnicos semicalificados en actividades económicas urbanas. Así, tanto en el campo como en las ciudades las activades intensivas en mano de obra tenderán a pagar bajos salarios y consecuentemente la economía, sobre todo de los estados sureños de la Unión Americana, se estimulará en beneficio de los consumidores en última instancia.[20]

Algunos Impactos Cualitativos de la IRCA

En nuestra encuesta de casos de quienes consiguieron documentos con la ley, el 29 por ciento considera que ahora tienen acceso a empleos mejor remunerados; aunque muchos mencionan que hay una exigencia mayor en la calidad de su trabajo; el 26 por ciento cree que una importante ventaja es el entrar y salir del país cuando lo deseen; el 21 por ciento piensa que otra ventaja importante es la obtención de prestaciones laborales; el 19 por ciento piensa que ahora pueden tener la posibilidad de conseguir trabajos menos pesados a diferencia de los del campo. A pesar de ésto, el 18 por ciento señaló como una desventaja de la IRCA que hay sobreoferta de mano de obra y, consecuentemente, mayor dificultad para conseguir empleo; pero poco más de la mitad consideró que la ley no tenía ninguna desventaja para los que consiguieron documentos.

Por otro lado, de los que no consiguieron documentos, (14 individuos en nuestra encuesta) sólo dos mencionaron que los habían desempleado y la mayoría considera que no hay ninguna dificultad para continuar emigrando. Además, de éstos la mitad declaró tener las mismas expectativas de empleo en Estados Unidos que antes de la ley.

Por lo que respecta a los que ya tenían documentos antes de la nueva ley, la mitad declaró que ahora sería más dificil conseguir empleos bien remunerados por la mayor oferta de mano de obra, y el resto piensa que no hay ninguna consecuencia para ellos.

En suma, se puede suponer, de acuerdo con las opiniones de los emigrantes, que la IRCA benefició a quienes consiguieron documentos; aunque esperan dificultades de encontrar trabajo y de bajos salarios.

A los entrevistados se les preguntó sus opiniones respecto a sus perspectivas futuras. De los que consiguieron documentos y fueron amnistiados, las tres cuartas partes piensan residir en Estados Unidos y la mitad piensa nacionalizarse. Mientras los que consiguieron permisos para trabajador especial agrícola, 50 por ciento piensa continuar su migración temporal y el 38 por ciento quisiera residir permanentemente en Estados Unidos; del total de este tipo de inmigrantes, la mitad desearía nacionalizarse.

---

[18]Cornelius (1988) tiene este punto de vista sobre todo para los nuevos inmigrantes de zonas expulsoras no tradicionales.

[19]Conferencia dictado en el Instituto de Estudios Económicos y Regionales, julio de 1987.

[20]El reporte de los asesores económicos del presidente R. Reagan en 1985 señala los efectos positivos que ha tenido históricamente la inmigración de trabajadores en la economía norteamericana (véase *Population and Development Review*, 1986:361–374).

De los que pensaban radicar en Estados Unidos, la gran mayoría (poco más del 80 por ciento) respondío que en Estados Unidos hay mejores condiciones de vida. Y aquellos que pensaban nacionalizarse establecieron como razón principal la obtención de mejores prestaciones y razones de tipo familiar. Por los resultados de las entrevistas a este respecto, tomando en cuenta las opiniones de los "informantes clave" y de otras personas, en cuanto a las pocas oportunidades de empleos suficientemente remunerados en México, de los efectos negativos de la crisis económica y de la falta de credibilidad y confianza en el gobierno, se puede suponer que existe un creciente "desarraigo cultural" de la población rural y semiurbana en nuestra área de estudio. Empero, también hay evidencia de que en el largo plazo una gran mayoría de inmigrantes tienden a regresar a residir permanentemente en México al final de su vida productiva. Se plantea este supuesto como objeto de investigaciones más amplias por parte de especialistas de este tópico.

Es necesario recalcar que los resultados que se presentan en este trabajo provienen de dos encuestas consideradas como de casos, esto es, no representativa estadísticamente y en este contexto debe evaluarse el análisis, el cual consideramos como una primera aproximación al estudio de esta problemática.

En la actualidad estamos llevando a cabo una encuesta representativa de hogares y otra de "informantes clave," en dicha área, que se enfoca sobre los impactos de la migración en al familia, la comunidad y el desarrollo regional, asi como sobre la IRCA dentro del contexto de la crisis económica nacional. Este estudio está diseñado para permitir algunas generalizaciones respecto de la migración de jaliscienses originada en zonas rurales y semiurbanas de fuerte rechazo poblacional. Consideramos que dada la rica heterogeneidad en esta área de estudio, puede ser representativa de muchas regiones en el Occidente de México de importancia migratoria hacia Estados Unidos.

CONCLUSIONES

1. La ley de inmigración ha involucrado a una mayor población de las comunidades rurales y semiurbanas motivando un aumento de emigrantes que de otra manera hubieran esperado más tiempo o no habrían podido emigrar.

2. La ley tiende a reforzar las redes y cadenas migratorias.

3. Aparentemente, contrario a lo que se esperaba, no se han experimentado retornos masivos o graduales a los lugares de origen, sino que más personas continúan enmigrando ya sea legalmente o ilegalmente.

4. La oferta de mano de obra de origen mexicano en Estados Unidos puede aumentarse como efecto de la IRCA, particularmente de personas calificadas.

REFERENCIAS

Alba, Francisco (1987), "La Dificil Tarea de la Nueva Ley de Inmigración de Estados Unidos," varios autores, *Foro Internacional*, XVIII (3), El Colegio de México, enero–marzo.

Arroyo, Alejandre J. (1989), "El Abandono Rural," Universidad de Guadalajara, Guadalajara, Jalisco.

Arroyo Alejandre, Jesús, Luis A. Velazquez, Aída Segovia, Mónica Gallegos, Fermina Robles, Salvador Carrillo, y Ramón Ojeda (1988), "Estudio del Subsistema de Ciudades Guadalajara-Ciudad Guzmán-Colina-Manzanillo," Universidad de Guadalajara-CONAPO (en revisión para publicación).

Arroyo Alejandre, Jesús (1986), "Emigración Rural de Fuerza de Trabajo en el Occidente-Centro de México: Una Contribución de Información Básica para su Análisis," *Cuadernos de Difusión Científica No. 6*, Universidad de Guadalajara, Guadalajara, Jalisco.

Arroyo Alejandre, Jesús, y William W. Winnie (1978), "La Migración de los Trabajadores Rurales de Jalisco hacia Estados Unidos," Ponencia presentada en el I Simposium Internacional sobre *los Problemas de los Trabajadores Migratorios de México y los Estados Unidos*, 11–14 julio de 1978 (mimeo.).

Bustamante, Jorge A., y Gerónimo G. Martinez (1979), "Undocumented Immigration from Mexico: Beyond the Border but Within Systems," *Journal of International Affairs*, 33:265–84.

Bustamante, Jorge A. (1987), "La Política de Inmigración de Estados Unidos: Un Análisis de sus Contradicciones," en Gustavo López Castro (ed.), *Migración en el Occidente de México*, El Colegio de Michoacán, México.

CENIET (Centro Nacional de Informacíon y Estadística del Trabajo) (1982), "Los Trabajadores Mexicanos en Estados Unidos. Resultados de la Encuesta Nacional de Emigración a la Frontera Norte del País y a los Estados Unidos," México, D.F.

Colegio de la Frontera Norte (1988), *El Correro Fronterizo*, año III, No. 4, septiembre–octubre, Tijuana, B.C.

Colegio de México (1987), *Foro Internacional*, XXVII (3), enero–marzo.

Consejo Nacional de Poblacíon (CONAPO) (1986), "Encuesta en la Frontera Norte a Trabajadores Indocumentados Devueltos por las Autoridades de los Estados Unidos," diciembre, México, D.F.

Consejo Nacional de Poblacíon e Instituto Nacional de Estadística, Geografía, e Informática (CONAPO-INEGI) (1985), "Proyecciones Estatales de Población," Guadalajara, Jalisco.

Cornelius, Wayne A. (1978), "Mexican Migration to the United States: Causes, Consequences and U.S. Responses," Center for International Studies, MIT, Cambridge, Mass.

Cornelius, Wayne A. (1988a), "Migrants from Mexico Still Coming and Staying," *Los Angeles Times*, domingo, 3 de julio.

Cornelius, Wayne A. (1988), "Implementation and Impacts of the U.S. Immigration Reform and Control Act of 1986: A Comparative Study of Mexican and Asian Immigrants, Their Employers and Sending Communities," San Diego, California.

Cross, Harry A., y James A. Sandos (1981), "Across the Border: Rural Development in Mexico and Recent Migration to the United States," Institute of Governmental Studies, University of California, Berkeley.

Dagodag, W. Tim (1975), "Source Regions and Composition of Illegal Mexican Immigration to California," *International Migration Review*, Vol. 9, No. 4, pp. 499–511.

Diez, Canedo, J. (1984), "La Migración Indocumentada de México a los Estados Unidos, un Nuevo Enfoque," Ed. F.C.E., México.

Gamio, Manuel (1930), *Mexican Immigration to the United States: A Study of Human Migration and Adjustment*, Chicago: University of Chicago Press.

García y Griego, Manuel (1987), "Origenes y Supuestos de la Ley Simpson-Rodino de 1986," *Foro Internacional*, Vol. XXVII, No. 3, enero–marzo de 1987.

162

García y Griego, Manuel, y F. Giner de los Rios (1985), "¿Es Vulnerable la Economía Mexicana a la Aplicación de Políticas Migratorias Estadunidenses?" *México–Estados Unidos, 1984*, El Colegio de México, Colección México–Estados Unidos, México.

INESER (Instituto de Estudios Economicos y Regionales) Arroyo Alejandre, Jesús, Luis A. Velázquez G., y Sergio Camarena (1987), "Guadalajara 2015: Reporte Técnico Prospectivo de la Zona Metropolitana de Guadalajara," Guadalajara, Jalisco (mimeo.).

International Labour Office (1987), *World Labour Report*, 1-2, Oxford University Press.

Massey, D., R. Alarcon, J. Durand, y H. Gonzalez (1987), "Return to Aztlán—The Social Process of International Migration from Western Mexico," University of California Press.

Mines, Richard (1981), "Developing a Community Tradition of Migration: A Field Study in Rural Zacatecas, Mexico and California Settlement Areas," Monographs in U.S.-Mexican Studies.

Mines, Richard (1984), "Network Migration and Mexican Rural Development: A Case Study," *Patterns of Undocumented Migration; Mexico and the United States*, Richard C. Jones, comp., Rowman and Allanheld, Totowa, New Jersey, pp. 136–155.

Population and Development Review (1986), Vol. 12, No. 2, junio.

Rodríguez, Maria (1989), "Los Efectos de la Migración en Cuatro Municipios del Sur de Jalisco," IES-Universidad de Guadalajara (mimeo.).

Taylor, J. Edward (1988), "U.S. Immigration Policy and the Mexican Economy," *Impacts of Immigration in California*, Policy Discussion Paper, The Urban Institute, Washington, D.C.

Taylor, Paul (1933), *A Spanish-Mexican Peasant Community: Arandas in Jalisco, México*, University of California Press, Berkeley.

The Council of Economic Advisors on United States Immigration, *Population and Development Review*, Vol. 12, No. 2, 1986, pp. 361–374.

Winnie, William W., y Adrián de León Arias (1987), "Regiones de Origen en la Migración de Mexicanos a Estados Unidos," Instituto de Estudios Económicos y Regionales, Universidad de Guadalajara, Jalisco (inédito).

Winnie, William W., y Luis Arturo Velázquez (1987), "La Encuesta de Hogares 1986," Universidad de Guadalajara, Jalisco, México.

LA LEY SIMPSON-RODINO: EL PUNTO DE VISTA DE LOS PUEBLOS EXPULSORES[1]

Gustavo López Castro
El Colegio de Michoacán

Sobre las enmiendas a la Ley de Inmigración y Naturalización de los Estados Unidos se ha comentado mucho, sobre todo en cuanto a la aplicación de las enmiendas en las regiones de destino de los inmigrantes mexicanos, y si algo se ha dicho sobre las comunidades que mandan a sus hombres a trabajar al norte es para hablar de los efectos nocivos que tendrá su aplicación en las economias locales. Sin embargo, poco se ha preguntado acerca de las percepciones de las gentes que se han visto acosadas por informaciones televisadas y noticiosas. La manera en que se percibe la aplicación de la Ley Simpson-Rodino (LSR) para llamarla coloquialmente, lo que tiene que ver con la propia familia o con la vida de uno está definida por múltiples mediaciones, entre las cuales me parece que las más importantes son las características históricas y actuales de los flujos migratorios de cada región y aún más, de cada pueblo, pues sabemos que dichos flujos migratorios tienen una gran variedad de elementos que los definen diferencialmente. Para abordar el problema decidimos incluir algunas preguntas sobre el particular en una encuesta que aplicamos en tres pueblos de lo que se conoce como el Bajío del país, Atotonilco el Alto,[2] Jalisco y Purépero, y Cieneguitas, en el estado de Michoacán.[3] El propósito de la encuesta era averiguar acerca de las características generales de los flujos migratorios de cada uno de los lugares con el fin de determinar si existían diferencias sustanciales, y a qué se debían. Con los resultados de las encuestas pudimos observar que a pesar de que la mayoría de la gente tenían información acerca de la LSR, paradójicamente no se tenían elementos suficientes para poder explicar de que se trataba, la mayoría no sabía que hubiera un programa especial para trabajadores agrícolas (SAW) y sólo se manejaba la posibilidad de poder obtener permisos de trabajo en los Estados Unidos.

Como se puede observar en la figura 1, en los tres pueblos estudiados, el porcentaje de las personas que respondieron conocer algo de la LSR es muy alto, ésto es básicamente debido a lo que habían escuchado en los noticieros televisados y radiofónicos, y en otra medida (aproximadamente el 40 por ciento), por lo que escuchaban decir a familiares y amigos, es decir, por lo que se comentaba en el ámbito social que se supone afectado por tales medidas. Al mismo tiempo, la percepción que se tenía del principal propósito de la LSR tiene diferencias en los tres pueblos según como les fue en la feria, es decir, la experiencia socializada de la migración a los Estados Unidos y las posibilidades reales de quienes podían calificar para la amnistía determinaron la visión general de la población respecto a las razones que se tuvieron para ponerla en práctica. En Purépero, donde una gran cantidad de emigrantes pudieron obtener permisos de trabajo temporal, la faceta más conocida e importante de la LSR fue la amnistía o

[1]Documento de debate preparado para la *Conferencia sobre los Efectos Internacionales de las Reformas a la Ley de Inmigración de los Estados Unidos*, The RAND Corporation y The Urban Institute, Guadalajara, Jalisco, mayo 3–5 de 1989.

[2]En realidad, Atotonilco estaria en la frontera entre los Altos de Jalisco y el Bajío propiamente dicho, aunque una parte de su economia estaria ligada a la producción de sorgo para los puercos de algunas zonas del Bajío y un poco de menos con los Altos.

[3]La encuesta mencionada se realizó en el verano–otoño de 1988, en tres pueblos del occidente del país con características diferentes en cuanto a sus actividades económicas principales, situación ambiental y ubicación geográfica, pero con una larga tradición migratoria a los Estados Unidos. Para ésta trabajo se contó con financiamiento del Conacyt, El Colegio de Michoacán y el programa de becas C. B. Smith, Sr., de la Universidad de Texas en Austin, a quienes agradezco su apoyo.

legalización de los indocumentados. La posesión de la mica es un ansia diferencial en los pueblos según sea que se trate de un documento indispensable para conseguir trabajo o no lo sea. En Purépero, donde una gran parte de los emigrantes posean su *tarjeta verde* de residencia en los Estados Unidos, tenerla significa la posibilidad de tener acceso a trabajos agrícolas y no agrícolas casi en cualquier región de aquel país, sobre todo cuando se emigra a las áreas metropolitanas de Chicago o Nueva York, donde el viaje aéreo es obligado. En cambio, el aspecto coercitivo de la ley fue privilegiado en Cieneguitas donde la mayor parte de los emigrantes son indocumentados y se sienten más vulnerables a los avatares de lo que no pueden controlar.

La mayor atención se concentró en estos dos aspectos de la LSR: la amnistía y el control. Sólo un 10 por ciento de los respondientes de Atotonilco y Purépero adujeron ambas razones como el propósito principal de la ley: "La ley Rodino mentada es nomás para tratar de acabar con los ilegales y que arreglen los que tengan cierto récord." Sin embargo es de hacer notar que el 44.6 por ciento de todas las respuestas son en el sentido de que la LSR es solamente un intento de control de la migración de indocumentados a los Estados Unidos. Asimismo, no deja de haber respuestas sugestivas en torno a un posible tinte de racismo y de sentimiento de despojo y ultraje en alguna de ellas, por ejemplo:

- Es una ley para quitarle el trabajo a los mexicanos ilegales y para pagarles menos a los emigrados.
- Es puro negocio del gobierno norteamericano para explotar más a los latinos.
- Es una ley para fregar a los ilegales y ayudar a los gringos.
- Es para echar [fuera] a los mexicanos y darles sus trabajos a los gringos.
- Es una ley que quiere beneficiar a los gringos y ponerlos en contra de los mexicanos.

Esta encuesta fue aplicada a emigrantes de los pueblos señalados así que saben de lo que hablan, o por lo menos es parte de su experiencia como trabajadores en los Estados Unidos.

Un mensaje importante que se manejó como efecto también importante de la LSR es que podría desalentar la inmigración de trabajadores indocumentados al hacer más difícil el encontrar empleo vía la sanción a los patrones; sin embargo ésto aún no se percibe así en los pueblos expulsores. En la figura 3 se puede observar que en total, el 46 por ciento respondío que a pesar de la ley intentaría pasar la frontera sin documentos a principios de éste año. La mayor diferencia entre los pueblos está en Cieneguitas donde el 67.8 por ciento respondió que se jugaría el albur de pasar sin papeles; también es el pueblo que tiene una mayor cantidad de inmigrantes sin documentos en su flujo migratorio.

Por otra parte, debido a que tal parece que las cosas no han cambiado, al menos como se le percibe en los pueblos expulsores, una gran parte de los entrevistados (88 por ciento) contestó que la LSR no los ha afectado; el restante (12 por ciento) respondió más bien en relación al temor de lo que podrá pasar en los próximos años. Uno de los temores más persistente está relacionado con el incremento de los precios de los *coyotes* y los papeles *chuecos*.

La utilidad de la LSR con respecto a sus objetivos percibidos es también un tema muy interesante. Para quienes consideran que el propósito fundamental de la LSR es la amnistía, la utilidad de la misma es a ojos vistas cabalmente cumplida; lo que se puede observar es que se dieron muchos permisos de residencia temporal y muchos indocumentados pudieron arreglar de una u otra forma su estatus legal. Asimismo se percibe como una manera de mantener los salarios en su nivel normal, "si hay mucha gente [buscando trabajo], pagan poco." Otros entrevistados se muestran más recelos acerca de que la LSR pueda servir de algo, debido a que en su vida como emigrantes internacionales han visto transcurrir muchas enmiendas y propuestas de reformas a la Ley de Inmigración de Estados Unidos; "otras no han resultado"; "de cualquíer manera se va a ir la gente"; "el nuevo presidente llega y entierra esas leyes"; "todo va a seguir igual, los mexicanos somos gente aventada."

En fin, la Ley Simpson-Rodino, hasta ahora, se percibe en los pueblos expulsores según las circunstancias históricas del desarrollo de la migración en ellos y según la experiencia cotidiana de los propios emigrantes; con la sabiduría popular que se acumula generacionalmente, hace poco me dijo uno de mis informantes que la LSR es mucho ruido y pocas nueces, lo que resume un pocas palabras el sentir de la población general.

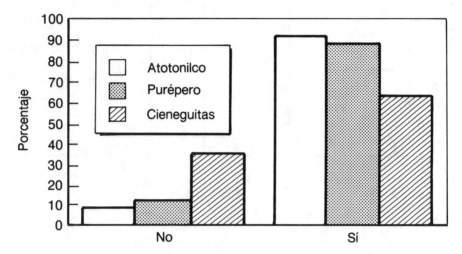

FUENTE: Encuesta efectuada por el autor.

Fig. 1—Conocimiento de la Ley Simpson-Rodino en tres pueblos del Bajío, 1988

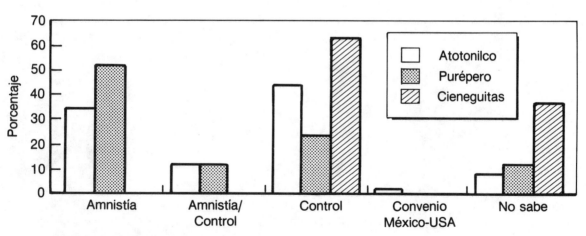

FUENTE: Encuesta efectuada por el autor.

Fig. 2—Percepción del propósito principal de la
Ley Simpson-Rodino en tres pueblos del Bajío, 1988

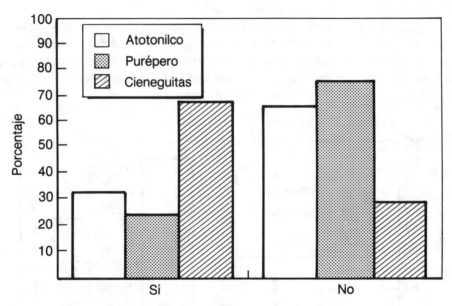

FUENTE: Encuesta efectuada por el autor.

Fig. 3—Porcentaje de quienes piensan ir a trabajar sin documentos a los
Estados Unidos a pesar de la Ley Simpson-Rodino, 1988

UNITED STATES–CARIBBEAN IMMIGRATION RELATIONS

Anthony P. Maingot
Florida International University

INTRODUCTION

It should come as no surprise that the thrust of the Immigration Reform and Control Act (IRCA) of 1986 should have been aimed at illegal immigration. The legislation attempts to deal with that hot political issue by imposing civil and criminal penalties on employers who knowingly hire undocumented workers. Typically, there was also "heart" in the legislation: Amnesty was offered to potentially millions of undocumented immigrants who had entered the United States before 1982.

With this legislation, the United States put itself in line with every major industrial country, all of which have, with different degrees of effectiveness, enacted employment prohibition laws.[1]

This paper discusses how IRCA might affect U.S.-English-speaking Caribbean relations in immigration matters and generally. It addresses these issues by analyzing areas important to understanding U.S.-Caribbean immigration relations: (1) relevant demographic trends; (2) the history and "structure" of Caribbean migration, and the dimensions and nature of known undocumented migration; and (3) specific problem areas.

RELEVANT SOCIAL AND DEMOGRAPHIC TRENDS

Taken as a whole, the Caribbean Basin has experienced one of the fastest population growth rates in history: from 55 million in 1940 to 166 million in 1980. This translates into an annual growth rate of 3 percent for four decades. The explanation lies not so much in increasing birth rates as in declining mortality rates, what demographers call the "death dearth." Improved standards of health account for much of this change. This has been especially true for the West Indies societies.[2]

The insular Caribbean has grown much more slowly than have Mexico and Central America. In 1936 Mexico had 36 percent of the Caribbean Basin's population size; this rose to over 42 percent by 1980. By contrast, during these years the proportion of the insular Caribbean fell from 25 percent to 18.5 percent of the total Caribbean Basin. As the data in Table 1 illustrate, the specific share of the West Indies is expected to drop from the present 4.15 percent of the total Caribbean Basin population to 3.3 percent by the year 2000. On some islands, populations are projected to actually decrease.

One explanation is the increased use of birth control methods. In Trinidad, 52 percent of women of childbearing age use contraception; in Jamaica the figure is 51 percent. Another part of the explanation, however, lies in the fact that emigration trends are calculated into projections; for example, most West Indian development scenarios are calculated according to

---

[1]U.S. Government Accounting Office, "Illegal Aliens: Information on Selected Countries' Employment Prohibition Laws," Washington, D.C., October 1985.

[2]Leon Bouvier and David Simcox, *Many Hands, Few Jobs*, Center for Immigration Studies, Staten Island, New York, CIS Paper 2, November 1986, p. 14.

Table 1

POPULATION PROJECTIONS FOR THE CARIBBEAN, MEXICO AND CENTRAL AMERICA,
AND THE WEST INDIES

Location	1985	2000	2025
Caribbean Basin[a]	133,690	185,971	—
Mexico and Central America	104,935	148,838	222,274
Insular Caribbean	28,755	37,133	53,195
West Indies[b]	5,554	6,135	—
Antigua/Barbuda	81	101	—
Bahamas	234	—	—
Barbados	253	260	—
Belize	169	215	—
Dominica	78	81	—
Grenada	102	98	—
Guyana	794	795	—
Jamaica	2,336	2,800	—
Montserrat	11.9	12	—
St. Kitts-Nevis	46	44	—
St. Lucia	139	128	—
St. Vincent/Grenadines	111	108	—
Trinidad/Tobago	1,199	1,259	—

[a]The World Bank, *World Development Report, 1986* (New York: Oxford University Press), 1986.

[b]Commonwealth Secretariat, *Caribbean Development to the Year 2000*, Summary Report, London, May 1988.

projections of migratory flows. The joint Commonwealth Secretariat and Caribbean Community Secretariat study of the Caribbean in the year 2000 is no exception. The dramatic impact of emigration flows on the rate of job creation is described in that study (see Table 2). Case "A" indicates the increase in the supply of jobs that the study believes will be necessary to reach full employment if emigration is eliminated. Case "B" shows the increase necessary to keep 1980 employment rates if emigration rates remain at the 1980 level.

Without calculating in emigration rates, it is evident that the growth rate of the labor force will be substantial, as Table 3 illustrates. It is difficult, indeed, to conceive of the economies of these countries—given their present structure—generating that many new jobs over the next decade.

Accompanying this increase in the labor force will be a qualitative change in the demographic and economic composition of the West Indies population: Urbanization is, and will continue to be, a dominant trend.

The annual rural growth rate will have decreased from 1.35 percent in the 1950–1960 decade to 0.71 percent during 1980–1990. The urban growth rate, on the other hand, will have risen from 2.93 percent in the decade of the 1950s to 3.18 percent during 1980–1990.[3]

The result is that an area already 54 percent urban will become even more so, some countries faster than others. Jamaica, for instance, already 78 percent urban, will experience a phenomenal 7.1 percent annual urban growth rate.

---

[3]Kempe Ronald Hope, *Urbanization in the Commonwealth Caribbean* (Boulder: Westview Press), 1986, p. 40.

Table 2

LABOR FORCE PROJECTIONS FOR THE YEAR 2000

Country	Case A[a]		Case B[b]	
	No. of Workers (In thousands)	Increase from 1980 Needed for Full Employment (In percent)	No. of Workers (In thousands)	Increase from 1980 Needed to Maintain 1980 Employment Rate (In percent)
Barbados	129	33	115	18
Belize	103	157	62	54
Dominica	41	93	29	38
Grenada	49	85	34	29
Guyana	405	115	235	25
Montserrat	6	43	5	23
St. Kitts-Nevis	22	54	18	23
St. Lucia	65	101	45	40
St. Vincent/ Grenadines	54	106	36	37
Trinidad/Tobago	624	93	43 [sic]	34

SOURCE: Commonwealth Secretariat, *Caribbean Development*, p. 11.
[a]Worker emigration not calculated into projection.
[b]Worker emigration rate held at 1980 level for calculations.

Table 3

GROWTH (IN THOUSANDS) AND AVERAGE ANNUAL GROWTH RATE (IN PERCENT) OF SELECT WEST INDIES LABOR FORCES, 1960–2000

Country	1965	1970	1975	1980	1985	1990	1995	2000
Barbados	89	90	98	107	115	125	133	143
	—	0.31%	1.67%	1.81%	1.44%	1.58%	1.41%	1.43%
Guyana	187	204	242	288	341	391	442	493
	—	1.73%	3.48%	3.50%	3.43%	2.91%	2.68%	2.48%
Jamaica	630	636	672	749	858	966	1,071	1,171
	—	0.18%	1.10%	2.21%	2.75%	2.48%	2.27%	2.07%
Trinidad/ Tobago	285	314	354	403	453	495	533	568
	—	1.92%	2.41%	2.63%	2.37%	1.87%	1.60%	1.38%
Total	1,191	1,244	1,366	1,547	1,767	1,977	2,179	2,375

SOURCE: International Labor Organization, *Labour Force Estimates and Projections, 1950–2000* (Geneva: ILO), 1977.

Can these societies provide jobs in the cities for these new hands, and even if they come close to doing so, can they keep these mobile, urban, and urbane people at home?

The history and "structure" of Caribbean migration to the United States tend to indicate that even if economic growth generates substantial numbers of new jobs, Caribbean people will probably still migrate. Six specific features of this migration appear to be important.

SIX STRUCTURAL FEATURES OF CARIBBEAN MIGRATION

It is calculated that during the late 1970s and early 1980s some 80 percent of all immigrants to the United States came from Latin America and Asia. Proportionally, however, the nations of the Caribbean Basin provided the largest share. Korea, with 41 million people, sent 29,248 immigrants to the United States in 1979; the nations of the Caribbean Basin (excluding Mexico, Venezuela, and Colombia) represent 39 million people but sent 92,000 legal immigrants to the United States that same year. Another way of putting it is that Korea sent on average 711 per million, the average for Europe was 125 per million, but the Caribbean Basin sent about 1,150 per million, a much higher proportion than that from Asia or Europe. While the European share of total legal immigrants fell from 59 percent in 1951–1960 to 19 percent in 1971–1980, the West Indies share climbed from 5 percent to 18 percent. The Haitian share, specifically, went from 0.7 percent in 1957–1961 to 3.6 percent in 1967–1971 and then down to 3 percent in 1972–1976.[4]

Evidently, the more vicious aspects of the racial bias that characterized so much U.S. immigration policy up to 1965 have abated visibly, and other less desirable legacies also appear today to be in fast retreat. Caribbean people visit the United States in truly extraordinary numbers, demonstrating voluntarily a preference for it over other possible destinations.[5]

It is good to remember, however, that despite past racial bias and the current increase in numbers of Caribbean immigrants, the movement has a long history. It takes time for any such movement to assume the structural features that Caribbean migration has today. We can identify six important dimensions—five are best characterized as giving shape to a "pull" syndrome, while the sixth points to the nature of the Caribbean immigrant.

(1) The Caribbean is a self-contained geographical space. No major mountain barriers or unmanageable bodies of water separate potential migrants from their North American destinations. Even the Caribbean Sea flows like a river from south to north as do the constant winds that are part of this stream. Historically, when and where Caribbean man and woman could not walk to their destination they rowed or sailed to it. That they still do is evident in the recent astonishing trek of a Haitian sailboat through the Bahamas to Florida and, even more improbably, as far as Guadeloupe. The Haitian case is particularly poignant. Despite an active interdiction program enacted in September 1981 by the U.S. Coast Guard, Haitians keep attempting the perilous crossing.

(2) Movement to the United States tends to be preceded by earlier moves, often to sites of U.S.-financed or managed job opportunities. For instance, the building of the Panama Canal drew large numbers of West Indians to that site. From Barbados alone 20,000 men were recruited, which was 10 percent of the island population and 40 percent of all adult males.[6] But as David McCullough writes, "For every man who was picked to go to Panama there were five or more others eager for the chance."[7] From Panama they moved to work in American-owned banana plantations and build British- or American-owned railroads in the rest of Central America. West Indians also worked on U.S.-owned plantations in Cuba and the Dominican

---

[4]U.S. Immigration and Naturalization Service, Statistical Analysis Branch, 1988.

[5]In 1986 there were 147,487 visitor visas issued to Jamaicans, 72,583 to Trinidadians, 69,514 to the Dominican Republic. The Bahamas, with a population of 230,000, sent 225,000 visitors to the United States.

[6]By the 1970s Barbados' Crude Emigration Rate (emigration as a percent of native-born inhabitants) to just the United States and Canada continued to be 10.5 percent despite a zero population growth rate.

[7]David McCullough, *The Path Between the Seas* (New York: Simon and Schuster), 1977, p. 475.

Republic.[8] It is an interesting footnote to the story of Caribbean migration that three of the significant protagonists of Grenadian politics in the 1960s, 1970s, and 1980s (Eric Gairy, Maurice Bishop, and Herbert Blaize) all either worked at the same time in Aruba's U.S.-owned oil refinery or grew up in Aruba. The man accused of murdering Bishop, Bernard Coard, is a graduate of Brandeis University.

This historical experience of West Indians with migration and with U.S. capital and business abroad created three additional characteristics, critical for an understanding of the "structural" nature of Caribbean migration:

(a) The very nature of the "open," export-oriented economies of the area familiarized Caribbean people with alien—especially American—people and customs. Even the lamentable expansionism and military interventions in the Caribbean, which have resulted in strongly negative ideological legacies and reverberations, have ironically also generated contacts and familiarity. It is a Caribbean-wide fact that the often virulent anti-Americanism of the intellectuals is rarely shared wholeheartedly by the majority and certainly not by the skilled workers and middle classes who are unambiguous in their preference for the United States as a destination. In the 1970s, between 60 percent and 70 percent of the Caribbean emigrants were professionals, managers, and skilled workers. The dramatic flight of nearly 11 percent of the Cuban population might well be repeated in the Nicaraguan case.

(b) A general attitude exists that migrating is the best avenue for success and that exercising such an option is a "right." There was and is today group approval for individual decisions to migrate and group expectations about remittances and future sponsorships of others. The so-called "guilt of abandonment" that sociologists hypothesize about is nonexistent in the Caribbean.

It makes no sense for Caribbean governments to ridicule or lament the "visa mentality" of their people, much less attempt to curtail its exercise. This was a lesson learned by some of the more totalitarian-minded of the PRG (People's Revolutionary Government) in Grenada, who toyed briefly with the idea of restricting immigration by creating a Cuban-style "army of work." The public's response quickly disabused them of any such plans.

(c) Because Caribbean migration is relatively old, there exist—in Miami and other regions—in the 1980s the necessary social-cultural enclaves and networks that attract others and facilitate their entry and success. These were built either directly in the United States or in the intermediate, U.S.-controlled areas in the Caribbean. As important as these latter "stepping stone" migration areas to the United States were, there was of course a significant direct movement from the West Indies to the United States, and this despite the racially biased immigration system in operation in the 1900–1910 period. During that decade, 30,000 arrived; in 1910–1920, some 60,000; and during the 1920s an additional 40,000. By 1930 West Indian blacks were about 1 percent of the U.S. black population and about 25 percent of the population of Harlem.

The presence of such "critical masses" was both the cause and effect of the third structural feature of Caribbean migration.

---

[8]José del Castillo found that in the 1920s British West Indians were second only to Haitians in the Dominican sugar estates (*La Inmigración de Braceros . . . 1900–1930*, Santo Domingo: Cuadernos del ENDIA, No. 7).

(3) Caribbean men and women have successfully assimilated. Thomas Sowell notes that as early as 1901, West Indians owned 20 percent of the black businesses in Manhattan and were represented beyond their numbers in the professions, and that second-generation West Indians have higher incomes than U.S. blacks and whites and have below-average unemployment rates. They also have lower rates of fertility and crime than either black or white Americans. Sowell's explanation that "West Indians were much more frugal, hard working and entrepreneurial" and that "their children worked harder and out-performed native black children in school"[9] describes many other immigrant groups.

The Harlem story has parallels all over the United States. For example, in Miami immigrant success stories are well known, as demonstrated by the success of more recent Caribbean migrants: Cubans and Haitians.[10] The important point is that these success stories tend to have two effects: They act as powerful incentives to the immigrant's fellow countrymen to move to the United States, and they propagate a favorable image of the immigrant in the host country. Assimilative capacity interacts positively with host society absorbability. It has been a positively reinforcing cycle in Caribbean migration.

(4) Ethnicity has a continuing role in international relations, both in official policy as well as in what is today known as transnational forces, i.e., forces that operate independently from official or governmental actions.

This is one of the most difficult areas to analyze. Although we are dealing on the one hand with attitudes and perceptions as realities, on the other hand there can be no doubt that official policy formulation continues to be important. It is evident, for instance, that the 1965 changes in immigration law were strongly influenced by the ideas of Lyndon Johnson's Great Society, which in turn had been influenced by the civil rights movement. American blacks forged the link between their gains in civil rights and the rights of foreign blacks to equal access to U.S. residence through immigration reform. This tendency to link foreign policy with immigration policy continues.

Regarding Florida, two fundamental aspects of that linkage deserve attention. The first aspect deals with race as it relates to internal U.S. politics. Caribbean migrants (both black and white) have been quick to recognize that while immigration is a *secular* issue in this society, race and ethnic matters are also, and very much so, *moral* issues. Even before they become citizens, immigrants learn the value of ethnic bargaining; they have made great strides in their own behalf through the use of U.S. laws generally and the civil rights movement specifically.[11]

It is important that the Caribbean Basin is predominantly black, mestizo, or mixed. Race and ethnicity will continue to play an important role in international politics and therefore also in U.S. thinking and actions on immigration policy.

The second aspect is geopolitical. The Caribbean Basin has been a traditional U.S. sphere of influence in which particular responsibilities and obligations transcend issues of immigration. The point is, of course, that these obligations have direct effects on immigration policy. Whether the immigrants are Cuban, Haitian, or Nicaraguan, the decision as to whether

---

[9]Thomas Sowell, *Ethnic America* (New York: Basic Books), 1981, p. 219.

[10]Alex Stepick says, "The Haitian business community has self-consciously attempted to repeat the earlier successes of the Cuban immigrant entrepreneurs." See *Haitians Released from Krome: Their Prospects for Adaptation and Integration in South Florida*, Dialogue Series No. 24, Latin America and Caribbean Center, Florida International University, Miami, Florida, 1984.

[11]Anthony P. Maingot, *Ethnic Bargaining and the Non-Citizen: Haitians and Cubans in Miami*, Report to the U.S. Coordinator of Refugee Affairs, Miami, Florida, 1981; also by Maingot on this subject, "Ideology, Politics, and Citizenship in the American Debate on Immigration Policy: Beyond Consensus," in Mary M. Kritz (ed.), *U.S. Immigration and Refugee Policy* (Lexington, Mass.: Lexington Books, D.C. Heath & Co.), 1982, pp. 361–379.

they are immigrants or refugees is never removed from political and geopolitical considerations.[12] Geopolitical considerations made by the federal government are particularly tricky for local governments; they suffer the consequences if the decisions go awry.

(5) The fifth characteristic of Caribbean migration is less permanent than the previous four but appears to have become enough of a part of U.S. thinking on immigration to be considered structural: In the United States both pragmatism and sentiment seem to provide strong and enduring support to the principle of family reunification as one of the centerpieces of immigration law. Family reunification takes on a mathematical dimension when we observe that the number of Caribbean people already in the legal immigration pipeline in the mid-1980s was substantial: 438,841 in all seven preference categories in 1982. Again, we note the demand from the West Indies by observing that the Hispanic Caribbean, with 32 times more people than the insular Caribbean, has less than 5 times its active visa applicants. Of course, this can change because of geopolitics or economic collapse in Central America. Be that as it may, the number of applicants under Preference 2 (spouses and unmarried sons and daughters of permanent residents) and Preference 5 (brothers and sisters of U.S. citizens) is a good indication of the strength of both the immediate and extended Caribbean family systems. This strength becomes part of the "structure" through its contribution to Caribbean networks, immigration success, and sense of "right" to migrate.[13]

These five features, therefore, are parts of a "pull" syndrome; they are mutually reinforcing, gaining strength as they interact over time. The sixth feature tells us something about the nature of the immigrant, specifically, that he or she has traditionally come to the United States through legal means.

(6) It is a critical aspect that these large numbers represent legal migrants, carefully screened by U.S. consular agents on each island. The available evidence indicates that illegal entry and staying over make up a relatively small part of the West Indian movement to the United States.

Although extremely difficult to assess, the numbers of illegals can be somewhat approximated. One way is to look at illegals in the 1980 U.S. Census figures. Estimates on the high side are those of Passell and Woodrow, who figure that Haitians, Jamaicans, and Trinidadians were 4.9 percent of all illegals counted in the 1980 census.[14] The U.S. General Accounting Office (GAO), on the other hand, placed the figure for that three-nation group at 2 percent.[15] If we agree that Haitians are probably the largest number in that group, we have an approximate sense of the West Indian numbers (see Table 4).

Another window is provided by the statistics on legalization applications under the provisions of the U.S. Immigration Reform and Control Act of 1986. Table 5 shows the comparatively small numbers of West Indians seeking amnesty as of May 20, 1988. The total from Jamaica (15,100) was equal to the legal migration to the United States from that island in 1970

---

[12]On the effects on international relations generally, see Myron Weiner, "On International Migration and International Relations," *Population and Development Review*, Vol. II, No. 3 (September 1965), pp. 441–455; on the refugee issue, see Michael S. Teitelbaum, "Immigration, Refugees and Foreign Policy," *International Organization*, Vol. 38, No. 3 (Summer 1983), pp. 431–449.

[13]It is interesting to see the spirited West Indian defense of the guest-worker program (H-2) in operation since 1942 and today hiring some 16,000 British West Indians to cut Florida sugar cane and pick New England apples. The program is generally regarded as "legitimately" West Indian just as Mexicans regard movement to the United States as historically legitimate.

[14]Jeffery Passell and Karen A. Woodrow, *Geographic Distribution of Undocumented Immigrants: Estimates of the Undocumented Aliens Counted in the 1980 Census by State*, U.S. Bureau of the Census, Population Division, Washington, D.C., Paper presented at the Annual Meeting of the Population Association of America, Minneapolis, Minn., May 3–5, 1984.

[15]U.S. Government Accounting Office, "Illegal Aliens," GAO-PEMD-86-9BR, Washington, D.C., April 1986, p. 7.

Table 4

ESTIMATES OF ILLEGAL ALIENS FROM HAITI, JAMAICA, AND TRINIDAD/TOBAGO,
IN SEVEN STATES

States	No. from Haiti, Trinidad/Tobago, Jamaica[a]	Legalization Applications I-678 and I-700[b]				
		Total Applications	No. Haitians	Percent Haitians	No. Jamaicans[c]	Percent Jamaicans
California	3,000	513,486	45	—	105	—
Florida	6,000	74,482	28,526	38.3	4,672	6.3
Illinois	2,000	50,634	81	0.2	61	0.1
Massachusetts	3,000	4,233	949	22.4	100	2.4
New Jersey	4,000	10,596	749	7.1	233	2.2
New York	70,000	49,781	4,637	9.3	2,337	4.7
Texas	1,000	146,468	18	—	109	—

[a]J. S. Passel and K. A. Woodrow, *Geographic Distribution of Undocumented Aliens Counted in the 1980 Census by State* (Washington, D.C.: Population Division, Census Bureau), 1984.

[b]U.S. Immigration and Naturalization Service, Statistical Analysis Branch, 1988.

[c]The only West Indian group listed.

alone (15,003). Even these illegals seem to have done well: Those seeking legalization under I-687 (in the United States prior to 1982) were mostly employed or students. Only a very small minority were listed as "unemployed or retired." However, there are yet some worrisome trends that can create serious problems for U.S.-Caribbean immigration relations.

POTENTIAL PROBLEMS

Generally speaking, one can conclude that West Indian migration to the United States has largely and historically been legal and productive. This puts West Indian claims to a disproportionate number of immigrant visas in a good light. Their sterling reputation has helped the bargaining that they, like other ethnic groups, partake in and that is an integral part of U.S. immigration policy.

This historical advantage gained from projecting a favorable "image" is being placed at risk by two problems that are making themselves all too evident. The first is the increasing awareness and concern in the Caribbean with the "brain drain."

To be sure, loss of talent is not a new phenomenon in the West Indies. Between 1962 and 1968, Trinidad lost 143 doctors and dentists, 170 engineers, 629 nurses, 784 teachers, and 909 other professionals, most in the productive 20- to 34-year age group.[16] Caribbean states are beginning to feel the pinch as the increasing loss of talent inhibits their development plans. Although there is really little West Indians can do to stem this tide, their increasing concern can become a source of friction with the U.S. government.

---

[16]*The Emigration of Professions, Supervisory, Middle Level and Skilled Man-Power from Trinidad-Tobago, 1962–1968*, Government Printing Office, Port-of-Spain, Trinidad/Tobago, 1970.

Table 5

ESTIMATES OF LEGALIZATION APPLICATIONS I-687 AND I-700
BY SELECT COUNTRY

Country[a]	No. of Applications	Percent of Total	No. of I-687	Percent of Total I-687	No. of I-700	Percent of Total I-700
Mexico	1,581,800	73.0	1,138,400	71.1	443,400	81.3
Haiti	50,400	2.3	16,800	1.0	33,700	6.2
Dominican Republic	24,700	0.7	13,100	0.8	1,600	0.3
Jamaica	15,100	0.7	10,800	0.7	4,300	0.8
Belize	4,900	0.2	4,900	0.3	100	—
Guyana	3,400	0.2	2,800	0.2	600	0.1
Trinidad/Tobago	2,900	0.1	2,500	0.2	400	0.1
Bahamas	2,100	0.1	2,000	0.1	100	—
Antigua/Barbuda	1,300	0.1	1,300	0.1	—	—
Barbados	1,000	—	900	0.1	100	—
Grenada	1,000	—	900	0.1	100	—
St. Vincent/ Grenadines	800	—	700	—	—	—
Dominica	600	—	500	—	100	—
St. Kitts-Nevis	600	—	500	—	100	—
St. Lucia	500	—	500	—	—	—

SOURCE: U.S. Immigration and Naturalization Service, "Provisional Legalization Application Statistics," Statistical Analysis Branch, May 20, 1988.

[a]Ordered by number of applications.

This trend, however, is not the most potentially damaging trend in the area. Criminality is.

The rise in criminality among some West Indian residents, evident in the rise of the Jamaican "posses" and "yardies," is a recent phenomenon tied directly to the increase in U.S. drug trade. Jamaicans, for instance, are now part of a much wider group of criminal aliens operating in the United States.[17]

John Shaw, Assistant Commissioner for Investigations, U.S. Immigration and Naturalization Service (INS), recently testified that "the large percentage of narcotics violators who are aliens moves the Immigration and Naturalization Service squarely into the narcotics enforcement area."[18] In fact, Shaw continued, two major pieces of legislation in 1986—the Anti-Drug-Abuse Act and the U.S. Immigration Reform and Control Act—thrust the INS "into the spotlight." Discussing the new ethnic groups that were forming themselves into criminal organizations, Shaw noted that they were "no different than traditional criminal organizations in their techniques or modes of operation."[19] He paid particular attention to one of the newest organized groups: the Haitians. Others have also noted the Haitian Connection.[20]

[17]U.S. General Accounting Office, "Criminal Aliens," GAO/GGD-86-56 BR, Washington, D.C., March 1986.

[18]"Haitian Narcotics Activities," Hearing, Caucus on International Narcotics Control, U.S. Senate, 100th Congress, May 21, 1988 (Washington, D.C.: Government Printing Office), 1988, p. 31.

[19]Ibid., p. 32.

[20]See, for example, Maureen Taft-Morales, "Haiti: Political Developments and U.S. Policy Options," Congressional Research Service (CRS) Issue Briefs (Washington, D.C.: CRS), March 14, 1989.

Fraud is another dimension of the problem. The evidence of the surge of criminality comes not only from U.S. police records but also in the number of illegal immigration schemes revealing themselves throughout the Caribbean. In Jamaica, fraudulent U.S. immigration visas are known to cost an average $10,000 Jamaican,[21] in Trinidad up to $5,000 U.S., and in Haiti the recent assassination of the head of airport security has been linked to his interference in a ring peddling fraudulent U.S. visas and passports.[22] The danger is that the historical and quite universal tendency to try to bluff or mislead local and U.S. immigration officials will be turned into a full-fledged criminal industry controlled by syndicates. The propensity to use fraud seems, if anything, to be spreading to otherwise law-abiding citizens. Examples are the large numbers of Jamaicans and especially Trinidadians who have recently been claiming "refugee" status in Canada, an outrageous claim given the human rights records of their countries.

Under section 212 (a) (23) of the Immigration and Nationality Act, U.S. Consul officials can deny visas to applicants suspected of being drug traffickers. Those suspected of *facilitating* drug traffickers, however, are not covered. Many Caribbean government officials and bankers involved in laundering money or turning a blind eye to other aspects of the drug trade regularly obtain U.S. visas.

The increase in such illegal activities has led to calls in the United States for a tightening of the visa-granting process. Note the following recommendation made by a Staff Task Force to the House Committee on Foreign Affairs:

> U.S. visa laws need to be changed to permit denial of visas to foreigners who are facilitators or money-launderers for drug traffickers. Current law does not specifically grant consular officers authority to deny visas on these grounds; thus, they are forced to grant visas to corrupt officials and other persons. Section 212 (a) (23) of the Immigration and Nationality Act should be updated to cover these offenses.[23]

Given the economic direction most Caribbean states have decided to take—services and free trade and manufacturing zones—an immigration atmosphere charged with suspicions and, consequently, barriers, could be very detrimental. International offshore banking and offshore manufacturing and transshipping all require open relations, movements, and communications.[24]

The irony of the present situation in the Caribbean is that it is precisely the openness, the cultural affinity, and the technical skills cultivated by contacts across the Caribbean and over a very long period that provide criminals with a transnational advantage. The illegal minority threatens the traditional good relations that generations of Caribbean migrants have helped shape.

What West Indians hope for is that the United States will be able to control the drug trade situation and deal with the minority who operate outside the law before the minority changes the climate of migration from the Caribbean. Migration is too vital to Caribbean/ West Indian development to allow a minority criminal element to destroy the preferential treatment Caribbean peoples presently receive.

---

[21]*The Jamaican Weekly Gleaner*, October 24, 1988, p. 12.

[22]*The Miami Herald*, November 12, 1988, p. 5A. In October and early November 1988, the INS was reported to be returning 20 Haitians per flight from Haiti because of fraudulent documents (*The Miami Herald*, November 21, 1988, p. 6).

[23]"U.S. Narcotics Control Efforts in the Caribbean," Report of a Staff Study Mission to the Committee on Foreign Affairs, U.S. House of Representatives (Washington, D.C.: Government Printing Office), December 1987, p. 2.

[24]Anthony P. Maingot, "The Drug Threat to Caribbean Nations" (Washington, D.C.: Congressional Research Service), April 26, 1989.

CHANGING THE RULES: THE IMPACT OF THE SIMPSON/RODINO ACT ON INTER-AMERICAN DIPLOMACY

Christopher Mitchell
New York University

Analysts of migration patterns are paying increasing attention to the role of the sending or receiving nation in shaping international population movements. It is less and less tenable to picture these national governments as simple bystanders and observers of a fundamentally *social* migration drama. Scholars are noting (1) the impact of entrance and exit rules upon population flows and (2) the tendencies of nation-states to use migration as an instrument in international dealings.[1] They are analyzing the countries' long-term influence on migration's role in the international political economy,[2] as well as how the conflicts of nation formation may generate and manipulate refugee flows.[3] Furthermore, they are exploring cases in which nation-to-nation bargaining has structured or even controlled international movements of people.[4]

One region in which the effect of national governments on international migration has grown and become better recognized during the past decade includes the Caribbean, Central America, and Mexico. As population flows from this area to the United States have increased in size, socioeconomic importance, and public recognition, both the United States and sending-nation governments have negotiated, lobbied, and revised their migration policies, hoping to gain advantage or mitigate damage from migration trends.[5] This paper will analyze the part taken thus far in these changes by a United States international initiative that happened to take the form of a legislative enactment: the Immigration Reform and Control Act of 1986 (also known as IRCA or the Simpson/Rodino Act, after its chief Congressional sponsors). This new legislation provided for (1) penalties against U.S. employers who hire undocumented aliens, (2) legalization of most aliens who had remained in the United States in violation of immigration law for more than five years, and (3) a more liberal "status adjustment" program for workers in certain segments of U.S. agriculture. Employment of undocumented workers

---

[1]On the first point, see Myron Weiner, "On International Migration and International Relations," *Population and Development Review*, Vol. 11, No. 3, 1985; and Alan Dowty, *Closed Borders: The Contemporary Assault on the Freedom of Movement* (New Haven: Yale University Press), 1987, which stresses the evolution of exit rules. On the second point, see esp. Michael Teitelbaum, "Immigration, Refugees and Foreign Policy," *International Organization*, Vol. 38, No. 4, 1984.

[2]Alejandro Portes and John Walton, *Labor, Class, and the International System* (New York: Academic Press), 1981; also see Robert L. Bach, "Political Frameworks for International Migration," in Steven E. Sanderson (ed.), *The Americas in the New International Division of Labor* (New York: Holmes and Meier), 1985.

[3]Aristide Zolberg, Astri Suhrke, and Sergio Aguayo, "International Factors in the Formation of Refugee Movements," *International Migration Review*, Vol. 20, No. 2, 1986; also Zolberg, Suhrke, and Aguayo, *Escape from Violence: The Refugee Crisis in the Developing World* (New York: Oxford University Press), 1989.

[4]Christopher Mitchell, "International Migration, International Relations and Foreign Policy," *International Migration Review*, Vol. 23, No. 3, 1989.

[5]Christopher Mitchell et al., *Immigration Policy and U.S. Foreign Relations with Latin America* (forthcoming); cf. Mark J. Miller and Demetrios G. Papademetriou, "Immigration and U.S. Foreign Policy," in Demetrios G. Papademetriou and Mark J. Miller (eds.), *The Unavoidable Issue: U.S. Immigration Policy in the 1980s* (Philadelphia: Institute for the Study of Human Issues), 1983. On patterns of international relations that developed around labor migration into some nations of Western Europe, see Tomas Hammar (ed.), *European Immigration Policy: A Comparative Study* (Cambridge: Cambridge University Press), 1985; and Barbara Schmitter Heisler, "Sending Countries and the Politics of Emigration and Destination," *International Migration Review*, Vol. 19, No. 3, 1985.

became illegal when IRCA was signed in November 1986, and technically the law entered into full effect in June 1988. The U.S. Immigration and Naturalization Service (INS), however, is only just beginning widespread enforcement of "employer sanctions" in mid-1989, following two years of informing employers about IRCA's provisions.

Simpson/Rodino has not been the only factor increasing migration's ranking on the international political agendas of regional governments. Other factors have included the rise of migrant remittances (in several sending nations) to the top ranks among foreign-exchange earners, greater publicity for the status problems faced by migrants in the United States, and country-of-origin sensitivity to the restrictionist mood that has influenced most U.S. immigration policy since the late 1970s. However, IRCA significantly accelerated the rise in immigration's foreign-policy priority for Western-Hemisphere sending nations. It did so primarily because it pulled together many of these nations' other immigration concerns and was seen as a threat to important country-of-origin interests.[6]

For the governments in most societies of origin, emigration has traditionally represented a developmental solution, not a problem. Departing migrants usually opened up jobs in hard-pressed local labor markets, and remittances from the United States helped bolster necessitous national accounts. Following this logic, source states preferred to treat migration as a matter of "low politics," seldom subject to discussion or bargaining with the receiving nation. Northward migration was viewed as a "tacit exchange" between sending and receiving nations. The latter benefited from inexpensive labor power and the former received hard-currency income and some relief from underemployment.

IRCA altered these calculations in two important ways. First, it created the perception that the U.S. government would sharply reduce the de facto benefits that had long been available through population movement, cutting net undocumented migration by enforcing the U.S. immigration code more strictly. Indeed, it was feared there might be massive repatriations of current undocumented residents of the United States. Second, IRCA tended to reduce the contrasts in migration interests between, on the one hand, countries that generated primarily economically motivated migrants and, on the other, those whose emigrants were primarily politically motivated. Simpson/Rodino's treatment of most recent undocumented aliens in their character as workers had a homogenizing effect on sending-state priorities. Threatened with expulsions or at least a decline in U.S. employment and remittances, both refugee-generating countries (e.g., El Salvador) and labor-sending nations (e.g., the Dominican Republic) had to focus on reducing the new law's effect on their political and developmental interests. Each gave up a prior motive for limiting the nation-to-nation discussion of migration issues: political embarrassment in the former case, and the economic benefits of laissez-faire in the latter.

This paper begins by reviewing briefly the key provisions of the Simpson/Rodino Act, together with data through early 1989 on patterns of legalization and some evidence on enforcement under the new law. This background will form a basis for the political analysis to follow. The paper then discusses the "first wave" of country-of-origin responses to IRCA, from late 1986 through early 1988. This discussion will focus on how Simpson/Rodino altered tacit migration exchanges for two sets of nations: traditional labor-suppliers (Mexico and the Dominican Republic), and sources of politically motivated migration (El Salvador, Guatemala,

---

[6]Analysts' views contrast sharply in evaluating this process, but they do not differ greatly in describing its basic mechanism. For a relatively uncritical view see Edwin P. Reubens, "Interpreting Migration: Current Models and a New Interpretation," New York University Center for Latin American and Caribbean Studies, *Occasional Paper*, No. 29, 1981. For a more radical analysis, cf. Robin Cohen, *The New Helots: Migrants in the International Division of Labour* (Aldershot, England: Avebury), 1987.

and Nicaragua). The paper will examine the international political tactics chosen by these governments, suggesting why they have not met with greater success.

The analysis then moves to the developments of the last 15 months. During this period, sending-nation governments (1) have tended to limit the demands they place on Washington in the migration field and (2) have usually brought pressure through bilateral rather than joint regional channels. Some of the most significant recent developments, it will be suggested, have been spurred by the impact of IRCA on politically motivated Central American migrants in the United States. Finally, the paper will look ahead to assess how hemispheric international migration dealings may evolve in the next few years. Though multilateral action by countries of origin remains a remote prospect, it will be argued that the need for bilateral negotiations may well be enhanced during IRCA's first years of application.

ELEMENTS OF IRCA

The major provisions of IRCA are set forth in Fig. 1. It is important to note that undocumented migrants who arrived after 1981 are ineligible for legalization, an exclusion which resulted from a legislative compromise. Since the current wars in Central America were just beginning at the start of the 1980s, the bulk of Salvadoran, Nicaraguan, and Guatemalan illegal migrants falls into this "ineligible" category, as do smaller proportions of labor migrants from other nations. This application of employer sanctions to most Central American undocumented residents in the United States, who do not enjoy significant access to amnesty, helps to maintain migration as a salient political issue for Central American states and helps to give their joint concerns an urgency not fully shared by other countries of origin.

Also to be noted is the provision for a category of "Special Agricultural Workers" (SAWs), who could have arrived as recently as May 1, 1985, before making application. This section of the law was inserted to meet the demands of U.S. agribusiness.

LEGALIZATION OF MIGRANTS FROM LATIN AMERICA AND THE CARIBBEAN UNDER THE TERMS OF IRCA

A strikingly clear trend is apparent among applicants for legalization under Simpson/Rodino: migrants from Mexico greatly outnumbered those from any other nation in applying for status as "temporary legal residents." Mexicans far outstrip not only migrants from Central American states (as might be expected, given the timing of migrant streams), but also those from nations with relatively long-standing labor migrations, including Jamaica and the Dominican Republic. Also noteworthy is the fact that Mexicans predominated in the SAW category, and among other nationalities only Haitians benefited notably from the less stringent cutoff date for agriculture. The data for nations in the Mexican-Caribbean-Central American region are set out in Table 1.

THE FIRST WAVE: EARLY COUNTRY-OF-ORIGIN RESPONSES TO THE PASSAGE OF IRCA

Initial press reports and forecasts on Simpson/Rodino in countries of origin tended to be alarmist and sometimes marked the advent of immigration as a major subject of public debate. Focusing (not altogether logically) on the start of the amnesty period as the effective date for

Employer Sanctions

- *Knowingly* employing unauthorized aliens is made unlawful.
- Escalating schedule of civil fines is created: from $250 to $10,000 per alien employed. Criminal penalties are also possible: not more than $3,000 per alien, or six months' imprisonment, or both. Higher penalties are possible for repeated offenses or a "pattern or practice" of violations.
- Employers must examine one relatively secure form of identification from the job applicant (suitably endorsed U.S. or foreign passport, naturalization certificate, "green card") or two less-secure forms (social security card, driver's license, birth certificate, etc.). Employers are not required to keep copies of documents examined.
- Extensive antidiscrimination provisions protect U.S. citizens and intended citizens against prejudiced hiring practices (unless the firm employs three or fewer workers). Upon reports of a widespread "pattern of discrimination" from the U.S. General Accounting Office (an investigative arm of Congress) and from a new administration task force, Congress could by joint resolution end employer sanctions within three months.

Legalization

- Temporary resident status is made available for those residing continuously in an unlawful status in the United States since January 1, 1982.
- Applications for adjustment were accepted only between May 5, 1987, and May 4, 1988, with limited additional time for submission of full documentation.
- Adjustment to permanent resident status is available after 18 months of temporary residence.
- Federal public assistance is not available to newly legalized aliens for five years (except for emergency, prenatal, and pediatric health care; aid to blind, aged, and disabled; Headstart and similar education services; and benefits to Cuban/Haitian entrants of 1980).
- $4 billion is appropriated for FY88 through FY91 to cover administrative costs of legalization plus state, local, and permitted federal health/welfare/education benefits to newly legalized aliens.

Provisions for Agricultural Workers

- A new category of "Special Agricultural Workers" is created. If such workers can demonstrate employment for at least 90 man-days in U.S. agriculture between May 1, 1985, and May 1, 1986, they will be granted permanent residence after a two-year period as temporary residents. If they can show such employment since 1983, they need wait only one year in temporary status.
- From FY90 through FY93, "replenishment workers" may be admitted up to the limits to be set by the Labor Department. They must wait three years in temporary status for permanent residency and during each of those years must work at least 90 man-days in U.S. agriculture to avoid deportation. To be eligible for naturalization, they must work at least 90 man-days in U.S. agriculture during each of five calendar years.

---

[a]The text of the law is available in U.S. House of Representatives, 99th Congress, Second Session, *Immigration Reform and Control Act of 1986* (Report 99-1000).

Fig. 1—Summary of IRCA's major provisions[a]

Table 1

NUMBERS OF IRCA LEGALIZATION APPLICATIONS BY
CITIZENS OF SELECTED COUNTRIES,
AS OF JANUARY 27, 1989

Country of Citizenship	Applications by Residents before 1/1/82	Applications for SAW status
Mexico	1,233,300	1,054,100
El Salvador	145,600	27,800
Guatemala	53,100	19,100
Colombia	26,500	6,400
Dominican Republic	18,000	9,100
Nicaragua	16,100	800
Haiti	16,000	49,100
Jamaica	13,000	6,800
Honduras	13,000	4,600
Belize	6,200	100
Guyana	3,200	1,100
Trinidad/Tobago	3,100	1,100
Costa Rica	3,100	600

SOURCE: U.S. Immigration and Naturalization Service.

the new law, Mexican newspapers speculated (for example) that several million migrants might be spurred to return from the United States; one major Mexican daily mistakenly headlined "State of Siege in the North" in early May of 1987.[7] "Fear in New York Dominican Colony," proclaimed a Santo Domingo news story,[8] while the foreign minister estimated that as many as 700,000 Dominicans might be in the United States illegally.[9] Radio Havana predicted that U.S. policy would require 3 million Mexicans to return home, together with an equal number of other Latins "who will surely settle in [Mexico]."[10] Ricardo Acevedo Peralta, then foreign minister of El Salvador, predicted that billions of dollars in refugee remittances might be lost to his country.[11]

In response to the terms of Simpson/Rodino, to the start of its enforcement, and to urgently worded press reports, the governments of significant countries of origin accorded the migration issue a priority it had seldom if ever enjoyed in the past. (This upgrading was probably motivated in part by a desire to find an outside force to share the blame for regional nations' considerable economic distress during the late 1980s.) Nation-of-origin governments also began (1) to alter their expressed preferences on the subject and (2) to explore new tactics for voicing their migration views to the U.S. government. Let us begin by reviewing alterations of policy stance by sending states in two cases of labor migration, the Dominican Republic and Mexico. We will then turn to the early effects of IRCA on the migration policies of El Salvador and other Central American nations, many of whose northern-bound emigrants cite political motives for their exit.

---

[7]*Excelsior* (Mexico City), May 12, 1987.

[8]*Utima Hora* (Santo Domingo), May 6, 1987.

[9]"Reid Pide OEA Intervenga para Evitar Repatriación," by Ary Moleón, *Listín Diario* (Santo Domingo), April 28, 1987. This figure may be compared with a range of estimates made by academic observers, which run from 70,000 to 120,000.

[10]*Foreign Broadcast Information Service—Latin America—Daily Report* (hereinafter FBIS/LA/Daily), June 26, 1987, p. A2.

[11]FBIS/LA/Daily, May 12, 1987, pp. P1–P2.

The Dominican Republic. The prospect of sharply reduced migration to the United States alerted many Dominicans to the ways in which their nation had benefited from northward population movements since 1962.[12] Approximately 380,000 Dominican migrants had established themselves in the United States, 80 percent in the New York region; remittances from "absent Dominicans" had become one of the country's two principal sources of dollar earnings, exceeding the proceeds from sugar sales; relatively easy access to the United States on visitors' visas (250,000 were in circulation) facilitated Dominican trade and dealings with foreign investors.[13]

Divisions of the Dominican state responded to IRCA in ways related to their degree of responsibility for international dealings: Segments of government traditionally distant from foreign relations tended to voice radical objections, while longer-established agencies of foreign policy chose more moderate lines of action. The Dominican Senate created a special commission to visit Washington, D.C., and press for a "more elastic" application of Simpson/Rodino, maintaining that "our nation should not remain silent in the face of this reality, which shows signs of injustice or at least demonstrates few humanitarian sentiments."[14] President Joaquín Balaguer expressed fear of a possibly "catastrophic" effect from enforcement of the new law. Foreign Minister Donald Reid Cabral, speaking in Washington, called on the Organization of American States to prevent the repatriation of thousands of Dominican workers. The rest of his speech contemplated more limited measures, however: "We appeal to the United States' high sense of justice and humanity, so that the [new immigration] measures are applied in a gradual and moderate manner...."[15] In March 1988, immigration was one of the issues President Balaguer raised with U.S. officials on a visit to Washington, even though from the American viewpoint the chief purpose of the visit was to discourage the granting of asylum in the Dominican Republic to Panamanian Gen. Manuel Antonio Noriega.[16]

Mexico. The government of Mexico had been reluctant, since the López Portillo administration, to include migration on the bilateral agenda with the United States.[17] That hesitation has been eroded, however, by what one observer described as the "strong rejection of the [Simpson/Rodino] law by all sectors of Mexican society."[18] Mexican legislators, who in the past have been more outspoken on migration matters than have government administrative spokesmen, signed a statement of concern that IRCA might lead to repressive police action,

---

[12]There were negative effects, as well, especially on aspects of Dominican development; see José del Castillo and Christopher Mitchell (eds.), *La Migración dominicana hacia los Estados Unidos* (Santa Domingo: Editorial UNAPEC), 1987.

[13]See Eric M. Larson and Wolfgang Opitz, "Sex Ratio-Based Estimates of Emigration from the Dominican Republic," paper prepared for presentation at the Conference on Dominican Migration to the United States, Santo Domingo, March 24–25, 1988; Franc Báez Evertsz and Frank D'Oleo Ramírez, *La Emigración de dominicanos a Estados Unidos: Determinantes socio-económicos y consecuencias* (Santo Domingo: Fundación Friedrich Ebert), 1986; and Max J. Castro, *Dominican Journey: Patterns, Context and Consequences of Migration from the Dominican Republic to the United States* (Ph.D. dissertation, University of North Carolina at Chapel Hill), 1985.

[14]*Hoy* (Santo Domingo), April 4, 1987.

[15]*Listín Diario* (Santo Domingo), April 28, 1987. The relative moderation of the Dominican cancillería (chancellery) on this subject results partly from their wish to avoid creating a precedent favoring undocumented Haitian migrants in the Dominican Republic.

[16]"Reagan y Balaguer tratan problemas comunes," *Listín Diario* (Santo Domingo), March 26, 1988, pp. 1, 13.

[17]Carlos Rico, "Punishing Friends? U.S. Immigration Policies and U.S.-Mexican Relations 1965–1986," draft essay prepared as part of a project on *Immigration and Foreign Policy*, New York University, April 1987. As Richard W. Day recounted in his keynote address to the Guadalajara conference in May 1989 (see Part I of these Proceedings), Senator Alan Simpson (R., Wyoming) tried vainly to initiate a dialogue with high Mexican officials during the early 1980s, when the U.S. Congress was considering the legislative draft of IRCA.

[18]Jorge Castañeda, panel presentation on "Migration as a Factor in U.S.-Mexico Relations," 10th Annual National Legal Conference, Center for Migration Studies, Washington, D.C., March 27, 1987.

undermining bilateral relations.[19] An experienced Mexican analyst speculated that "since the *fantasma* [of a massive decrease in net migration from Mexico to the United States] is taken as real by many in Mexico, in a sense it *becomes* real both for Mexico and for the United States."[20]

A new channel for dialogue on immigration between the United States and countries of origin (especially Mexico) was opened by the provisions of IRCA itself. The new law created a Commission for the Study of International Migration and Cooperative Economic Development (CSIMCED) to examine ways in which U.S. aid might be better distributed to help relieve migratory pressures in sending nations. Commission chairman Diego Asencio, former U.S. ambassador to Colombia and to Brazil, stated: "Our charge is unique, for we are mandated to work with the nations from which illegal immigration occurs and to examine trade, investment, and economic development programs which might stem the flow."

The Commission focused its early attention on Mexico, with results that some staff members described as "a breakthrough." President de la Madrid met with the Commission at length in December 1987. According to Mexican press reports, de la Madrid

> demanded the U.S. Government's cooperation in controlling the excessive flow of Mexican migrants to that country, not only by supporting existing programs, but by establishing frameworks within which bilateral trade can be broadened and diversified to occupy a larger number of workers.[21]

The Mexican Population Council was designated to work directly as the Commission's Mexican counterpart; 14 specific study projects have been agreed upon.[22] In visits to Haiti, the Dominican Republic, and all five Central American nations, the Commission has provided informal communication channels between officials of the United States and those of countries of origin.

El Salvador and Other Central American Nations. On April 10, 1987, President José Napoleón Duarte wrote to President Reagan formally requesting that Salvadorans illegally in the United States be granted "extended voluntary departure" (EVD) status. (EVD is a legal condition that may be granted by the U.S. Attorney General, permitting migrants to remain temporarily in the United States on the grounds of unsettled political conditions in their home societies.) President Duarte based his petition on the importance of migrants' remittances to the Salvadoran economy and on the ineligibility of most Salvadoran migrants for legalization under IRCA. "My government estimates," Duarte wrote, "that the total value of remittances is some place between $350 million to $600 million annually, and is thus larger than the United States Government's assistance to El Salvador. . . . The enormous cost of the war, the destruction the guerrillas have caused, the reduction of our sugar exports, the loss of the cotton market and the plummeting of coffee prices all bode ill for the Salvadoran economy in the coming year. To eliminate remittances from the United States would be yet another blow that seems counterproductive to our joint aims of denying Central America to Marxist-Leninist regimes." Duarte was careful to contend that "the improved human rights situation does not justify the granting of political asylum by the United States to Salvadoran illegals."[23]

---

[19]Federation for American Immigration Reform (FAIR), *Immigration Report*, Washington, D.C., December 1986.

[20]Jorge Bustamante, presentation at *Seminario de Estudios México-Estados Unidos*, Querétaro, Mexico, May 16, 1987.

[21]*Unomásuno*, Mexico City, December 4, 1987, p. 3.

[22]CSIMCED, press release, September 22, 1987; CSIMCED, "Report of the First International Consultative Mission to Mexico," Washington, D.C., December 1987; *Commission Newsletter*, No. 1, February 1989.

[23]"Duarte Appeals to Reagan to Let Salvadorans Stay," by Robert Pear, *New York Times*, April 26, 1987, pp. 1, 14. It is interesting to note that Dominican leaders frequently cite the danger of domestic political instability as a concern in opposing full implementation of Simpson/Rodino, while President Duarte's international and ideological commitments deter him from making most such arguments. By early May 1987, before the U.S. reply to his letter, Duarte

It is interesting that the Salvadoran rebels also attacked the new U.S. immigration law, because of its purported effect both on refugees and on their home society. Rubén Zamora, speaking for the insurgent Frente Democrático Revolucionario (FDR), anticipated that Simpson/Rodino would reduce the $700 million to $1.3 billion that he estimated is sent home from the United States each year by Salvadoran refugees. "These are funds that go directly to the families . . . and therefore they help somewhat to improve the very hard conditions in the country." Zamora described the new legislation as "a very unjust law that all Salvadorans must condemn" on the grounds that the United States finances the war that generates refugees and then denies them the chance to work.[24]

Somewhat surprisingly, the official Salvadoran request was supported by the U.S. State Department in interagency consultations in Washington. Assistant Secretary Elliot Abrams, who had vigorously opposed EVD when it was advanced on human-rights grounds, supported it out of concern for the Salvadoran economy.[25] Arguments by the Justice Department and by members of Congress including Senator Simpson, however, prevailed. President Reagan rejected Duarte's request on May 14, also noting in his message that "it is unlikely that a large-scale exodus of Salvadorans will occur."[26]

In addition, the governments of Guatemala, Honduras, and Nicaragua all criticized IRCA's provisions for employer sanctions, and the presidents of the first two nations directly lobbied the White House for delays in enforcement against their citizens, without success.[27] Nicaragua announced that it viewed Simpson/Rodino as a violation of human rights, which would afflict the Central American economies if massive deportations took place.[28]

Along with these newly explicit (and probably newly formulated) policy positions on migration, the foreign policies of countries of origin began to explore new tactics including regional cooperation. As we have noted, there was considerable logic behind this evolution. Differences tended to disappear between the immigration-policy interests of countries from which labor migrants originated and those whose societies generated refugees. As governments of both categories anticipated that net migration to the United States would be reduced, there seemed less potential benefit in playing down the migration process, and sending nations tended to become more unified as well as more vocal.

The Guatemalan government took the lead in regional moves in Central America. In late May of 1987, all five Central American labor ministers (or their representatives) signed a declaration in Guatemala City jointly appealing to the United States "concerning the implementation of immigration measures and the protection of the rights of Central Americans who remain in that country. . . ."[29] President Balaguer of the Dominican Republic, a source of labor migration to the United States, supported the initiatives of Guatemalan President Vinicio Cerezo toward forging a common front among countries of origin.[30]

---

was hoping for a 3-to-5-year delay in the enforcement of Simpson/Rodino affecting Salvadorans. "My goal is to get a space for the Salvadoran migrants in the United States through the executive branch." FBIS/LA/Daily, May 12, 1987, pp. P1–P2.

[24]FBIS/LA/Daily, May 8, 1987, pp. P1–P2.

[25]The positive U.S. State Department view of EVD for Salvadorans has continued, at least in the San Salvador embassy. In early 1989 U.S. Ambassador William Walker told Congressional staff members that he supported President Duarte's position on "safe haven." National Immigration, Refugee, and Citizenship Forum, *Action Alert,* Washington, D.C., March 7, 1989.

[26]Federation for American Immigration Reform, *Immigration Report,* Washington, D.C., June 1987, p. 1.

[27]FBIS/LA/Daily, May 19, 1987, p. P8 and May 22, 1987, p. Q1.

[28]FBIS/LA/Daily, May 26, 1987, p. P14.

[29]FBIS/LA/Daily, May 26, 1987, p. P1.

[30]Federation for American Immigration Reform, *Immigration Report,* Washington, D.C., June 1987, p. 1; also "El Embajador de EU afirma que la ley de inmigración será aplicada con justeza," by Miriam Abreu, *El Nuevo Diario* (Santo Domingo), April 28, 1987, p. 2.

These lobbying efforts—both separate and joint—had almost no impact on U.S. policy or administrative actions. The reasons are not difficult to discern. The U.S. administration had labored long and hard for a new immigration law and had little relish for granting far-reaching exceptions to it. Moreover, the countries of origin tended to use tactics that avoided the best paths to exercising leverage in Washington. For the most part, they simply asked the executive—usually the Chief Executive!—not to enforce IRCA in relation to their compatriots, ignoring the potential benefits of seeking allies in Congress or among pro-migration interest groups.

Only the Salvadoran government adapted in a moderate way, endorsing (by July 1988) an initiative in the U.S. Congress by Representative John Joseph Moakley (D., Massachusetts) and Senator Dennis DeConcini (D., Arizona) to grant "temporary safe haven" to political migrants from El Salvador and from Nicaragua. The Salvadoran Christian Democratic government backed this bill in a letter to then Senate Majority Leader Robert Byrd (D., West Virginia). Shifting his ground of argument from the earlier appeal to Ronald Reagan, President Duarte expressed the fear that FMLN (Farabundo Martí National Liberation Front) guerrillas would "find recruits . . . among the Salvadorans who may soon be forced to return to their country. . . . I am convinced that temporary safe haven is the single most important initiative the United States can now take to help my nation achieve this aspiration [democracy and peace in El Salvador], which the people of El Salvador and the United States have shared for so long."

Perhaps ironically, the only national case in which effective U.S. administrative action provided relief from employer sanctions and other IRCA provisions was that of Nicaragua, whose government had not specifically sought such action. In July of 1987, Attorney General Edwin Meese instituted a policy of leniency in granting political asylum to Nicaraguan applicants, thus nationalizing a policy that had existed for more than a year in the Miami area.[31] The effect of this policy (whose long-term significance will be discussed in the next section) is dramatically evident in Table 2.

THE SECOND WAVE: CHANGE AND DEEPENING OF RELATIONS BETWEEN SENDING AND RECEIVING NATIONS

During 1988 and early 1989, significant changes took place in Western-Hemisphere international relations on the subject of migration, influenced in part by experience with IRCA's implementation. The sending nations' most immediate fears of Simpson-Rodino's consequences were not realized, as formal and effective deportations from the United States to regional countries remained near historical levels. One important country—Mexico—even began to cooperate officially with the U.S. Justice Department's efforts to slow undocumented migration from Central America. Under these circumstances, sending-nation interests tended to diverge, and specific migration concerns came to prominence in place of the shared wariness that prevailed in 1986 and 1987.

This trend seemed to represent only a temporary downgrading of migration as a subject of inter-nation concern, however. Equally important, this period witnessed a blending of immigration issues with other important political considerations, especially for Central American nations. Chief among those issues was the treatment of politically motivated migrants, and

---

[31]*New York Times*, July 20, 1987, p. A18.

Table 2

NUMBERS OF ASYLUM APPROVALS AND DENIALS, RESULTING FROM APPLICATIONS TO DISTRICT DIRECTORS OF THE INS

Fiscal Year	El Salvador			Nicaragua		
	Approved	Denied	Percent Approved	Approved	Denied	Percent Approved
1983–1986	641	17,495	3.5	2,602	15,856	14.1
1987	29	776	3.6	1,867	357	83.9
1988	110	3,822	2.8	2,786	2,455	53.2
1989 (1st quarter)	86	2,130	3.9	652	761	46.1

Fiscal Year	Guatemala			Honduras		
	Approved	Denied	Percent Approved	Approved	Denied	Percent Approved
1983–1986	14	1,461	0.95	6	234	2.5
1987	7	178	3.8	2	39	4.9
1988	24	447	5.1	10	125	7.9
1989 (1st quarter)	9	247	3.5	1	135	0.74

SOURCE: National Immigration, Refugee, and Citizenship Forum, based on figures from the U.S. Immigration and Naturalization Service.

Central American anxieties about this question were heightened by the effects of employer sanctions after IRCA went into full effect in June 1988.

The first year of Simpson-Rodino's implementation—when the INS deliberately stressed public education over workplace enforcement—did not bring the nightmarish planeloads of expellees that some countries of origin had envisioned. As seen in Table 3, persons deported or formally "required to depart" were scarcely more numerous than in past years, though the government's enforcement effort showed the same unequal pattern according to nationality that was evident in asylum figures.

Immigration relations between the United States and Mexico entered a period of mixed signals. Mexican officials voiced dismay at the symbolism implied in plans for a four-mile anti-truck ditch at the heavily used border between Tijuana and San Ysidro, California. On the other hand, Mexico's new administration had many economic and political motives for maintaining good working relations with the United States, and in early 1989 it was revealed that INS agents were being permitted to operate within Mexico in an attempt to slow the northward flow of Central American migration. Negative public opinion in Mexico obliged the government of President Carlos Salinas de Gortari to end this joint enforcement effort.

The Mexican government of late 1988, however, showed no interest in cooperation of another sort: mutual lobbying in Washington by countries of origin. In Central America, as well, the initiatives of 1987 stagnated, as individual countries focused on nationally specific aspects of the immigration issue. For the Honduran state, the departure of the anti-Sandinista

Table 3

NUMBERS OF DEPORTATIONS AND IMMIGRANTS REQUIRED TO DEPART, BY SELECTED COUNTRY

Country of Nationality	FY84	FY85	FY86	FY87	FY88
El Salvador					
Deported	2,619	3,078	3,690	2,585	2,711
Required to depart	1,842	2,307	2,357	2,407	1,828
Guatemala					
Deported	851	1,649	2,369	1,881	2,049
Required to depart	882	1,083	1,133	890	813
Honduras					
Deported	455	771	1,074	1,033	1,312
Required to depart	492	566	445	331	218
Nicaragua					
Deported	54	134	174	87	36
Required to depart	228	262	211	228	173

SOURCE: U.S. Immigration and Naturalization Service.

Contras—either to Nicaragua or to the United States—was of primary concern.[32] Guatemalan officials at this time showed little interest in the migration of their compatriots to the United States; their attention focused on the situation of Guatemalan displaced persons in Mexico. Nicaragua expressed a willingness to reintegrate many of its citizens who had fled from war, economic distress, and political polarization. Only political leaders in El Salvador—including President-elect Alfredo Cristiani of the right-wing ARENA party—continued to press hard for a go-slow policy in the enforcement of IRCA.

At a less evident but probably influential level for the long term, migration issues were becoming interlocked with other major considerations in inter-American relations, especially in the dealings between the United States and Central American countries. IRCA was involved in the most dramatic of these "issue interpenetrations."

In late 1988 employer sanctions began to have a significant impact on the situation, perceptions, and behavior of many undocumented Central American migrants and potential migrants.[33] With access to the U.S. job market subject to rather effective new restrictions, many Central American migrants in the United States turned to the only North American administrative process that could still provide them with work authorization: filing asylum applications.[34] IRCA's impact in this regard is outlined vividly by a recent report of a field visit in Los Angeles:

---

[32]For example, the standing committee of the Honduran Congress sent a request to the U.S. Senate in early 1988 asking that funds be approved to permit the Contras' departure from Honduras. Oscar Armando Melara Murillo, Secretary of the Honduran Congress, contended that if the U.S. Senate endorsed the Esquipulas II agreement "then the U.S. should take in the Nicaraguans fighting the Sandinista government." FBIS/LA/Daily, February 9, 1988, p. 13.

[33]This finding supplements the research reported by Keith Crane and Beth Asch in their contribution to these Proceedings (see Part II, Session I). As of mid-1989, the prospect of employer sanctions appears to be exerting a reputational or psychological effect (at least in the case of Central American undocumented migrants), even in advance of widespread enforcement efforts.

[34]This analysis implies no prejudgment as to the previous eligibility of these applicants for political asylum status. They had to work, their work situation changed as a result of IRCA, and a large increase in asylum applications ensued.

The INS estimates that approximately 50,000 persons filed affirmative asylum applications at the Los Angeles District Office alone during calendar year 1988. This represents an unprecedented increase from the previous year when 26,000 affirmative applications were filed nationally. The applications began in late spring of 1988, reached [their] height during that summer, and have continued to date at approximately 125 per day.[35]

Near U.S. borders, the "steering" effect of employer sanctions, which boosted asylum applications, acted in combination with a higher outflow of migrants from Nicaragua. These emigrants were spurred by a combination of military, political, economic, and natural calamities that "seemed . . . to have provoked a general despair."[36] The formerly obscure INS office in Harlingen, Texas, is estimated to have received 30,000 asylum applications between September 1988 and February 1989. Migrants both from Nicaragua and El Salvador obtained work authorization in South Texas for the period of asylum-application processing, then moved on to South Florida or to Texas cities and Southern California. Measures undertaken by the U.S. government to slow this growth in asylum requests (which had been encouraged in part by the Reagan administration's open leniency toward Nicaraguan petitioners) had some counterproductive as well as some intended results. When asylum applicants were forbidden to leave Harlingen, a temporary restraining order against the INS was obtained. This provided a few weeks of safe passage which probably encouraged some northward population flow,[37] though reinstatement of "rapid-fire" asylum processing in late February deterred many migrants from crossing the Rio Grande.

Both receiving and sending nations face significant dilemmas resulting from this aspect of IRCA. Authorities in the United States confront protest from border areas affected by the new detention policies of the INS, a growing backlog of asylum cases, and the prospect of continuing public criticism for (variously) harshness, leniency, and inconsistency. El Salvador, Nicaragua, Guatemala, and Honduras must cope with a situation of restricted access to the U.S. labor market; more compatriots imprisoned, homeless, or economically "underground" in the United States; and possibly diminishing hard-currency remittances.

It is unclear, however, whether the common elements of these problems are likely to be addressed in a constructive joint manner by the nations concerned.[38] There is evidence that while Central American states are willing to consider cooperative action on the needs of refugees and other "displaced persons" remaining *within* Central America, neither regional governments nor Washington is currently disposed to make migration to the United States a subject for multilateral debate. In late May 1989, an International Conference on Central American Refugees (CIREFCA) was held in Guatemala City, convened by the five Esquipulas countries plus Belize and Mexico. With delegations at the ministerial level, and the office of the United Nations High Commissioner for Refugees serving as secretariat, CIREFCA considered a series of specific projects to aid the displaced, with the hope of attracting funding from governments and agencies outside the region.[39] In conference deliberations, potential donors emphasized that the Central American nations should fulfill commitments they made in

---

[35]James Morsch and Diane Kuntz, "Report on Trip to Los Angeles, Dallas, and South Texas," Washington, D.C.: Refugee Policy Group, April 7, 1989, p. 2.

[36]Nina M. Serafino (Congressional Research Service), testimony before the Commission for the Study of International Migration and Cooperative Economic Development, Washington, D.C., April 21, 1989, p. 3.

[37]See the excellent participant reports by Guy Gugliotta of a "coyote"-aided Nicaraguan migrant group rushing to "beat the deadline" in late February, *Miami Herald,* February 26–March 1, 1989.

[38]In this sense, of course, migration is similar to many other inter-American issues, including trade, drugs, and sovereign debt; see Mitchell, "International Migration, International Relations and Foreign Policy."

[39]Testimony of Elena Martínez, United Nations Development Program, Hearing of the Commission for the Study of International Migration and Cooperative Economic Development, Washington, D.C., April 21, 1989.

1987 to reduce the refugee problem before looking with any confidence for outside aid to tackle remaining difficulties.[40] While the U.S. government is favorably disposed toward CIREFCA's pragmatic approach to refugee dilemmas, it decided, in agreement with the Central American countries, that it would not attend CIREFCA and that migration to the United States would not be discussed at Guatemala City.

Under these circumstances, the way remains open—but difficult—for bilateral negotiations between Washington and the countries of origin in Central America. There is considerable regional precedent for nation-to-nation agreements regulating migration flows; the United States has concluded such bargains with both Cuba and Haiti. Under these accords, sending nations undertake to restrain emigration in return for concessions that may include economic aid for and political toleration of a local regime (Haiti) or political dialogue and normalization of immigration dealing (Cuba). These compacts bring to bear the sometimes-unsuspected administrative ability of sending nations to regulate population outflows.

SOME RECOMMENDATIONS

Some prerequisites for the conclusion and viability of bilateral agreements with other nations—e.g., Mexico, the Dominican Republic, and those in Central America—may be suggested. First, formal agreements should supplement IRCA rather than supplant or undercut the new law, and they should be perceived to do so. Legislators in the United States (and members of the executive branch in the long run) are likely to reject intergovernmental deals that do not use IRCA's provisions for their basic ground rules. Second, both sides should perceive undocumented migration as a problem that is damaging their national interests. This damage, though it strikes individual migrants first and foremost, also affects more general social concerns, through "issue interpenetration" and other policy linkages and tradeoffs. Third, countries of origin should have the capacity and political will to alter the undocumented migrant flow effectively and humanely. Concessions by the United States will not endure if the migration pattern is not at least modified once new agreements are in effect.

Here are a few examples. If appropriate incentives from the United States were available in the form of practical development aid for grassroots employment, both Nicaragua and El Salvador might be able to reduce out-migration considerably, and Guatemala might better regulate population flows through its territory by instituting visa requirements for Central Americans. If U.S. preferential sugar purchases from the Dominican Republic could be increased, Santo Domingo might be assisted in restarting the engine of development, which would tend to retain labor over the long run.

At the same time, it must be stressed that such negotiations and national regulations would be a harsh and hollow sham if not accompanied by peace settlements of both the international and domestic conflicts that currently wrack all Central American nations except Costa Rica. The Central American wars of the 1980s exemplify foreign policy as an accelerator of migration; perhaps an embracing, humane, and constructive set of foreign policies can also act to slow this wrenching social process.

---

[40]*New York Times*, May 29, 1989, p. 3, and June 4, 1989, p. 17.

Appendix

CONFERENCE PARTICIPANTS

Jesús Arroyo Alejandre, Director
Instituto de Estudios Económicos y
    Regionales
Universidad de Guadalajara
México

Beth J. Asch
The RAND Corporation
United States

Diego C. Asencio
Commission for the Study of International
    Migration and Cooperative Economic
    Development
United States

María Basilia Valenzuela V.
Centro de Estudios México-EEUU
Universidad de Guadalajara
México

Frank D. Bean
The Urban Institute
United States

Jorge A. Bustamante
Colegio de la Frontera Norte
México

Gustavo Cabrera
Colegio de México
México

Juan Cantu Gutiérrez
Consejo Nacional de Población (CONAPO)
México

Leo Chavez
University of California at Irvine
United States

Keith W. Crane
The RAND Corporation
United States

Richard W. Day
Subcommittee on Immigration and
    Refugee Affairs
U.S. Senate Judiciary Committee
United States

Rodolfo O. de la Garza
Center for Mexican-American Studies
University of Texas, Austin
United States

Adrian De Leon Arias
Centro de Estudios México-EEUU
Universidad de Guadalajara
México

William Diaz
The Ford Foundation
United States

Sergio Diaz-Briquets
Commission for the Study of International
    Migration and Cooperative Economic
    Development
United States

Michael Dino
U.S. General Accounting Office
United States

Jorge Durand
Universidad de Guadalajara
México

Thomas J. Espenshade
Princeton University
United States

Edgardo Flores Rivas
Director General de Protección y Servicios
    Consulares
México

Manuel García y Griego
Colegio de México
México

Guadalupe Gomez Maganda de Anaya
Camera de Deputados de la República
México

Victor Johnston
U.S. Immigration and Naturalization
 Service
United States

Charles B. Keely
Georgetown University
United States

Gustavo López Castro
Colegio de Michoacán
México

David Lyon
The RAND Corporation
United States

Flora MacDonald
Queen's University, Kingston
Canada

Anthony P. Maingot
Florida International University
United States

Douglas Massey
University of Chicago
United States

Kevin McCarthy
The RAND Corporation
United States

Christopher Mitchell
New York University
United States

William Moore
U.S. Embassy
Mexico

Jaime Navarro
Quantum
México

Mario Ojeda Gomez
Colegio de México
México

Andrew W. Oltyan
Department of State
United States

Victor H. Palmieri
The Palmieri Company
United States

Carlos Rico F.
Colegio de México
México

Edward Rivera
Commission for the Study of International
 Migration and Cooperative Economic
 Development
United States

Hector Rivera Estrada
Secretario Particular de la C. Directora
 General
Dirección General de Servicios Migratorios
México

Manuel Rocha
U.S. Embassy
Mexico

David F. Ronfeldt
The RAND Corporation
United States

Irwin Rubenstein
U.S. Consulate-Guadalajara
Mexico

Raul M. Sánchez
The Ford Foundation
México

Alan Stapleton
U.S. General Accounting Office
United States

Michael Teitelbaum
Alfred P. Sloan Foundation
United States

Georges Vernez
The RAND Corporation
United States

Michael J. White
The Urban Institute
United States

Ofelia Woo
Colegio de la Frontera Norte
México

Esther Lee Yao
Commission for the Study of International
    Migration and Cooperative Economic
    Development
United States

Sergio Zendejas
Colegio de Michoacán
México